D1293556

JOHN STAINER

JOHN STAINER

and the Musical Life of Victorian Britain

PETER CHARLTON

DAVID & CHARLES
Newton Abbot London North Pomfret (Vt)

British Library Cataloguing in Publication Data

Charlton, Peter
  John Stainer.
  1. Stainer, John   2. Composers — England —
  Biography
  I Title
  780'.92'4   ML410.S/

ISBN 0-7153-8387-6

Typeset by Typesetters (Birmingham) Ltd
and printed in Great Britain
by Redwood Burn Limited, Trowbridge, Wilts
for David & Charles (Publishers) Limited
Brunel House   Newton Abbot   Devon

Published in the United States of America
by David & Charles Inc
North Pomfret   Vermont 05053   USA

Contents

To the memory of Owen Franklin

Foreword

John Stainer was a well-known name in musical life in the early 1880s. He was Organist of St Paul's Cathedral and an influential figure in various branches of musical education. At the same time he was a prolific composer – too much so, as will become apparent – and a successful writer of educational texts. *The Daughter of Jairus* had already been written for and performed at the Worcester Triennial Festival (the forerunner of the Three Choirs' Festival) in 1878 and had received wide public acclaim and attention. Still to come were *St Mary Magdalen* and *The Crucifixion*, in addition to much church music, songs and books; and he was yet to hold the professorship in music at Oxford and, as a part-time Her Majesty's Inspector in Education, take an important role in the training of teachers in elementary schools.

He died at the early age of sixty, having already relinquished most of his musical work. Stainer was tireless in all his activities and had literally worn himself out. But he had had a full and happy life: he had held key appointments, enjoyed a highly successful marriage and a happy family life, and was himself a product of a devoted and loving family background.

Today the name of John Stainer is familiar enough in musical circles and fairly well known outside; but little seems to be generally known about the man himself except that he was the composer of the popular work *The Crucifixion*. Although aware of his three main appointments, at St Paul's Cathedral, Oxford and the Board of Education, I did not realise until I began to look into his activities in some depth just how important a national figure he was. His achievements, his reputation (somewhat bedevilled because of *The Crucifixion*) and the lack of adequate previous research made John Stainer an attractive person to study; his interests are my own to a great extent, and although I could never be a strong champion of all his music, I must say that he has suffered unfairly over the years, partly through neglect but

7

also owing to the unintelligent remarks of those who should know better.

Whatever his status as a composer in the general view, when I presented my research I felt that if I were to write about his life and his achievements without a survey of his compositions, as well as of his educational and other literary publications, the picture would not be complete. But this section proved to be larger than I intended and I thought such a thorough exposition would be out of place in a published work intended for general musical interest. Accordingly, I have treated this particular aspect in a far briefer and less detailed way here. I have dealt with general stylistic features in Stainer's compositions and looked at a few of them in later chapters; I have also taken the opportunity to mention those larger-scale works which were very popular at the time but are now totally forgotten, and to comment on *The Crucifixion*.

However, it ultimately became clear to me that his life and work for music were more valuable than I could have imagined. It is true that, to some extent, I was at a disadvantage in not being able to trace any diaries or engagement books, but his character and great industry were revealed in other ways. Stainer's published writings have all been studied in an attempt to gauge both the man and his mind. Although I was aware of the some-what flattering kind of literary style used in the press in the latter half of the nineteenth century, the fact that Stainer was one of the most helpful and kindest of men was still apparent, and the extent of his activities was both unquestionable and almost unbelievable. Of course, I have had to rely on the testimony of others a good deal, but I consider that collectively such testimonies have helped me to portray a fair assessment of John Stainer as a man.

It is with much gratitude that I dedicate this book to the memory of Owen Franklin, formerly Assistant Organist of York Minster, Organist of Doncaster Parish Church and Director of Music, Heathfield School, Ascot. Whatever success I may have enjoyed in the music profession I owe to his constant encourage-ment and advice from my boyhood and onwards. He was an outstanding example of kindness and integrity, and influenced generations of young people.

Peter Charlton
Clifton, Bristol.

1
Early life

John Stainer was the eighth of nine children born to Ann and William Stainer. Three children – William (born 1824), Sarah (1830) and Frederick (1832) – died in infancy leaving six, two of whom were also christened William and Sarah. Mrs Stainer (née Collier) could claim descent from an old Huguenot family that had settled in Spitalfields as silk weavers.[1]

Stainer's father, William, was born at Wing in Buckinghamshire on 22 March 1802, spending his early years in Markyate, Hertfordshire, before moving, while still a boy, with his parents to settle in Southwark. It was intended that he should take up a profession in law and he was articled to a solicitor in King Arm's Yard, King William Street, in the City of London. He spoiled any chance he might have had in that line by entering into a runaway match with Miss Ann Collier, the daughter of the proprietor of the Rose Hostelry. They were married on 9 November 1823 when William was twenty-one and Ann twenty years old. There is some doubt as to whether the marriage was a clandestine one, but it does appear to have had elements of secrecy about it since there were no Stainer family signatures bearing witness to the marriage when it was registered at Christ Church, Spitalfields, although there were two witnesses from the Collier family.

Now having a wife to support, William joined his brother John (who had already completed his apprenticeship) in a small cabinet-making firm in Web Street, Southwark, and there is every reason to suppose that he was reasonably successful in this work. However, he suffered some ill-health and for this reason applied for and was appointed vestry clerk and registrar of births at St Thomas's School on 8 June 1830, holding the further appointment of parish school master from 1834. He remained there until 1854 when he benefitted under the will of his cousin, Mary Stainer of Wimborne.

William Stainer appears to have been 'a clever if not a very clever man'. He was of a nervous retiring disposition but was constantly brought up to scratch by his wife who was rather the opposite in temperament. William was an enthusastic lover of music, 'gifted but not trained, had a bad touch on the piano and delighted in thumping out hymn tunes, his performances were of the slow and sure kind'. He was an excellent flautist – one of the best in London, according to William Clark – and he often played at civic functions at the Guildhall in London. William Stainer had other talents also: he was especially gifted in mathematics and at one time intended to publish a book on Euclid but the work was never completed. He studied French and Italian and kept up his interest in these languages to the last; latterly when he was practically paralysed he was often taken by his friend, the musician William Clark, to hear the French services at St Martin-le-Grand Church. He was a keen antiquarian and a collector of old books and china. As a teacher he is described as being patient and 'very clear, making everything attractive and interesting both to his pupils and also to his own children'.[2] William Stainer died at Wimborne – where he eventually had settled on leaving London – on 27 April 1867, at the age of sixty-five, and was buried in the minster churchyard where his wife joined him in March 1884, at the age of eighty-one years.

From this account of his parents, one can trace certain inherited characteristics in John Stainer. He was a highly cultured man with both artistic and literary ability, something not generally associated with English musicians of Stainer's time, and this side of him came from his father. From his mother came an extremely industrious disposition and a great courtesy towards and concern for other people. Of his surviving brothers and sisters, the elder son, William, became an important figure in the education of the handicapped, his life being devoted to the welfare of the deaf and dumb; he was subsequently ordained and became chaplain to the Royal Society for the Deaf and Dumb in London. Ann was organist of the chapel in Magdalen Hospital, Streatham, for over fifty years. She is said to have had a very bright and vivacious personality and never missed a single Sunday service during her tenure at the chapel.[3]

BIRTH OF JOHN STAINER AND HOME LIFE

John Stainer was born on 6 June 1840, although for some unknown reason his father (by then a registrar of births, one might add) registered the event as taking place on 12 June. He was born at home, 2 Broadway, Southwark, a little thoroughfare which belied its name and ran parallel to and north of St Thomas's Street, Southwark; London Bridge railway station now stands on the site of Broadway. John, as a child, shared the qualities of a kind and sympathetic nature that were already apparent in William and Ann (respectively fourteen and fifteen years older than John), the latter recalling John as the 'sweetest, most darling little mite in the world' with a singularly affectionate disposition. At first he was a delicate boy and clearly Ann's maternal instincts were directed towards him as she described him as being 'my constant care and delight' during his childhood. When he was five years old, John lost an eye as a result of an accident, the details of which are not known. Although he led a normal healthy life afterwards, this defect in his vision must have proved, both in conducting and organ playing, a serious obstacle but he never made it apparent. However, as will be seen, it did have an effect on his later professional life.

Ann describes their house in Southwark as at one time possessing five pianos, one with a full compass range of pedals, and a small chamber organ with a fine polished mahogany case and gilt pipes. Shortly before his death Stainer sketched this organ, one without pedals but with a lever on the right-hand side which was pressed to supply the wind. It was on this instrument that John had his first lessons in keyboard playing from his father. Ann recalls:

John used to watch him as he played the organ, and at the slightest indication of any hesitation he would say, 'Five shillings for a wrong note, dad!' My father always instilled into us that 'duty was the first thing' and this we have tried to carry out. As for my dear brother John, I cannot say anything too good about him.

A contemporary of Stainer's described the Stainer home as a very modest house:

. . . no green grass, no budding trees, no sound of singing birds about that neighbourhood! But inside that humble dwelling place, perfect love,

11

perfect harmony, and exuberance of mirth existed. It was a perfect holiday for me to go to tea with Stainer. His father was a schoolmaster of the old type. Wearied with his work among the unruly lads of that locality, he would come in, snatch up his violin and solace himself with playing a hymn-tune! Little Johnnie frequently came in at such a time, and would sit down at the pianoforte and accompany the good old father with his evening hymn. Of course, there was plenty of merriment over it; but I could see clearly enough that the old man was led by the influence of the little beloved disciple. Full of fun himself, a clever punster even at that early age, he nevertheless was the little child that seemed to lead them − his loving and devoted parents. His dear mother was devotedly fond of her boy, and it would be difficult for me to name amongst my acquaintances a more devoted, loving family than the Stainers. To know them made you better.[4]

The writer of this extract considered that Stainer's happy and ideal home life subsequently influenced him in writing such tunes as he wrote to the hymns *There's a Friend for little children*, *The Saints of God*, *Jesu, gentlest Saviour* and many others of deep religious feeling.

EARLY MUSICAL TRAINING

As a boy, John was keenly interested in church and religious music. His father often took him on to St Olave's Church, Southwark, when their own service at St Thomas's had finished so that he could hear the choral music and the organ being played. (There was no organ in St Thomas's at that time.) H. J. Gauntlett[5] was organist there but William Pole (Gauntlett's brother-in-law) often played and a chance meeting with Pole on one occasion was the beginning of a long and lasting friendship and professional relationship.[6] At that period Pole made great efforts 'to introduce music practically unknown'.[7] He wrote out the manuscript parts himself and had 'parties in his house to sing Bach cantatas (not easy to get at that time) [and music by] Mozart and early Italian composers'.[8] Stainer recalled that he used to go there and sing them as a child and 'I recall the pleasure he gave to many. He was a pioneer in the difficult task of teaching people what they ought to like . . .'[9] At one of these parties, on 6 March 1852, there was given the first complete performance in England of Bach's *Magnificat*. Pole recalled that he was 'amazingly struck by it' when he first saw it and arranged and wrote out the parts himself. Twenty-five singers took part, 'and on that occasion the alto part was kindly sung by Master John Stainer, a chorister at St Paul's, with whose skill and talent we were all delighted'.[10]

There is no record of what early musical or general education Stainer received apart from that which his father gave him. But as a chorister he attended the choir school at 1 Amen Court, the house in which he afterwards resided when he became organist of the cathedral. He recalled later that, despite the lack of the more favourable conditions that were to come about, the choirboys were really educated and that he owed it to the dean and chapter of St Paul's Cathedral that he never had to open a Latin or Greek grammar when he was reading for his arts degree at Oxford.[11] What is clear is that Stainer had uncommon musical ability, and at the age of seven he became a probationer in the choir of St Paul's Cathedral. In actual fact he was probably nearer to eight years old because his probationary period would not have exceeded one year and the fact is recorded that he was fully admitted to the choir (in those days informally in the Dean's Vestry) on 24 June 1849 at the age of nine.[12] Stainer, with an autobiography in mind, unsuccessfully tried to ascertain the date of the beginning of his probationary period, but records in those days were scantily preserved and improved slightly only when the Rev J. H. Coward became a minor canon of the cathedral and responsible for the education of the choristers, in June 1848.

At the time of his entry into the choir Stainer was already a competent young musician with varied musical skills. He had sufficient keyboard ability to play the Overture to Handel's oratorio *Acis and Galatea* and J. S. Bach's *Fugue in E*, the one referred to by Samuel Wesley as 'The Saints in glory fugue'. As to his actual singing ability we know little except that it was described as 'a pretty voice'[13] and that he was for a long time one of the soloists in the cathedral choir. Grove subsequently described Stainer as being, on his entry into the choir, 'already a remarkable player and an excellent sight-singer'.[14] As Stainer himself recorded, his success as a solo singer could have ruined his digestion for life, owing to the 'crowns, half-crowns and even half-sovereigns' that came his way after services from grateful members of the congregation following a favourite solo:

13

'Immediately after the service', said Sir John with a smile, 'I used to cross the road to the nearest pastry-cook's – our usual tuck-shop – followed by a crowd of boy friends; whose friendship at the moment was perhaps not altogether disinterested. We then found our way into the back parlour, and open and three-cornered tarts and lemonade were a few of the good things which crowned the entertainment' . . .[15]

The lifelong friendship between Stainer and the Rev Arthur Whitley began when Whitley expressed his admiration of Stainer's voice after hearing it at a service.[16] Charles Steggall[17] was also impressed and, on the recommendation of Mr Coward, master in charge of the cathedral choristers' education, Steggall used him for the performance of his degree exercise in Cambridge in 1851. Steggall obtained BMus and DMus in the same year, but this particular exercise was the one performed for his doctorate. Steggall recalls this occasion as his first acquaintance with Stainer although Stainer himself later recalled meeting Steggall earlier through The Bach Society (constituted in 1849 under William Sterndale Bennett):

Dr. Steggall certainly played sometimes – I cannot of course say always. But I admired Steggall's playing very much and I remember being for the first time introduced to him at one of those early rehearsals. Also I remember that he laughed heartily when I asked him whether he had *pedalled* all the running bass part of the chorus, 'Let lightnings and thunders'.[18]

However, Steggall recalled that:

Not only his [Stainer's] beautiful voice, but his general personality and manner, made a great impression in the University town, and I remember Professor Walmisley being much taken with him. Looking at him admiringly during lunch after the rehearsal, he turned to me with, 'What a sweet child it is, and what a pretty little pipe it's got!'[19]

In this exercise Stainer had to sing a long sustained high B flat. Steggall also recalled how impressively Stainer behaved at the dinner his father gave, following the performance of the degree exercise, to the London contingent of singers (several from the Royal Academy of Music) with Sterndale Bennett and others who had come to hear his work:

. . . he [Stainer] was noticed by everyone and how readily he answered a question in Latin, jokingly made by an undergraduate who showed his appreciation by handing a half-a-crown across the table . . . he had – even at that early age – a remarkable facility in extempore playing in the style of Bach, and very wonderful it was. [20]

Steggall, when he lectured on the subject of church or other choral music, invariably asked Stainer to assist him in the vocal illustrations.

Stainer sang, at the age of thirteen, in the first public performance in England of Bach's *St Matthew Passion*, 125 years after the time of composition. This – and his participation in the *Magnificat* at Pole's house – gave him the privilege of singing in two first performances in England of Bach's works. Stainer wrote an account of the preparations and performance of the Passion music, which took place under the auspices of The Bach Society in the Hanover Rooms, London, on 6 April 1854; Sterndale Bennett conducted. Stainer, writing to F. G. Edwards some forty years later, recalled:

I was only nine years old when The Bach Society was founded. I was one among the very first of those who regularly attended rehearsals, to which I was escorted by an elder sister.

The rehearsals were held in Store Street, or sometimes in Tenterden Street. But I have a most vivid recollection of a series of rehearsals held in Gray and Davidson's organ factory. At these Dr Steggall accompanied us splendidly on the organ, and once or twice, in the unavoidable absence of Dr Bennett, we were conducted by Oliver May. The Misses Johnston attended regularly and the *Passions-Musik* was in process of translation by them, fresh sheets of lithographed music being produced at each rehearsal. It was at one of these rehearsals at the organ builders that Hogarth said, 'Mr Bennett – couldn't we have a little expression in the chorales?' adding words to the effect that they were too beautiful to be sung at one dead level of sound. Bennett replied, 'Oh! yes, by all means: there are none in the original but I see no objection to some being introduced.' They were accordingly introduced but always included in a parenthesis (p) (f) etc and I think were so printed in the first English edition folio. This was the veritable origin of that over-done expression which ultimately turned these congregational chorales into fastidious part-songs, a genuine misfortune and a blot in the otherwise fine performances (in which I often took part as cembalist) in Westminster Abbey, Exeter Hall (under Barnby) and elsewhere. But I restored the chorales to their proper position in St Paul's when we produced it in 1873: making, of course, some contrast between the verses, and some expression in the lines but not enough to be a stumbling block to grand congregational singing.

But it may interest you to know that the public had become so accustomed to the 'part-song' treatment that my Dean (the late Dr Church) was told by a well-known amateur that I had utterly ruined the performances of the St Matthew Passion by not following *the varied marks of expression as given by Bach in the original score*!!! Fortunately the Dean mentioned to me the next day that a complaint had been made to this effect by Mr — so I soon had an opportunity of justifying myself. I have luckily preserved my card of thanks for taking part in the first performance. It is very tasteful.

My recollections as to the first performance are limited, and (worst of all) it was wretchedly rendered from beginning to end. Those troublesome little choruses led off by a rush of violins had been insufficiently rehearsed and were a series of catastrophes. The entrance of the strings when over-lapping the pianoforte in the Recits. was nearly every time a bungle.[21]

Stainer subsequently asked Edwards to suppress the remarks about a poor performance from the article in preparation for *The Musical Times* but thought that some credit should be given to Goldschmidt's first performance in England (1876) of the *Mass in B minor* in the Royal Albert Hall 'when Germans were brought over to play on their new long straight instruments' [German trumpets] . . .[22]

CHILDHOOD

Stainer's contemporary friends during his days as a cathedral chorister were Henry Gadsby (later to be an assistant vicar-choral under Stainer and also a minor composer) and Arthur Sullivan, although he was a Chapel Royal chorister and not in the cathedral choir. Gadsby later recalled some of their childhood pranks on their way home from the day school in Amen Court, there being at that particular time no boarding establishment for the choristers:

One of our chief diversions on our way home from school was to dance about on the timber logs seasoning in the river by Southwark Bridge, and allow ourselves to be rocked on them by the wash occasioned by the river steamers — and it was a miracle that we did not end our career in a watery grave.[23]

16

It was John Stainer's custom to travel from his home to St Paul's by steamboat on the River Thames which also provided many hours of leisure with Sullivan.[24] He and Sullivan were also organ pupils of George Cooper[25] who, by that time, had succeeded his father as sub organist at the cathedral. The lessons were given in St Sepulchre's Church, Holborn Viaduct (now known as the Musicians' Church) where Cooper was also organist. He saw the potential of the two young boys and predicted a great future in music for them, should that be their wish. One day, when he was giving a lesson to Stainer, he allowed Sullivan to be present and gave them a difficult theme on which to extemporise. Both worked it out to the 'intense satisfaction of the old organist, who exclaimed, ''I should like to live to see the race you two will run; for both of you will do something great'' '.[26]

But it was not all serious study; Gadsby remembered how he and Stainer were once caught jumping over chairs in the cathedral and on another occasion hiding in the pulpit; there were also light-hearted musical moments. Gadsby further recalled:

I well remember the happy musical evenings we used to spend together as boys at his father's house in St Thomas's Street; little Johnnie playing the Inventions and easy Fugues of John Sebastian on the pianoforte. We also used to play pianoforte duets – one of the favourites being the 'Hailstone Chorus'.[27]

As will be described later, the music during the 1850s at St Paul's was of a low standard and declined even further up to the time of Stainer's tenure as organist. He was later to recall the bad and slovenly attendance of the vicars-choral and minor canons, anthems performed at services with poor voices – and sometimes completely missing vocal parts – and to recollect how Handel's *Hallelujah* chorus was sung by 'a handful of boys and two men'.[28] But there were occasions that left their mark, such as the funerals of J. M. W. Turner in 1851 and the Duke of Wellington the following year. Also there were people at the cathedral who made a profound impression on him, namely John Goss and George Cooper who were responsible for his music teaching, and his masters, William Bayley, under whom he also studied harmony from the text-book written by Goss, and Mr Coward.

MUSICAL STUDIES AND MEETING WITH OUSELEY

There is no record available of Stainer's departure from the choir, but it is evident that he retained his association with the cathedral, occasionally playing the organ for services there. His lessons in organ playing continued under George Cooper, at Miss Maria Hackett's expense,[29] and at the age of sixteen he secured the appointment of organist at the old Wren church of St Benedict and St Peter, Paul's Wharf, where Mr Coward was also the rector and George Cooper had been a previous organist. He had, even at this time, a remarkable facility in extemporising on the organ in the 'manner of Bach'[30], and Mr Coward was much impressed by his musicianship and virtuosity.

It was probably at this time that he decided to study seriously for the musical profession and went to Charles Steggall for lessons in harmony and counterpoint.[31] Why he wrote much later that he never had a *'lesson* in the art of composition in my life, and have never had any one to whom I could go for advice'[32] is not quite clear. One assumes that no element of composition entered into these lessons from Steggall.

Undoubtedly the turning point in the career of the young Stainer was his acquaintance with Sir Frederick Ouseley, at the time Professor of Music at Oxford as well as Precentor of Hereford Cathedral, in those days both little more than titular offices.[33] Some years later Stainer recalled those early days in an after-dinner speech at the Royal College of Organists:

I first made his [Ouseley's] acquaintance when a small chorister boy in St Paul's Cathedral. He came to examine the choir boys and a few words of kindness, advice and encouragement which he spoke to me on that occasion were valuable to me for the rest of my life. I saw no more of him for some years until one day I happened to be playing deputy at St Paul's Cathedral (sometime in 1856) in the unusual absence of both Goss and Cooper. It was fortunate that those great lights were extinguished for that day. Sir Frederick Ouseley had come to ask whether either of them could recommend a young organist, and he came up into the organ loft, where he found me getting on very comfortably, and so, in the evening of that day, he wrote me a very kind letter, asking if I would play his organ . . .[34]

Stainer also recalled that at his first meeting, at the examination of the choristers, he was very nervous but managed to play 'a

Prelude and Fugue by Bach, from the "forty-eight", by memory . . .'[35]

Sir Frederick Arthur Gore Ouseley was born in London in 1825, son of the Rt Hon Sir Gore Ouseley, Bart, GCB, FRS, and succeeded to the title in 1844 while an undergraduate at Christ Church, Oxford. He took both arts and music degrees, obtaining his doctorate in 1854. His appointment to the professorship at Oxford in 1855 met with opposition from those who described him as a musical amateur, although he raised the standard of the degrees in music to a higher level than ever before and, even though a non-resident professor, spent more time in Oxford than his predecessors and also lectured more regularly. His compositions, in the main church music, were closely allied to those of Crotch, and while Stainer was later to comment on his brilliant gift in improvisation, the flair Ouseley showed there was lost when he attempted formal written composition. He was a keen and ingenious writer of canons, attempted more as a leisurely intellectual exercise than anything else. However, he is remembered now for the foundation, at his own expense, of St Michael's College, Tenbury, near Worcester, where the object of the foundation, as set forth in the printed statutes, was 'to prepare a course of training, and to form a model for the choral service in these realms; and for the furtherance of this object to receive, educate and train boys in such religious, secular and musical knowledge as shall be most conducive thereto'.[36] There, to an almost non-existent congregation, the services were rendered as beautifully as possible 'for the glory of God, and the offering would be none the less acceptable to Him because it came from an out-of-the-way spot in a remote country district'.[37] The college was founded in 1856 and Ouseley himself became the first warden; Stainer arrived there the following year succeeding the college's first appointed organist, Hanbury, who held the post for a few months only.[38]

Ouseley, a bachelor, devoted to the cause of church music, proved to be Stainer's 'fairy godfather' whose 'life was irreproachable, his example noble; in the sphere of historical knowledge of his art probably no contemporary surpassed him'.[39] Stainer, for his part, was extremely able and conscientious, and proved himself not only to be an efficient contributor in the running of the college but also a devoted and life-long companion to Ouseley, from whose vision, as Long says, he seems to have drawn life-long inspiration. His duties at St Benedict and St Peter's Church kept him in London until Michaelmas, 1857, when he became the organist at Tenbury at the age of seventeen.

ST MICHAEL'S COLLEGE, TENBURY

Stainer recalled his days there in the tribute he made to Ouseley shortly after his death:

In 1857 I found myself, after a railway journey to Worcester and then twenty miles on the top of a coach, settled in the charming building which he [Ouseley] had raised at his own cost for the advancement of church music. From it a short cloister led into a church of beautiful design, rich in carved woodwork and stained glass, containing a fine organ, and served by an admirable choir. Here, day by day, choral services of a high standard of excellence were maintained.[40]

To Stainer the life, at first, seemed primitive and medieval. Meals were served for the staff at high table with the boys in the body of the hall. He gave piano lessons to the boys in the afternoon and after evensong he studied or practised, often spending the evening with Ouseley. In Ouseley's music library[41] there was a collection of Italian masses in manuscript and in old clefs. Stainer played them to Ouseley, observing the master's critical remarks and learning much from them and him. He recalled that he gained much from the almost unique chance of studying the vocal writers from 1550 to 1700. At one stage Ouseley gave Stainer a guitar and arranged Bach's Prelude in C (from Book 1 of the 48 Preludes and Fugues) expressly for him and bearing this title: 'Bach's 1st Prelude. Arranged, for the guitar and carefully fingered by F.A.G.O.' At the end of the autograph copy Ouseley wrote in Latin: 'Ad usum amici Johannis Stainer aptatum praeludium hoc, quo melius quantum organis tantum etiam cithara praeter omnes emicaret D.D.D. amicus citharoeda Michaelensis'. (This prelude, adapted for the use of his friend John Stainer, in order that he might excel on the guitar no less than on the organ, was presented to him by his friend the guitarist of St Michael's.)

Apart from this aspect of his studies Stainer continued to work at the organ and piano and wrote a good deal of music, including several anthems; *I saw the Lord*[42] and *The righteous live* are the most notable. And he was fond of sporting activities and played cricket and tennis with boys and masters.

The Rev John Hampton, who succeeded Ouseley as warden, remembered Stainer when he arrived there:

He looked too young for the post, which we considered to be so very important. However, Sir Frederick assured us that 'he would do' and we soon found out that was true. All the while he was here I believe he was most sincerely loved by us all, and he was forward to help everyone with whom he came in contact. The curate, a first-rate mathematician, read with him and formed a very high opinion of his capabilities. We thought him bumptious, but we soon found that we were mistaken, for he was humble enough and seemed glad to be plainly spoken to by any whom he conceived had a right to speak. We were all right sorry to lose him and sincerely glad whenever he came to visit us.[43]

It was while organist at St Michael's that Stainer prepared for the BMus degree at Oxford, there being no residence qualification at that time. The exercise was completed on 19 October 1858 and performed on 9 June 1859 with the degree awarded on the following day. The text was part of Psalm 103, *Praise the Lord, O my soul*,[44] consisting of two five-part choruses, a quartet and semichorus and scored for flutes, oboe, clarinets, horns, trumpet, bassoons, timpani, strings and organ. It attracted little attention and was never published. As will be seen, his exercise for the doctorate took Oxford more by surprise.

2
Oxford, 1860–72

The next stage in Stainer's career begins with his taking up residence at Oxford, as Ouseley had done, to read for an arts degree. Again, through Ouseley's influence, Stainer was to be considered for the post of organist at Magdalen College. The president of Magdalen, Frederic Bulley, invited him for interview a few days before Christmas 1859, when, incidentally, the choir was still in residence, which gives some indication of the arduous nature of the task of those connected with chapel worship in those days. What Stainer had to do at the audition is not clear, but he was evidently viewed very favourably. Writing to Ouseley, the president said that of the three candidates to whom he had given leave to compete for the position of organist, Stainer was the one who appeared to be most suitable, being 'a person of good taste and judgement and capable of considerable development'.[1] The duties also required some teaching and training the choir, and to see how he acquitted himself in both, he was appointed first on a trial period of three months. The stipend was £120 per annum, increasing by £10 each year to £150. When Stainer left in 1872, it had in fact been increased to £200 per annum.

Bulley recommended that Stainer should matriculate at some other college because he could not be placed in the Commoners' list at Magdalen for some time and the expenses were too heavy, probably considerably more than Stainer could afford, 'the Commoners being for the most part people of independent means, tho' the system pursued is economical considering the class for whom it is intended'.[2] Bulley advised Stainer to matriculate at St Edmund Hall[3], but said that if he wanted to postpone this until he had been formally admitted as organist, that is, after the probationary period, Bulley would provide him with lodgings; he took these lodgings in Merton Street, at the house of Bulley's servant, Skinner, with the option of dining in hall at his own expense. Stainer took up residence for duties, beginning at early

22

prayers (when the communion service was sung) at 8.00am on the last Sunday in January 1860.[4] He was required to agree to resign anytime up to Christmas 1860 should the president request this and he was obliged to attend chapel on Fridays (when the services were sung without organ accompaniment) to direct the choir. The organist was required to instruct the choristers if no chaplain was available to do it but, in actual practice, the *informator choristarum* seems to have generally acted as organist, also receiving a stipend for his work in each capacity.

The period for which the choir was obliged to be in residence each term was longer than the statutory university term. The duties for Stainer were demanding and restricting in the sense that not only had he to conduct boys' practices and later the men (an Order of College was made on 7 May 1860 requiring the men 'to attend the practisings of the Quire when required by the Organist') but he also had to attend matins and evensong every day, except Wednesday when there was no morning service. There are no service lists available for the period of Stainer's tenure at Magdalen College Chapel, but in December 1857 the music there, directed by his immediate predecessor, Benjamin Blythe, included works by Ouseley, Crotch, Mendelssohn, Spohr, Handel, Boyce, Haydn, Hayes, Batten, Wesley, Green (sic) and Elvey, and there is every reason to suppose that Stainer would have widened the repertoire considerably, especially after full choir practices were instituted. The vast number of services that were required to be sung in the chapel over the course of a year would have required a large and varied repertoire.

One can only speculate what trouble may have arisen among the singing men at Magdalen when Stainer wanted to institute regular full choir practices. He may have received every consideration and co-operation as was to happen later at St Paul's, for contemporary accounts indicate that Stainer got on well with the choir and Parratt later stated that Stainer's major contribution to Oxford music was in Magdalen College Chapel. It is, therefore, strange that Parratt's biographer recalled that 'some of Stainer's troubles with the Magdalen choir fell to his successor to conquer'. His evidence for this is a letter from Parratt to his mother which would not seem to be conclusive and certainly does not indicate that Stainer left things in a state of disarray but rather that Parratt found the lay-clerks a trial at the beginning:

I have had some trouble with the lay-clerks and have had to be very sharp
with them. There are two specially disagreeable men who miss practices
and misbehave generally. Last night we had a frightful service . . . [when
it was discovered that one of the men was drunk] I see some months of
rather disagreeable work before me but I see after that a considerably
improved choir.[5]

How much time Stainer was able to get for choir practices is
not known, but one can assume that the boys were readily
available. The pattern in 1895 may give some indication: boys'
practices on Monday, Tuesday, Wednesday and Thursday,
10.50am to noon; one practice for men and boys, Friday,
2.00pm. There was a weekly total of sixteen hours spent on
services and practices.[6] The college chapel organ, on which
Stainer seemed to excel, had been installed by Gray and Davidson
in 1855 and incorporated no previously used pipework. It was not
a large instrument but 'singularly complete':

Indeed it would be difficult to mention another organ of which the
comparatively small contents are made to go so far, or in which, as
limited a number of registers place, by judicious contrivance, an equal
amount of effect in the hands of the solo performer.[7]

Stainer seemed to get on well with his university colleagues and
made a name for himself early on within university circles. In the
local newspaper he was referred to as 'the newly appointed and
highly accomplished organist'[8] and an old Magdalen chorister
wrote to Lady Stainer in the following terms in a letter of
condolence after Stainer's death:

One of the very first to see and know 'Mr' Stainer at Magdalen was
myself. Directly we choristers saw him and heard him we adored him
and did so ever after. Over and above his unapproachable playing, he was
one of the very few touched with the radiance of the inner life of sacred
music.[9]

This was the type of tribute paid to Stainer throughout his life.
He was a kind and considerate man who evidently had a way with
his colleagues and subordinates which got the best out of them.
He must have realised that he had this gift early on in his
Magdalen days, just as it was here confirmed to him that his real
forte was in church music. A career of some importance awaited
him. The *Manchester Guardian* commented much later on his

24

great success at Magdalen College, asserting that it was there that his extraordinary ability as a choirmaster had really become apparent and 'he raised the choir to a higher standard than had hitherto been known in the Anglican Church'.[10] In the earlier days there he had the additional burden of pursuing his classical studies for an arts degree. As already mentioned, Stainer's successor at Magdalen, Parratt, considered that his major contribution to Oxford music was in Magdalen College Chapel, which alone says much for his success there, especially in view of the valuable reforms he made later as professor of music.

On the death of Stephen Elvey, Stainer, then twenty, became on the recommendation of the vice chancellor, Dr Joune, Organist of the Church of St Mary the Virgin, the university church.[11] The post was linked at that time with the position of university organist and to receive it was no mean distinction for one so young. The university church was an important one in Oxford and had become particularly associated with the Oxford Movement, something which directly influenced the order of the services in St Paul's Cathedral in the 1870s.

ACADEMIC DISTINCTION

In 1861, Stainer went into residence at St Edmund Hall in order to read for his arts degree, with the result that he obtained his BA in 1864, proceeding to the Master's degree in 1866. He continued to work at his musical studies and on 7 November 1865 he was granted the Grace by the president of Magdalen College to enable him to proceed to the Doctorate.[12] The musical exercise was his oratorio *Gideon* and a selection from it was performed on 8 November. He received the degree on the following day.

It had been intended to perform the exercise in the hall of Magdalen College. In the event, interest was so great, and so many people turned up, that audience, soloists, instrumentalists, along with instruments, music and the rest, had to be moved in procession to the Sheldonian Theatre. Contemporary accounts of the proceedings showed that there was great excitement:

The exercise, however, being of a much more elaborate character than usual, it excited great interest; the Hall, consequently, was crowded before the appointed hour, the staircase was packed, and the cloisters were rapidly filling when the Vice Chancellor, who had had considerable difficulty in effecting ingress, adjourned the performance to the Theatre, it being next to impossible for all the performers to make their way through the crowd. The galleries of the Theatre were soon well filled and Mr Stainer, the Vice Chancellor and Sir Frederick Ouseley were warmly cheered on entering.[13]

There was not entirely universal acclaim for the work, although Oxford itself could find nothing to criticise either in the work or its first performance. One account described it as being 'of great merit and exceedingly well performed'[14] and another stated that: 'Throughout the piece the master mind of the composer was developed, which was illustrated by the rounds of applause drawn from the audience, comprising the musical talent of the university and city.'[15] The principal soloist was Miss Emma Jenkins from London 'whose solos thrilled her hearers with delight', and the choruses, sung by members of the university, were described as being perfect.[16] Mr Reinagle led a group of instrumentalists, some coming from London. Of the proceedings, the *Oxford Chronicle* perhaps gave a more picturesque account, but one which nevertheless did nothing to minimise the amount of public interest Stainer's *Gideon* had created:

Mr Stainer could not possibly squeeze in his band, although a rev. friend who assisted skilfully with the drums amused us with one or two attempts to beat a passage with his drum sticks. In his dilemma, Mr Stainer appealed to the Vice Chancellor, who, with his usual good nature, proposed an adjournment to the Theatre, inviting all who wished to hear the exercise to avail themselves of the opportunity. It was somewhat amusing to see, as the company passed up High Street, some of the undergraduates in their zeal shouldering the music stands in the 'flit'.[17]

This was the first large-scale choral work of John Stainer; no later works of a similar scale were to achieve such an 'exciting send off' as this one had done,[18] although the others did have a somewhat longer life. *Gideon* did not achieve notice nationally except for a scathing review in *The Orchestra* which dismissed the work as worthless and underlined the reviewer's contempt by giving more space in praise of a fifty-year-old exercise by Crotch:

26

Oxford has lost much ground in music. Take the exercise of fifty years ago, the 'Palestine' of Dr Crotch – and look at it well. Much of it is alive to this hour, and it is so because it is real honest work; genuine in its design, and felicitous in its execution; and what is still more important, the style is always dignified and elevated. There is no Zampa-like overture in the oratorio of 'Palestine'. In the oratorio under review there is no harmony, no dignity, no elegance; nothing to show solid acquirement, extensive reading or erudite research . . . 'Palestine' yet lives. 'Gideon' is dead.[19]

Members of Magdalen College, including the Rev H. R. Bramley and the Rev L. S. Tuckwell, both of whom were afterwards to become editorially associated with Stainer,[20] presented their organist with his doctor's robes, and the following letter signed by all his Magdalen friends:

We beg to offer you our warmest congratulations on your recent degree, and to request your acceptance of the appropriate robes, as a mark of sincere personal regard for yourself and high appreciation of your most successful efforts to sustain the musical reputation of this College and of the University of Oxford. With our united good wishes for your future happiness . . .[21]

MARRIAGE

The year 1865 was a momentous one in another way for Stainer in that he became closely attached to Eliza Cecil Randall (who was four years older), only daughter of Alderman and Mrs Thomas Randall of Oxford. There exists in manuscript a song which he wrote for and dedicated to her in February 1865, *'To sigh, yet feel no pain '*; with the propriety of the period Stainer sent it first to Eliza's mother with the following letter:

My dear Mrs Randall,
   I send with this a song which I have this morning indited for your young lady. The words are very old and very beautiful – the author's name is – I am sorry to say – unknown.
   If she doesn't 'fancy' it tell her to commit it to 'the devouring element'. It is to be sung at a 'goodish' pace. I hope your cold is better.
   Ever yours sincerely,
                                            John Stainer
P.S. Ask the young lady to withold her verdict till she knows it quite well.

Evidently she did like the song – and its composer – for she and John were married on 27 December 1865 at St Aldate's Church, Oxford, by Ouseley. It was a highly successful marriage both emotionally and domestically. Stainer wrote her long affectionate letters when he was away, showing he was capable of talking about domestic trivia, and they shared an interest in foreign travel, travelling extensively in Europe and making a visit to North Africa and to Egypt on their annual holidays.

Seven children were born to the Stainers, all of whom survived with the exception of one, Frederick Henry, who died in infancy. The eldest son, John Frederick Randall (1866–1939), although not a professional musician, could be described as an amateur musicologist of some distinction. He graduated in law at Magdalen College, Oxford and subsequently held a position in the public trustee's office. Elizabeth Cecil – Cecie – (1867–1937) was the author of *A Dictionary of Violin Makers* and, with her elder brother John, later helped Stainer with his work published in 1899, *Dufay and his contemporaries* and *Early Bodleian Music*. The other children were Ellie (1868–1928), Edward (1869–1948), Charles (1871–1947) and William (1873–1932). Edward married Rosalind Flora Bridge, the daughter of Sir Frederick Bridge, in Westminster Abbey on 1 June 1907. Bridge became deputy organist of the abbey in 1875 and succeeded Turle as organist in 1882. He and Stainer had been acquaintances for some time.

WORK IN OXFORD

After his marriage Stainer was to remain in Oxford for a little over five years before returning to London. During this time his musical activities widened. He became conductor to Magdalen College Musical Society[22] and founded the Oxford Philharmonic Society, conducting its first concert in June 1866[23] (the first Oxford public performance of Mendelssohn's *Elijah*), after which he handed the conductorship to James Taylor, New College. He also revived the Oxford Choral Society.[24] Additionally he was conductor of the Exeter College Musical Society and held similar posts in connection with the University Amateur Musical Society and the Oxford Orpheus Society which he founded in 1865. In 1870, in appreciation, the Oxford Orpheus Society presented to

Stainer a signed testimonial 'as a mark of their esteem, and as a trifling acknowledgement of his valuable services as the honorary conductor of the Society since its establishment'. They also presented him with an engraved silver inkstand mounted on a polished stand of black bog oak on two circular plates of silver, one on either side of the ink vase. When Stainer left Oxford, W. T. Allchin succeeded him as conductor of this society.

In March 1864, it was recorded that the Exeter College Musical Society had had a very poor year and was unable to give a concert; a large number of boys had arrived into the choir with little or no knowledge of music. Stainer was asked to help out and take over the conductorship, and in June 1865 the college commemoration concert was 'one of the most successful ones ever given in Exeter'. Stainer then handed over the conductorship to the college organist, F. S. Clark, but he proved to be unsatisfactory and at the society's meeting during the Lent term 1866, Stainer was again elected by a large majority to be in charge of their music. Such references as 'great energy', 'efficient conductor . . . had golden opinions both from audience and performers' and 'whose earnestness and zeal are always so conspicuous' bear witness to Stainer's success. He continued his relationship with the college until just before he left for London when he handed over his music charge again to James Taylor of New College.[25]

The beginning of Stainer's relationship with Hubert Parry took place through this society, Parry being an undergraduate at Exeter College. It was for the society's concert on 8 June 1869 that Stainer adapted, for performance in English, Schumann's *Das Glück von Edenhall* (The Luck of Edenhall), composed some fifteen years earlier. Stainer conducted the first public performance of this cantata in this country, Parry accompanying 'of course excellently' on the piano.[26] He also conducted a concert in June 1868 which included music by Parry (then still an undergraduate) and Mendelssohn, and he conducted more of Parry's music in April 1869, Parry commenting, 'Little Stainer conducted wonderfully'.[27] Stainer's interest must have been a great encouragement to the young Parry in his days as a student.

Other works presented by Stainer during those days with the College Musical Society included Mendelssohn, Choruses from *Antigone*; Purcell, *Come, Ye Sons of Art*; Haydn, *Spring*

Cantata; Mendelssohn, Overture *Ruy Blas* (piano duet arrangement with Stainer playing one part); Mendelssohn, *Athalie*; and Mendelssohn, Andante from *Reformation Symphony* (piano duet) – 'first time heard in Oxford and almost new to London'. Stainer often played piano duets with Parry at these concerts and on one occasion they played the piano duet version of Rossini's Overture to *William Tell*.[28] Through his connection with the society, Stainer became firm friends with Professor Donkin, FRS, a good amateur violinist, and Stainer was later to dedicate to him a string quartet, a work which is unpublished but which has received some performances in Oxford.

In June 1870, at the commemoration celebrations connected with the installation of the Marquess of Salisbury as chancellor of the university, Stainer and Corfe shared the conducting of the morning concert on 18 June, in a programme which included Beethoven's *Pastoral* Symphony and his *Violin Concerto* with Mendelssohn's Overture to *A Midsummer Night's Dream* and Weber's *Jubilee* Overture.

The undergraduates requested the orchestra to play something. They turned their attention to the platform where Sir Frederick Ouseley, Dr Corfe and Dr Stainer were seated in their dress robes. Sir Frederick and Dr Corfe were loudly cheered and a tremendous burst of applause greeted the mention of Dr Stainer whilst at the same time a wag lightly requested that the Choragus (at that time Dr Corfe) give the company a Corfe mixture![29]

The humour of this situation becomes more complete when it is revealed that Corfe, when playing the organ for services at Christ Church, invariably used the same organ stops. These were left drawn when the organ was not in use, in readiness for the next service. Not realising that one day Ouseley and some of his undergraduate colleagues had changed the drawn stops to the mutations (which he never used), Corfe began to accompany the psalms on those mutation stops, which included the mixture.[30]

Stainer was equally busy and successful in the musical activities of the town. He conducted performances of Handel's *Messiah* and Mendelssohn's *Elijah* and *St Paul* at important public concerts. He also did much charity work, organising and conducting concerts, the proceeds of which went to people in need. For instance, in February 1868 he organised a concert for Mr Grimmett, a player in one of the local amateur orchestras, and later in that year, on 8 June, he conducted a concert of vocal music, the proceeds going this time to the widow of Gwilym Carter, a college servant. One week later, with Magdalen College Chapel Choir, he gave a concert in aid of the Headington Church restoration fund.[31]

MADRIGALS AND GLEES IN OXFORD

During his Oxford period Stainer renewed an interest in madrigals and glees that had begun at Tenbury. He succeeded Blythe (the former Magdalen College Chapel organist) as the conductor of the College Madrigal Society which, in addition to singing for its own amusement, sometimes sang outside college. For instance, in November 1866 a concert was given in the university music room in aid of a new organ for St Giles's Church, for which £30 was raised.[32] He published a collection of eight madrigals in 1864,[33] one written for two choirs of five voices and the remainder for five, six and eight voices. His interest in this music was not restricted to composition: on 7 February 1865 he also founded the Maltese Glee Club and became the first conductor. There were twelve members; they met on Fridays, singing their first glee at 9 and the last at 10.30pm. Their rules included the proviso 'that the refreshments be limited to beer or other malt liquor and that they be provided at the expense of the host for the evening.'[34] Later they instituted the practice of having supper and inviting friends. Stainer conducted six concerts between 17 February and 31 March 1865 but on 19 May resigned in favour of Dr Corfe as 'my hands are so full of work'. W. A. Barrett, to be associated with Stainer in so many ways both at the cathedral and at the Board of Education, was also a member. The Maltese Glee Club ceased to function on 2 March 1866, still with Dr Corfe as conductor.[35]

Of a longer duration were The Magdalen Vagabonds, founded by the Rev Compton Reade, a one time chaplain at Magdalen College. They were Vagabonds 'for they wander from place to place; and the object of their wanderings is to obtain as much Coin of the Realm as they can extract from the pockets of the natives of the various places which they visit'. The first concert was in 1862 and the last in 1899, during which time hundreds of concerts were given and thousands of pounds donated to charitable objects. Stainer took part in the first concert at Titchfield, Hampshire, in July 1862, but it is not clear whether as conductor or as a member of the choir although the indications would seem to point to the former. Certainly he conducted concerts later until he was eventually succeeded by Walter Parratt. A tribute appeared to him in this connection with the following words:

For some years Dr Stainer joined us on our wanderings: and we do not know which to admire most in this gentleman, whether it was his distinguished musical talents, or the quiet and unaffected manner in which he displayed these talents.[36]

The choir numbered from sixteen to twenty singers, to whom were added on a few occasions some half a dozen of the choristers and a few musical friends from outside the college, but as a rule the group consisted of past and present members of the choir. Between 1862–75, on two occasions each year, after the Gaudy and after Christmas Day, they gave their concerts, visiting more than fifty towns including Romsey, Ryde, Yeovil, Leamington, Basingstoke, Rugby, Lutterworth, Birmingham, Bridgnorth, Folkestone, Glastonbury, Hereford and Taunton. During this period they collected more than £2,000. 'On the whole it may be said that the very noblest specimens of English glees and part-songs were performed',[37] and an example of the kind of programme they gave is shown in their first concert at Titchfield in 1862:

Part I

1	Madrigal	Adieu, adieu, my native shore	Pearsall
2	Part-song	I love my love in the morning	Allen
3	Song	How fair art Thou	Abt
4	Glee	The Bells of St Michael's Tower	Knyvett
5	Part-song	Spring	H. Smart
6	Part-song	Hydeldee	Marschner
7	Trio	Ti prego	Curschmann
8	Part-song	For the new year	Mendelssohn
9	Madrigal	Allen-a-dale	Pearsall

Part II

1	Madrigal	Down in a flowing vale	Fesca
2	Trio	L'addio	Curschmann
3	Song	Legend of the Avon	Dowland
4	Part-song	The Victor's return	Mendelssohn
5	Glee	Myn heer van Dunk	Bishop
6	Song	Come in to the garden	Balfe
7	Duet	The sailor sighs	Balfe
8	Part-song	Ave Maria	H. Smart
9	Part-song	The Hardy Norseman	Pearsall

WORK AS AN EXAMINER

Stainer was appointed a university examiner in 1867 and later became Examiner in Music for the Oxford Local Examinations. All these activities were additional to his duties at Magdalen College; and he was beginning to compose church music in a more extensive way than before. The evening canticles in E and E flat came from this period as did his edition of *Christmas Carols New and Old* (1872).

In Stainer's work as a university examiner, Hubert Parry was in the first batch of candidates to come before him; Ouseley and Corfe were also examiners. Parry was still a boy at Eton when he came to Oxford to take his BMus and Stainer recalled that 'we all thought him bright, intelligent and talented'.[38] There seemed to be a mutual affection between the two of them and Parry dedicated to Stainer a set of evening canticles in D major, written while still at Eton. Another candidate in that year (1867) was William Pole. He came to be examined for his doctorate in music. Stainer met him socially at Dr Corfe's house and it was on this occasion that Stainer mentioned to Pole that he thought there ought to be a 'musical society on the same lines as our learned societies'. This was the beginning of the (Royal) Musical Association, of which body Stainer subsequently served as president. In Stainer's own words, Pole 'encouraged the idea, and I promised that if ever I lived in London I would try to carry it out'.[39] This was the start of a long association with Pole even though Stainer was the younger by twenty-six years.[40] As mentioned earlier, Stainer, when a boy, had sung in Pole's concerts in the 1850s.

The music degree examinations in this period of Stainer's

Oxford life took place in the ancient 'Schola Musicae' which, like the other ancient examination rooms, was on the ground floor of the Bodleian Library. Stainer himself was examined in the same room in 1859:

... but I had the interesting experience of being examined in Law and History in the old 'Schola jurisprudentiae'. All these rooms are now part of the Bodleian. All examinations take place at the new examination Schools, High Street. It was in this Schola Musicae that the splendid musical library was stored; in cupboards fronted by wire-work over green baize! The cupboards were constantly left unlocked and the books were so neglected that it's a wonder any have come down to us. Dr Heather (founder of the Professorship) left all his books as a 'start' to it.[41]

Apart from his university duties and his work at Magdalen, Stainer was in constant demand elsewhere and there are frequent references to him in *The Musical Times* 1864–71 accompanying choral services and festivals and taking accompanying parts on the organ or harmonium in oratorios. When the foundation stone of Keble College was laid on 25 April 1868, Stainer was given the responsibility of the musical arrangements for the service. On 7 November 1868, he gave the first of many organ recitals at the Crystal Palace Saturday concerts. He played organ solos at these concerts, introducing Prout's *Organ Concerto in E minor* in October 1872 and Gadsby's *Concerto in F* in January 1874.[42] It was an innovation in 1868 to introduce organ recitals into the Saturday concerts, and it was through Grove's insistence that Stainer gave the first one.[43] He played Bach's 'Great' *Prelude and Fugue in G minor* (BWV 535) and Mendelssohn's *Fourth Organ Sonata in B flat* which met with much approval, as the following report indicates:

The experiment of an organ performance was entirely successful, thanks to the admirable playing of Dr Stainer. The Organist of Magdalen College is a master of his instrument. Neither the Sonata of Mendelssohn nor the Fugue of Bach presented any mechanical difficulties that were not conquered with perfect ease; while in point of style and finish there was nothing of which hypercriticism could complain. We may especially instance the Allegretto in the Sonata, and the whole of the Fugue as examples of the pure legato execution which is the *sine qua non* of organ playing. The works themselves are well known enough not to require description, and it therefore only remains to be said that Dr Stainer was applauded with marked emphasis at the close of his task.[44]

There is little doubt that although Stainer was a fine all-rounder, well respected as an academic musician and liked as a conductor, his real forte at that particular time was his organ playing. Hubert Parry, for most of his life responsible for keeping a diary, on his first meeting with Stainer wrote of him playing the organ 'gloriously'.[45] When he actually arrived in Oxford as an undergraduate it was Stainer who impressed him most as an organist in comparison with the organists at New College and Christ Church.[46] Alfred Hollins, the blind organist, also recalled Stainer's superb organ accompaniments to oratorios at rehearsals of the Royal Albert Hall Choral Society (to become the Royal Choral Society in 1888) as being 'wonderfully fine'.[47]

Even in his Oxford days Stainer acted as consultant in the building of organs and his advice was often sought by cathedral organists. In 1867 he assisted at St Cuthbert's Church, Doveridge, Derbyshire, when the whole building was reseated with open pews. 'The organ, built by Steele & Kay of Stoke-on-Trent, was placed on the west side of the Church; it was designed by the great Church musician, John Stainer, who often used to stay at Doveridge Hall with his friend Lord Waterpark.'[48]

REID PROFESSORSHIP AT EDINBURGH

When the Reid Professorship at the University of Edinburgh became vacant in 1865 it was hoped by many that the appointment would go to Stainer as one who appeared to possess the qualities the university authorities were looking for. There were twenty-one candidates for the post, among them Prout, Macfarren, Hullah, Gauntlett and Stainer.[49] Hullah, Macfarren and Stainer were all strong contestants and it was both a surprise and a shock when Herbert S. Oakeley, then comparatively unknown, was appointed by Mr Gladstone, chancellor of the university and chairman of the elective body, on his own casting vote. Stainer had 'a high professional reputation as a performer' and possessed the gift of extempore fugue playing in a degree 'by no means common at the present day' commented one newspaper supporting Stainer's claim.[50] It appeared later that S. S. Wesley was responsible for supporting Oakeley; Stainer had little time for Wesley whom he once described as a grumbler. Of H. J. Gauntlett he wrote: 'Like many other of these high-flyers, he thought *grumbling* was as good as work. Wesley was another; he was at three cathedrals and left each in a worse musical state than he found it.'[51] Oakeley's brother's account is a little different regarding the single casting vote giving the appointment to Oakeley, but it is clear that Gladstone had used his influence and powers of persuasion to 'resolve the at first somewhat discordant views of the University Court into a final concord of unanimous agreement.'[52] But Stainer was not a man to harbour resentment, and later he became a personal friend of the Gladstones as he subsequently related:

Mr Gladstone and his dear wife were most kind to me and mine when we were in London, 1872 and onwards, and I was very much gratified to receive an invitation from the Gladstones to attend the funeral [of W. E. Gladstone in 1898] as a *friend of the family.* I had one of the best seats in the Abbey . . . I travelled from Aberdeen (500 miles) on the night of Friday to attend the funeral on Saturday and returned to Glasgow (400 miles) the same night.[53]

MAGDALEN COLLEGE CHAPEL

Had the offer not come for Stainer to go to St Paul's Cathedral in 1872, at the age of thirty-one, it seems very likely that he would have secured some other preferment, either in academic life or as a cathedral organist. He was eminently suited and qualified to follow either career. His influence in Oxford itself was considerable and he certainly assisted Ouseley to bring respectability to the music faculty there.

In the first instance, however, he came to look after the music in Magdalen College Chapel and he probably regarded this as his main duty. Canon Scott Holland recalled how in his own Oxford days the quality of the music in chapel was outstanding: ' "fragrance" and "magic" are the words that again bring back to me the tone of that wonderful music'.[54] Sir Hugh Allen considered, as Parratt had done, that when one reviewed the main achievements of three earlier Oxford professors of music, Ouseley, Stainer and Parry, Stainer was to be remembered during his first Oxford period particularly for the way he improved college musical life, not only in chapel but in secular music also.[55] Edward Chapman's account, to follow, is further evidence of the quality of the musical performances in Magdalen College Chapel.

It is strange, therefore, that Stainer's successor, Walter Parratt, should have found difficulties when he went to Magdalen and also that at one stage towards the end of his time there, Stainer himself should speak somewhat disparagingly of the choir. When J. F. Bridge (later Sir Frederick) was Organist of Manchester Cathedral and became interested in the idea of, at sometime, succeeding Stainer at Magdalen, he was told by Stainer that:

... although Magd. ought to consider you a real 'catch' – if you give up your present position for my old shoes I should consider you nothing short of a donkey. Nothing like plain speech! You would have half the income, a worse choir! and twice the responsibility coupled with a most expensive place to live in. This is private.[56]

In view of this letter it is surprising to learn that Stainer urged Parratt to apply for the Magdalen post[57] even though there was some doubt whether, financially, he could do as well at Oxford. He was slightly older than Bridge and although he held an important parish church appointment at Wigan, he had not been a cathedral organist. Bearing in mind also that Manchester had been a cathedral city for only twenty years and had, therefore, not established a musical tradition comparable with Magdalen's, it is difficult to understand why Stainer should try to deter Bridge moving to Oxford. If the Magdalen choir was worse than that of a new cathedral, it seems curious that it should attract so much praise from intelligent men.

Edward Chapman, MP, one-time tutor at Magdalen, described Stainer as the 'life and soul of several musical societies' in the city and university, and one who did much for reviving an interest in madrigals and the singing of part-songs. But what impressed him most was Stainer's manner of accompanying the chapel choir at college services. His accompaniment to the psalms received special mention and his extemporisations 'exceed in beauty any of his written compositions'. As to the psalms:

The chant first simply played through, say, on the choir organ, would then become a wonderfully harmonised interpretation of the words, no brilliant or dashing execution; but if I may call it an inverted and dispersed harmony on the solo or choir organ, no two verses alike, but sustaining and truly accompanying the choir ...[58]

Chapman also spoke of Stainer as a man of deep piety and devotion, as one who felt himself to be very much part of the worship to which he was contributing.

On leaving Magdalen, Stainer was presented with a clock with matching drawing-room ornaments. The presentation was made in Stainer's rooms in the presence of senior members of the college, when it was said that Stainer's 'kindly disposition and affability of manner endeared him to all who had the pleasure of knowing him.'[59] The testimonial from members of college, meeting on 12 March 1872, expressed 'their sense of the great zeal and ability' Stainer had shown as their organist.

3
Music in St Paul's Cathedral

In each position that John Stainer held he established higher musical standards. Nowhere was this more impressively exemplified than at St Paul's after his return to the cathedral as organist in 1872. This was a time of great change in the cathedral, and in the space of two years a new chapter came into existence determined to see whether the full capacities of the building might not be brought into the service of splendid worship. Stainer was fortunate to return at a time when he knew that he would have the support of the dean and chapter in his reforms, and his policy and determination fitted in nicely with the new circumstances.

Canon Scott Holland, on the occasion of the unveiling and dedication of the memorial to Stainer in December 1903, spoke of Stainer's boyhood in the cathedral when slackness was at its height – 'they were weird crabbed days, when the boys could roll their pennies in a race from the Dome to the West Door, down the gaunt, solitary Nave, without fear of obstruction.'[1] From that time things were to get worse; the careless approach to and lack of dignity in worship was to reach its peak in the last days of Goss as organist there. And then the revolution came and a reversal took place. As Scott Holland described it:

The music had hitherto been a tiny trickle of sound tinkling along in a dim corner to the favoured few. It was to become a tidal flood, possessing and pervading and ensouling the entire fabric with the spirit of praise and thanksgiving. The old school of music could not conceive the task, and it withdrew in dignity and honour in the person of one who will always be revered in St Paul's – Sir John Goss. Stainer was given a free hand to do all he could by a Chapter that entirely trusted him. The wonderful thing is the pace at which he accomplished his work. By help of his personal fascination and flawless temper he had brought it all about within a year. He started the Choir School himself; the Choral Eucharist filled the Dome; the Voluntary Choir for the great Evening Service was drawn together by personal attachment to him; and within hardly more than a year he had already attempted the great 'Passion' music of Bach.[2]

39

Such is the summary of Stainer's contribution. The difficulties that beset him and how he overcame them must now be described. Here again it will be seen how inseparably Stainer's success as a musician was bound up with the warmth and humanity of his character, and with the love and respect he inspired in others by his tact and through the example he set in the unassuming and diligent way he tackled his work. There are many musicians within the Church – and not only musicians – who forget the operative word 'church' in their work; Stainer was not one of these. His bearing and example were those of other great Christian men and it is, perhaps, above all as an exemplar that he can be justly set above most other musicians of his time.

THE OXFORD MOVEMENT

Stainer came to St Paul's at a crucial moment. Had the chapter not changed significantly, it is doubtful whether he would have left Oxford at all. He would have known that the musical improvements he wanted to make would have been impossible without the strong support of a dean and chapter. But the style of worship was changing and a consequence of the Oxford Movement within the Church was that it brought more dignity to worship, paying more attention than before to the liturgy, one side effect of which was to give some importance to the value of music within the service. There were sound theological reasons for the changes in emphasis away from the evangelical approach to one which put the Holy Communion service foremost in its worship, but it was the importance given to beauty and dignity in worship that brought about the changes in the standards of musical performance. As Professor Owen Chadwick summarised:

Certainly the principal changes which it brought in English life were changes in the mode of worship, or in the understanding of sanctity, or in the consequent methods of religious practice; and the changes of theological or philosophical thinking were by comparison less far-reaching.[3]

Another factor which contributed to the introduction of more music into the services (though not in itself responsible for improving the standard of it) was the mass production of musical scores. Vincent Novello, through his connection as organist at the Portuguese Embassy Chapel in South Street, Grosvenor Square, London, became conscious of the difficulties entailed in performing Viennese masses and began to think seriously of their publication in England. From this idea there was eventually established the publishing house of Novello, who realised that music sold in large quantities could be made inexpensive. By introducing type-setting to replace engraving, his firm was able to begin publishing cheap octavo copies of choral works in 1846.[4]

THE STANDARDS OF CATHEDRAL MUSIC

During the four hundred years that have elapsed since the Prayer Book was first introduced, daily choral services have taken place within English cathedrals. The statutes and endowments of the cathedrals provide for such choral services and, apart from the Cromwellian period, they have continued unbroken. The low musical standards associated with the eighteenth and nineteenth centuries significantly coincided with the decay of spiritual and religious life of the Church of England;[5] the progress of recovery in the cathedrals was inevitably slow.

When cathedral deans took pains to appoint clergymen who were interested in the musical side of the cathedral services, the services tended to improve in standard. In the early part of the nineteenth century Bumpus recalls the evidence of one worshipper in Norwich Cathedral who spoke highly of the canons who sang the services:

Well do I remember the delight with which I used to listen to the service in Norwich Cathedral, when the minor canons, eight in number, filed to their stalls. Precentor Millard at their head, whose admirable style and correct taste as a singer I have never heard surpassed; Browne's majestic tenor; Whittingham's sweet alto, and Hansell's sonorous bass . . . Walker's silvery tones and admirable recitation found their way into every corner of the huge building . . .[6]

In contrast to this situation we have that in Rochester Cathedral in which only one minor canon attended the services each week and the versicles and responses and prayers were not intoned by him although the choir did actually sing the responses. Two services, *Aldrich in G* and *Rogers in D*, had been sung in rotation for a twelve-year period preceding 1790 when Ralph Banks was appointed organist.[7]

An early clerical reformer in matters relating to dignity in worship was Bishop Hamilton, whose name is closely associated with cathedral matters of that period. W. K. Hamilton (1808–69), appointed Canon Treasurer of Salisbury in 1841 after having acquired parochial experience at St Peter's in the East, Oxford, subsequently became Precentor and then Bishop (in 1854) of Salisbury. He played an important part in the early reforms of cathedral establishments, and during his time as precentor he took meticulous care in the service music and conduct of the services. As his biographer, H. P. Liddon, recalled: 'Every chant and anthem that was used during his precentorship was selected by himself, and upon the principle of making the music and anthems, so far as might be, illustrate the Church's seasons, or the prominent features of her teaching, in the daily services.'[8] Hamilton also gave much time to making friends with the boys and men in the choir at Salisbury, 'with a view to leading them to feel their high privilege in taking so prominent a part in the worship of God, and to replacing the perfunctory and irreverent spirit which is too common in cathedral choirs, by a sincere and earnest devotion.' Later it was at Hamilton's suggestion that choristers live together in one of the houses in the Cathedral Close under the care of a clergyman-schoolmaster; prior to this taking place they had lodged at different houses within the city of Salisbury.[9]

Hamilton attended the daily services in the cathedral with unfailing regularity and set a good example to others in this respect; wherever he instituted a new service he made himself responsible for the performance of it and he strongly held that the dean and residentiary canons should not have outside livings. During this period at Salisbury, evensong during the week (except on Tuesdays) was always attended by a residentiary canon, one vicar-choral (presumably at that time a clergyman singing in the choir), five laymen, eight choristers and two probationers,[10] which would seem to be a more orderly and effective arrangement than in most cathedrals of the day.

Sebastian Wesley, alongside Bishop Hamilton, was an important musical reformer. Following the surveys of Jebb on cathedral music,[11] Wesley gave some words of advice to cathedral authorities in his *A Few Words on Cathedral Music and the Musical system of the Church, with a Plan of Reform*. The basic plan, although too idealistic, had elements in it which St Paul's and Stainer were to adopt later on. The main points were:

1 That every choral foundation should provide for at least twelve men, salary £85–150 per annum so that they need not take up further employment. Selection should be by the cathedral organist and two other nearby cathedral organists. There should be three deputy choirmen in case of sickness and other emergency. Enthusiastic and competent amateur singers could on occasion augment the professional choir.

2 'The Cathedral Organist should, in every instance, be a professor of the highest ability', elected by seven nearby cathedral organists. The annual salary should be between £500–800 and higher for the organists of St Paul's Cathedral and Westminster Abbey. 'The artists [cathedral organists] are the bishops of their calling . . .'

3 A college should be founded for the training of all types of cathedral musicians.

4 There should be adequate financial resources to cover education of choristers, music and the upkeep of organs. Every cathedral should have its own full-time music copyist.[12]

ST PAUL'S CATHEDRAL – EARLY NINETEENTH CENTURY

Much of the trouble in St Paul's Cathedral, as elsewhere, emanated from the clergy themselves. Their attendance was far from adequate and gave every scope to the choirmen to behave in a similar way. While the attendance of the boys was satisfactory, though not their general demeanour, the men took advantage of the situation until they had almost established for themselves a right to be absent even on their attendance days. At St Paul's, the dean[13] in the 1830s was also Bishop of Llandaff and, therefore, was often absent at his see. His interests could by no means be said to be concentrated on St Paul's Cathedral.

In addition to the singing being quite undisciplined there seemed to be no general order. No regular weekly music lists were published at this time, and sometimes anthems, often inappropriate to the season, were chosen during the service, the choice itself being made with the object of showing off individual voices in the choir. For this reason verse-anthems were preferred and at certain periods full anthems were seldom or never heard. Because of the lack of choir practices the solo singing might have been admirable but the interspersed choruses in anthems were lacking in precision and finish.[14]

The music in the cathedral was at its lowest ebb from the time of Thomas Attwood's latter years there and during the period when John Goss was organist. There was little they could do to stop the decline, although soon after his appointment Goss wished to introduce some 'salutary reforms into the services which were carried on in a most perfunctory manner. But his suggestions, though kindly listened to by Sydney Smith and other members of the Chapter, were never acted upon.'[15] In any event, the organist's duty lay solely in playing the organ for cathedral services; what training there was of the choir (and then never the men) was not his responsibility. There was no proper recruitment of the boys and the overall direction of the music within the cathedral lay, in actual practice, in the hands of no single person. When Stainer was appointed, the attitude of the chapter had changed and plans were made immediately to regularise all that pertained to the choir and the music. Had Attwood and Goss had this support they would probably have done better. Stainer thought that Goss certainly would have.

CHANGES IN THE CATHEDRAL CHAPTER

The initial turning point was the appointment of the Rev Robert Gregory to a canonry of St Paul's in December 1868. He recalls that his installation took place 'on a specially dark evening of the shortest day of the year'[16] after evensong, only his family being present. He describes it as 'a more miserable and disgracefully slovenly service I never saw'. He was advised that St Paul's was 'an Augean Stable that nobody on earth can sweep, therefore let things take their course and do not trouble about them'.[17]

Gregory appreciated that example must come from the dean and chapter attending the services regularly, and that this would be a good influence on all the others on the staff, clerical and lay alike. He was aware of W. K. Hamilton's work at Salisbury and determined to follow his example in ideal and method. Gregory's own first impression was confirmed by everything he saw afterwards in those early days. Neither clergy nor choir wore cassocks under their surplices, and there was little or no order of movement. The canon came from his vestry, the minor canons and choir from theirs, and they met at the mouth of the choir, latecomers taking their seats as they arrived. Continuing in Gregory's own words:

The choir was wretched; it consisted of six or eight boys and two, three or four men, just as they happened to turn up. The appointed music had sometimes to be changed, because there were not men of the right voice to sing what was appointed . . . No voluntary was played as the clergy and choir entered the church; and the choir men read letters and talked during the service.[18]

Gregory was not popular with the chapter, who suspected him of having too much energy. He refused to hold any ecclesiastical living other than his canonry, although it was still the custom for the clergy to do this, and he was determined to give all his time to the cathedral and improve the state of things. During his month of residence in 1869, incensed by the fact that at the two services on All Saints' Day, a major festival of the Church, there were only two choirmen present at either of the services, he summoned the choir and told them that he thought that the services were becoming a public scandal and that it was a weighty question as to whether the services had not better be discontinued.[19]

I was in residence and, being very much annoyed at the miserable attendance of choirmen on All Saints' Day, on the following morning, instead of following the virger into the Dean's vestry after the conclusion of the service, I turned the other way when coming out of the choir and accompanied the choir into the south aisle, where they vested; then, closing the iron gate, I asked all present to remain for a few minutes as I had something to say to them. I then spoke of the disgraceful attendance of the singing men, and the miserable services we had in consequence. I then proceeded as quickly as I could to a meeting of the Ritual Commission which met that morning, thinking no more of what had happened. Returning home from the Ritual Commission, I saw to my surprise on the placards of the evening papers at the news shops the announcement of 'Extraordinary proceedings at St Paul's'. I instantly procured a paper, and then read all that I had said to the choir. This seemed to attract general interest, as it was copied into newspapers all over the country. I had papers with it in sent me from distant parts of Scotland. My colleagues were much scandalised at the publicity thus given to the state of things at St Paul's, and Archdeacon Hale proposed that we should revive the discipline Chapter that for many years in old times used to sit every Saturday. This was done, and that Chapter has very usefully sat on every Saturday since that time, and has taken note of all lapse of duty during the preceding week. [20]

Small improvements came by tighter control of the vicars-choral; they were told that from 28 November 1869, the choir and clergy would form a procession in and out of service with an organ voluntary on each occasion and that there would be a record kept and a note made of unpunctuality and absenteeism. But at this stage only small reforms could be initiated and the music continued to be unworthy and badly received.

In 1870, H. P. Liddon was appointed a canon of St Paul's, a post which he held until his death in 1890. Earlier in 1870 he had given some lectures at St James's church, Piccadilly, where 'in spite of the abnormal length of each lecture the church was thronged, and the effect on the educated people of the west end of London was profound'. [21] Apparently the crowds that had listened to him there came to hear his first sermon at the cathedral and filled the choir which at that time was the only part of the cold and uninviting cathedral that was used for anything other than very big services. On the second Sunday in September 1870 Liddon 'moved out to a pulpit under the dome and thus forced the change, which has since become permanent, of using the main body of the Cathedral for all services'. When Dean Church was appointed he evoked Liddon's loyalty and 'he threw all his ardour into the revival of the full devotional use of the cathedral'. [22]

Early in January 1871, the chapter sought legal advice in the form of counsel's opinion as to the power of the dean and chapter 'to punish Mr Francis [a vicar-choral] for disobedience to their injunctions' and to examine 'the proper means of giving legal force to such rules as the Dean and Chapter may hereafter prescribe for the regulation and government of the Choir'. [23] There was also a move to examine the freehold of the vicars-choral in order to attempt to restrain them from holding similar appointments in other foundations such as Westminster Abbey and the Chapels Royal, [24] often a reason for the vicars-choral either being late for service or leaving early. Later in the year Canon Gregory made formal plans for a 'musical service appropriate to the Season in the Cathedral during Holy Week'. The performance of the *St Matthew Passion* of J. S. Bach in Holy Week began in 1873

46

under Stainer and has continued for over a hundred years.

Two final changes on the cathedral staff in 1871 helped to make Gregory's vision of a new St Paul's more nearly a reality. On the death of Dean H. L. Mansel, who had been dean for only three years, R. W. Church was appointed, and following the resignation of Goss, John Stainer was appointed organist. Both appointments provided the chance for more rigid control of the choir and improvements in the standard of worship. Church, after an academic life at Oxford, had become Rector of Whatley in 1852. From all accounts he was a quiet man, conscientious in parish work yet retaining his academic pursuits. He was not the kind of man to expect or pursue preferment and was surprised to be offered the deanery by Mr Gladstone. Dean Church was associated with the Oxford Movement, though not at its beginning, and wrote a history of it in 1891. Through this appointment, along with those of the other new canons, St Paul's came to be regarded as 'High Church', a reproach also levelled against Stainer. Other outward signs were the introduction of choral celebrations of the Holy Communion services, candles on the altar and 'increased elaboration of Christmas and Easter decorations' [25], all these features receiving critical attack in the press at the time.

Writing to his friend, Dr James Mozley, on 31 August 1871, Church shows that he had a full knowledge of the situation at the cathedral; it would be a 'very tough practical business, and I am not to be as other Deans have been'. The task, as he saw it, was to set the cathedral in order to fit it to be in the eyes of the country *the* great English cathedral. This is what Gladstone had in view and what canons Liddon, Gregory and Lightfoot expected of Dean Church. He set himself three tasks: to put the financial side of things in order, to carry out the architectural restoration at the cost of about a quarter of a million pounds, and 'to fight and reduce to order a refractory and difficult staff of singing men, etc., strong in their charters and inherited abuses. I don't mean that all this is to be done single-handed, but the responsibility will fall upon the Dean'. [26] Later, writing to his friend Dr Asa Gray, the American botanist, Dean Church said:

St Paul's is a big ship to command. I hope things are mending a little in it, but there is much to be done, and much to fight about, which is not much in my line. But I must be satisfied if I leave it a little, only, better than I found it. I hope I may do that. [27]

47

4

Stainer at St Paul's

It is possible that Stainer may have had some warning of the impending departure of John Goss and some hint of the likelihood of succeeding him. Stainer's correspondence with Bridge appears to suggest this[1] and there seems little doubt that the cathedral chapter would wish Goss to go so that it could effect improvements in the service music without delay. The resignation of Goss was accepted by the chapter on 2 December 1871. He gave as his reason the increase in the number of services, which he felt he could not cope with at the age of seventy-one, especially as he had other commitments. The dean and chapter agreed to his retaining 'the name of Organist of St Paul's on the condition that he in no way interferes with the organ or choir of the Cathedral; and that he be permitted to retain his office of vicar-choral without being responsible for any of its duties'.[2] This was to affect Stainer's own position on appointment. Goss had received £250 per annum salary but the chapter increased it for the new organist to £400 per annum, providing 'he undertakes the whole musical instruction and superintendence of the Cathedral Choir and that he is available whenever his services are needed at the Cathedral and that he accepts no other appointment'.[3]

George Cooper, who had been assistant to Goss since his appointment in 1838 and had been Stainer's own organ teacher, applied for the post of organist at, he said, the suggestion of Goss.[4] He would appear to have been well qualified through his long association with the cathedral from the time of the Attwood period. He was, also, organist at the Chapel Royal. From the appointment of Goss to the appointment of John Dykes Bower in 1936, George Cooper was the only assistant organist (or sub organist as the post was often designated) who was not elevated to the post of organist. However, the final minute of the meeting which had considered Cooper's application said: '*Resolved* that Dr John Stainer be elected Organist of St Paul's Cathedral at a salary of £400 a year commencing at Lady Day next'.[5]

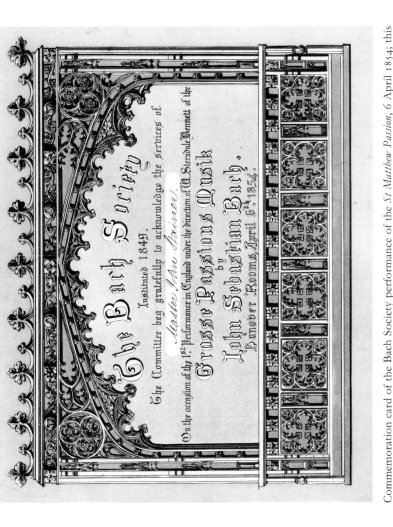

Commemoration card of the Bach Society performance of the *St Matthew Passion*, 6 April 1854; this was the first occasion the work had been performed in England. Stainer was thirteen at the time and a singer in the choir

(above left) Sir Frederick Ouseley, Bt (1825–1889), Stainer's great patron and lifelong friend. The founder of St Michael's College, Tenbury Wells, he appointed Stainer college organist in 1857 (the approximate date this picture was taken); *(above right)* Stainer (seated) in 1864, the year he obtained his BA at Oxford. Beside him is Robert Brown, an Oxford don; *(below)* The Magdalen College Chapel Choir, 1865. Stainer is standing, second row on left, wearing a boater

It is possible that Ouseley may have put Stainer's claims forward – this was suggested at the time by a correspondent to *The Musical Standard* who referred to Stainer as 'a member of a university and a protegé of the Reverend Baronet'[6] – but it is not quite clear how much influence Ouseley had upon his fellow clerics. The chapter may have preferred to appoint someone who was known to them rather than listen to any outsiders. George Cooper had not only the apparent support from Goss but was also favoured by some of the vicars-choral who referred to his 'great experience and undoubted abilities' making him the 'proper successor' to John Goss.[7] However, the chapter were evidently wanting someone more able to carry out their reforms and its members would have been able to see the advantages in appointing someone outside the cathedral circle.

One wonders whether Stainer really wanted the post. He was thirty-one years of age, married with a young family, firmly settled in Oxford life and well thought of there. He would have known only too well the state of music in the cathedral and that reform would be an uphill task. On the other hand, a man of Stainer's energy must have needed a challenge at this time and most probably would not have felt able to resist this once he knew that the chapter wished to appoint him. Furthermore, the majority of his compositions at that time were for the Anglican Church services and St Paul's would give him wider opportunities than a college chapel. And a move to London would put him into the heart of things.

However, there seems little doubt that it was Canon Liddon who was largely responsible for Stainer's being appointed to St Paul's. When he first went to Oxford he became a member of St Edmund Hall in order to read for his arts degree, and it was there that Stainer later came into close contact with Liddon with whom he studied. The two men had become firm friends. *The Guardian*, in an obituary article contributed by Canon Scott Holland,[8] spoke of that period:

In 1870–2 three men were gathered together in St Paul's who were of one mind, and were determined to show what a cathedral could be in the midst of a city like London. There were Dean Church, Canon Gregory and Dr Liddon. When Sir John Goss resigned in 1872 they needed the services of an organist who would appreciate the work for their ideal, and they found what they wanted in the organist of Magdalen.[9]

51

Whatever the circumstances leading up to the appointment, Stainer attended the chapter meeting on 28 December 1871, and 'having received from the Chapter all needful explanations signified his acceptance of the office of Organist'.[10] It was said that Stainer had declined to accept the appointment unless he was offered the first vacant vicar-choralship. He held a freehold office (an appointment for life) at Magdalen, but the post offered at St Paul's was not a freehold one as it was not then mentioned in the statutes. The custom had arisen whereby to safeguard his position, the organist was given additionally the post of vicar-choral; although the chapter wanted this custom to cease, rather than lose Stainer they gave way on this point.[11] So Stainer accepted the appointment on the understanding that he would also be appointed vicar-choral as soon as there was a vacancy. The chapter hoped that Stainer would retain George Cooper as assistant organist, at £100 per annum, but the decision was left to him.[12]

Stainer's appointment was well received although 'like most reformers, Stainer had to face a certain amount of opposition on his appointment from those who worked with him.'[13] And now that Goss was going, his faults did not appear so great. He certainly left in a blaze of glory for one of his last acts was to write a *Te Deum* to be sung at a thanksgiving service for the recovery of the Prince of Wales. (Gounod wanted a *Te Deum* of his sung, but this was declined.) The service took place on 27 February 1872, just one month before Stainer's arrival on 25 March, after which Goss received a knighthood from Queen Victoria and became the only knight living in Brixton, as he was fond of remarking. Stainer was present at the thanksgiving service. *The Musical Times* hoped that Goss would not give up composition: 'the service-music of so consummate an artist can scarcely be too much multiplied . . . .'. Stainer they welcomed as an 'able musician and excellent organist; little doubt could exist that he would conscientiously fulfil his duties and worthily uphold the dignity of the responsible position as Organist at St Paul's'.[14] Another welcoming notice said of him that 'as an extempore fugue player he stands in the foremost rank' and much applauded the fact that he possessed an arts degree in addition to having passed the 'usual musical examinations'.[15] *The Times* welcomed Stainer and did not doubt that he had the capacity to effect 'the much needed improvements in the choir and musical services'.[16] The paper described his brilliant powers as an organist with which 'no Oxford resident during the last twelve years can be entirely unacquainted', and, because of his book, *A Theory of Harmony* (1871), he held a high reputation as a scientific musician within the profession. In common with other welcome notices, mention was made of his youthfulness and boundless energy.[17] The journal *The Choir*, in congratulating both the chapter and Stainer, described him as a 'profound musician, a facile composer and a very fine executant'; they considered him one of the most accomplished organists of the day. His playing in Magdalen College Chapel on Sundays was 'well known as one of the most constant subjects of attention among musical residents and visitors'. In the selection of music for chapel he took a moderate attitude to the old and new styles of church music; and in the singing of the psalms at service, where he had a special interest, they hoped to see much improvement at St Paul's 'where, at present, this most important portion of the services has reached the lowest point of slovenliness. The choir, as they showed last Sunday afternoon, cannot even sing the Amens with ordinary care and decency . . .'[18]

The Musical Standard also welcomed Stainer's appointment and congratulated the dean and chapter on their selection and also on the manner of making the appointment:

Competition is of very questionable use, even when it is desired to test the abilities of unknown men; but in the case of filling the vacancy at St Paul's it is entirely unnecessary. Public opinion would not tolerate an obscure man as organist there, and to attempt a competition among gentlemen at the head of the profession would be fruitless.[19]

But some criticism of the appointment denounced the lack of open competition. The editorial view in this instance, however, seems very sound. It went on to acclaim Stainer as a thorough churchman, 'an accomplished player, a thoughtful and original writer, whose compositions, both for organ and choir, display considerable skill', and concluded by saying that his appointment 'reflects credit on the authorities who have made the selection'.[20]

The great writer of hymn tunes, the Rev J. B. Dykes, who had worked with Stainer in their revisions of various editions of *Hymns Ancient and Modern*, writing to his brother, Frederic,

53

expressed much pleasure at Stainer's going to St Paul's saying that 'as a churchman and a musician he is the very man for the post . . . he will be very much missed in Oxford'.[21] Stainer's own thoughts at the time are summarised in a letter written to his friend, the Hon J. S. Egerton, on 12 March 1872:

Many thanks for your very kind letter. I ought to have answered it before – but I have had so very much to do. I trust to be able by steady and quiet work to make the services at St Paul's something like what they should be. The Dean and Chapter (best in England) are prepared to back me up to any extent. The responsibility of the post will not be shirked by me, I assure you. In a few years, if I am spared, I hope with God's help to let you hear a really fine performance there. Funds are being squeezed out of the Eccles:' [Ecclesiastical] Commissioners for a very large Choir – probably three times as numerous as now. Only time is required for such vast changes.

The organ will be very fine – and although not encumbered with spare room in the organ loft I shall hope to see you up with me some day.

We have got a house in town – 7, Upper Montague Street, Russell Square – and after May 1 we hope to have ejected painters, bricklayers, etc. You must not fail to look us up.[22]

<h2 style="text-align:center">EARLY REFORMS BY THE CHAPTER</h2>

A significant early reform of the choir was that its members were expected to attend all daily morning and evening services throughout the week between the sixth Sunday in Lent and Easter Day, that is Holy Week, in 1872, and in subsequent years.[23] (Stainer arrived in Holy Week, 1872.) It was an important step, for not only did the chapter exercise their rights as employers, they also showed that the Lenten and Easter services, as a first stage, should be a model for others to follow. At this time, in addition, Liddon's fame as a preacher was even greater and he continued to attract very large congregations. As Canon Gregory summarised: 'The choir was made to attend somewhat more regularly; the services were more reverent, and it was felt that a new spirit was beginning to stir in the Cathedral.'[24] The chapter continued to tighten their grip during 1872, next ensuring that future vicars-choral should hold no similar appointment with another choir; this left them without an excuse for leaving before the end of the service.[25] This was, indeed, a revolutionary step. When Frederick Bridge was appointed organist of Westminster

Abbey in 1875 (although not yet officially with that title) the choirmen left officially before the sermon in order to sing in other churches. Westminster's difficulties continued for longer than St Paul's.

Then, on the occasion of the cathedral's being prepared for the thanksgiving service to be held on 27 February 1872 for the recovery of the Prince of Wales, the vicars-choral asked for holiday leave during the time that statutory services were not being held in the cathedral, from 5 February. The chapter had, however, previously made arrangements for the services to be held in Christ Church, Newgate Street, and felt unable to agree that advantage be taken of the closing of the cathedral 'to discontinue services in which the whole metropolis is interested and by which they trust the glory of God is advanced when a very suitable church for the continuance of the services of the Cathedral is placed at their disposal.' [26] However, the vicars-choral declined to comply with the order on the grounds that the chapter had no power to require them to sing outside the cathedral, [27] and most provided deputies for the whole period until the cathedral was reopened on 24 March 1872, Palm Sunday – one day before Stainer arrived. A few days later the chapter insisted that the choir should begin and end the service with a prayer, which caused some of the men to complain that they would miss their accustomed train home! [28]

The disruption of the statutory services was something which the chapter wished to avoid as far as possible. Consequently, the annual service for the charity children, which had for many years been held in St Paul's each June, was abandoned after 1871 on the grounds that it seriously disrupted the regular services in the cathedral. The charity children (from schools in the London area) undeniably provided each year an impressive musical festival, which had been held since 1704 and in St Paul's Cathedral since 1801. [29] Indeed, both Haydn (in 1792) and Berlioz (1851) attended the festival and were deeply impressed with the singing. But the occasion required the closing of the cathedral for weeks beforehand so that elaborate staging and galleries could be put up, which in the chapter's view interfered 'with the now improving services and worship'. [30] Because of the later changes in the school system the gatherings ceased altogether in 1877. Presumably Stainer, as a cathedral chorister, had experience of singing in these festivals. But however much he might have favoured them, it is unlikely that he would have been happy about the loss of the daily services for such a long period.

When Stainer undertook his duties in Holy Week, 1872, he apparently asked the chapter to say nothing critical to him for two years, at the same time giving his guarantee that at the end of that period they would find that the music of the cathedral was in good order.[31] In the two-year period the chapter could not have been anything but highly satisfied with his work there, for there was never any question but that Stainer would continue in charge of the music at St Paul's.

One of the deputy vicars-choral in the choir at the time of Stainer's coming recalled that the day after his arrival he requested that the gentlemen of the choir should meet him for a few minutes after the service because he wanted to speak to them, as it turned out, about the singing of the responses and also 'that beautiful Ely confession', as Stainer himself described it, which they used in services at that time. As the account of the meeting revealed: 'We then tried whatever he wished, and the men seemed to take the matter in good part, though they were not accustomed to choir practices, but then Stainer had such a charming way with him.'[32] The men had never been in the habit of practising with the organ and the boys, for they evidently considered themselves professionals beyond any need of rehearsal.

There was a further trial of Stainer's tact when he decided that he must rid himself of people he did not require. There are, for example, accounts of Goss playing the organ while members of the choir conducted, and in the Voluntary Choir Goss took a secondary role to another conductor. Also Mr Winn, one of the vicars-choral, had for many years conducted the Festival of the Sons of the Clergy, held annually in the cathedral in the form of a musical extravaganza, which he did for the last time in Stainer's first year at the cathedral. Stainer, not unnaturally, wanted to take all the cathedral music under his care, and would find such a state of affairs quite unacceptable.

SUNDAY EVENING CHOIR

Stainer's apparent winning ways with the vicars-choral, however, were at first lost on the Voluntary or Sunday Evening Choir who sang the second evensong on Sundays at 6.30pm. They resigned in a body and on the following Sunday 'sat in a row in the front of the Dome expecting a breakdown'.[33] Some singing friends came to Stainer's rescue on this occasion and the anticipated collapse in the musical part of the service did not happen. The dean and chapter supported Stainer and made it quite clear that only he could prescribe the form and conduct of all musical services. He was responsible for the reconstruction of the choir 'in such a way as he may think will best conduce to its efficiency'.[34] Any existing members of the Voluntary Choir who wished to continue their singing under Stainer were asked to get in touch with him to learn the conditions on which their further services would be acceptable. This meant a virtual reformation of that particular choir. Once the troublemakers had gone and the remaining members had got to know him, the choir was constantly very loyal and its relationship with Stainer was a very good one.

At the end of 1875 the members invited him to dinner and presented him with a handsome baton of ivory and gold, accompanied by an illuminated address on vellum. A year later they met again to dine and reminisce. They spoke of Stainer's 'self-denying love; his genial manner' and the report added that Stainer was a 'great favourite with the choir' and his late entrance at this particular function, because he had been attending another meeting earlier, was marked 'with great applause'. In the account of the speech given by the chairman it is interesting to note their change of attitude to Stainer and how he had improved things in a short period:

I can remember the old Sunday Evening Choir; things are indeed changed. We were then located in a gallery over the south door: we had to buy our own music and surplices, and the admission for the public [to these special services] was by ticket; we asked for one each to admit a friend – we were told we might have one by paying the expenses of printing them. But now how different. We are seated in the proper place in the choir, all music and surplices found, and everything done to make us comfortable; the whole of the Cathedral free to the public, and a thoroughly congregational service . . . Dr Stainer and others have said we are not the same choir, musically speaking, we were a year ago; all thanks to Dr Stainer for that. We could not then have sung such music as Antigone and other such music, and the best proof we can give Dr Stainer of our gratitude is by regular attendance at the weekly rehearsals.[35]

The Voluntary Choir continued to be successful, as the Church commissioners subsequently pointed out: 'The volunteer choir, which is under the direction of Dr Stainer, has never failed or fallen off during the last seven years'.[36] The choir also took part in the performances of Mendelssohn's *St Paul* and Bach's *St Matthew Passion*, to be described later.

There were minor complaints during Stainer's time such as when the choir did not sing an anthem; others took exception to the fact that the congregation was unable to join in the chanting at what was intended to be a congregational service. But the complaints were trivial and, by and large, Stainer's work here was appreciated.[37] His startling innovation to replace the boys by lady singers who were in some way attached to the cathedral also caused some indignation but in time it became generally accepted.

RESTRUCTURE OF APPOINTMENT
AND TENURE OF THE VICARS-CHORAL

It is clear, however, that one of the most pressing problems in the cathedral was the vicars-choral. They abused their position and privileges and held, to say the least, an irresponsible attitude to their duties. Although their duty was to sing, no provision was made for their resignation when their voices were no longer useful in the cathedral services; they retained their income as long as they lived. Consequently, on Stainer's appointment, nearly half the men were totally inefficient simply from old age. For example, the voice of one of the men, Mr James Shoubridge, was considered to be seriously 'failing' and he was requested by the cathedral chapter 'to appoint a permanent deputy to be approved by the Organist'.[38] Ironically, Shoubridge died before the end of the year and it was Stainer himself who was elected to the vacant post of vicar-choral in accordance with the conditions of his cathedral appointment. The deputy system had also been much abused and often when a vicar-choral could not attend he found a replacement though not necessarily of the same voice, which upset the balance of the choir considerably.

Two further instances give some indication of the general position. Charles Lockey had become a vicar-choral in 1844 but owing to the loss of his voice had been served by a deputy since 1859. He died in 1901 so, because of the type of freehold existing prior to Stainer's arrival, for more than forty years a permanent replacement could not be provided. An even worse example of abuse of freehold concerns the cathedral precentor, the Rev C. A. Belli. He had been appointed in 1819 and in the earlier days of his precentorship he was a frequent preacher at Sunday morning services, as the Preachers' Book testifies. Later, however, so rarely had he been seen in the cathedral that when he made his appearance at the funeral of the Duke of Wellington on 18 November 1852, he was unknown to any of the cathedral officials and was actually refused admittance.[39] As precentor he had been theoretically responsible for the chief direction of the cathedral music for upwards of half a century. For many years he lived at his living of South Weald, Essex, and was under no obligation to reside in the cathedral precincts.

In October 1872, the position of future assistant vicars-choral, as they became known, was regularised and eight additional men were appointed after open competition. Age at entry into the choir was to be under thirty, retirement age was fixed at sixty and there was a contributory pension scheme. Various conditions on appointment would be imposed on the assistant vicars-choral and disciplinary measures and fines levied against those men who were absent or late for service. No other appointment could be held (for instance, at Westminster Abbey or the Chapel Royal). When the regulations were revised in 1888, contrary to today's ecumenical spirit, the assistant vicars-choral could not take part in musical services held in 'or on behalf of Roman Catholic or Protestant Dissenting Chapels'.[40] Sir John Goss helped in the judging of candidates, who were asked to sing a prepared solo and do some sight-reading – altos from the alto clef and tenors from the tenor clef. Stainer presided and was also assisted by Mr Webber, one of the vicars-choral. The interviewing committee sat under the cathedral dome to hear the candidates. The successful men were formally admitted into the choir with effect from 25 January 1873 and, from that same date, Stainer's salary was increased by £100 to £500 per annum.[41]

That the choir became a more cohesive and disciplined body is obvious from the musical standards it achieved. The resentment and friction among the assistant vicars-choral became less apparent and they showed greater willingness to work with the cathedral authorities rather than take their former defensive or opposing role. The clergy, for their part, set a good example, and they were more friendly towards the choir. Canon Liddon frequently had the assistant vicars-choral to dine with him once he got to know them. But there was a stormy beginning when he had to complain to the men about their behaviour at the Holy Communion service and stated that it should be the chapter's intention to have 'religious men first; then if we could get them, accomplished musicians'.[42] He did not lay all the blame on the choir, feeling that the clergy themselves still needed to set a better example. He wrote to Canon Gregory in these terms:

They [the Choir] took what I said well, I hope; anyhow I could not but say it. Every time I reside, the hollowness and mockery of our services strikes me more and more; it must be unspeakably offensive to Almighty God, and I know how much it does to produce in the minds of half-believers and unbelievers, a conviction that our whole work is based on hypocrisy and insincerity. Of course, people of that kind do not distinguish.

I wish that we Canons could enter into a compact (1) not to talk on secular subjects in the vestry before Service, and (2) to avoid all lounging and looking about while we are in the Choir. Do you think I might mention this, without offence, at a Chapter? We cannot hope to get our subordinates to be reverent if we do not take pains to be reverent ourselves; they are quick to observe in us what they do not dare to mention. Speaking for myself this morning, I freely acknowledged to them the imperfections and shortcomings of my own service; I am sure we shall only win them by downright sincerity of this description with ourselves.[43]

However, there was a far better atmosphere and, as the cathedral succentor pointed out, the good feeling all-round was to 'a considerable degree due to the influence and tact of Dr Stainer, whose zeal and high principle was combined with so much kindness and patience.'[44]

There was a gradual improvement in the choir's work at services which became close to absolute perfection after Stainer had been at the cathedral for five years. Dean Church recalled the consecration of Dr E. W. Benson as the first Bishop of Truro in April 1877, which he described as a memorable day because it was one of the first occasions in St Paul's when a great religious ceremony was carried out 'with all the order and beauty of a perfected musical service'.[45] Dean Hole of Rochester preaching at St Paul's in the 1880s commented: 'I was thoroughly delighted with St Paul's, such a dignified service, and such sublime music.' He referred especially to Stainer 'who is the chief source and strength [and] is so humble and unselfish'.[46] Similarly, in an article contributed to *The Musical Standard*, Bumpus stated that 'for beauty of music, dignified and impressive yet simple ritual, and facilities for accommodating an immense congregation, the services now at St Paul's will challenge comparison with any other English cathedral'.[47] The unaccompanied services on Fridays were 'a very great treat, and the singing thereat will challenge comparison with that of the Pope's celebrated choir in the Sistine Chapel at Rome'. Bumpus spoke also of the great beauty of the sung celebration of the Holy Communion service on Sundays and considered generally that the state of the cathedral music (in 1881) was 'worthy of the great Cathedral of the greatest city'.[48]

THE RECRUITMENT AND TRAINING OF BOY CHORISTERS

Plans regularising the entrance of choirboys were outlined at the chapter meeting which determined Stainer's appointment as organist, and the first entrance examination was planned to take place at Christmas 1872. The chapter concerned themselves with the welfare of the choristers and, in addition to gradually increasing the number of boys, wished to provide new residential accommodation for them all, ensuring that their general education was not neglected through their singing duties.[49]

Some idea of their long day can be gleaned from a report of 1836. They were up at 7.30am in the summer and 8.00am in the winter and before breakfast (consisting of milk, bread and butter), rehearsed the set psalms for the day. They went to matins in the cathedral for 9.45am and after a short break proceeded to have music lessons and singing practice from 11.00am until 2.00pm (except for the six senior boys who had lessons in Italian, paid for by Miss Hackett). They had lunch of vegetables and '½

pint of beer to wash it down, and more if they required it'. At
3.15pm they sang evensong after which they had some
recreation, their main actual school work taking place from 5.30
to 8.00pm on four weekdays; they were taught reading, writing,
arithmetic and the church catechism. The boys ate their supper at
8.00pm (bread, butter and beer again), after which they went to
bed at 9.00pm although sometimes they went out to sing
oratorios. On Wednesdays they had free time and they were
allowed to go home after Saturday evensong until Monday
morning, although they had to come in on Sundays to sing the
services. Apparently their linen was changed at least twice a week
and they slept two to a bed. They attended cathedral services
every day in the year but were free from school work for three
weeks after Christmas, two after Easter and four in the summer.[50]
After this, for three years from Michaelmas 1845, the boys lived
together in the Chapter House but this did not prove successful
and subsequently they lived at home with their parents, or with
friends if they came from outside London.

The situation had improved by the 1870s as a contemporary
account by Canon Liddon shows. When he was first appointed to
the cathedral, the choristers, as just mentioned, were living at
home or with friends. They came to the cathedral for matins (by
that time it had been changed to 10.00am) and the time between
that and evensong (at 4.00pm) they spent 'partly in school, partly
at dinner, and partly at play'. They went home after evensong.[51]
The danger was that on their way to and from the cathedral for
services they were 'getting into mischief and evil of every
description'. One of the least evils, it appeared, was singing in the
music halls, where the choristers were highly paid and the money
welcomed by their parents who, generally speaking, were 'often
not well off'. So, at great expense, a residential school was
completed in 1875 for these boys, largely to prevent their being
exposed to evil and partly because of the demanding cathedral
work.[52] The school accommodated forty boys, all cathedral
choristers. The total cost of this building was about £20,000 and
it was erected almost on the site of the original school of Anglo-
Saxon foundation; it opened on 26 January 1875, one year after
the laying of the foundation stone. There were studies,
dormitories, a large dining-room and a practice room where
Stainer took the boys' practices; where possible, separate sets of

music were provided to avoid them being moved from school to cathedral. A playground on the roof was provided, in a large wire cage, where the boys could play football. At this time it cost the dean and chapter £70 per annum for each boy; the education was free of all charges, parents having to provide only clothes, travelling expenses and pocket money. Four of the city companies provided scholarships to enable deserving choristers to continue their education elsewhere after leaving St Paul's, and later more funds were to become available. At the age of eighty-nine Miss Hackett was shown round the almost-complete building by the dean and Stainer.[53] So, at last, Maria Hackett saw a boarding school for the choristers established and cathedral services rendered in a magnificent way.

Stainer attached great importance to the careful education and thorough training of the choristers and was instrumental in making this choir school a model for all other cathedral choir schools in the country. On completion of the school all the boy choristers resided there, and in 1876 the chapter looked into the possibility of providing the education of the Temple Church choristers on a day-boy basis, but nothing came of this. When the school was opened boys living outside London suburbs were no longer prevented from becoming choristers just because of this fact. As a direct consequence of these changes, however, the type of boy that was admitted altered. Formerly almost all of them had been sons of tradesmen, but the cathedral authorities now wished to encourage 'sons of gentlemen, chiefly of poor clergymen'.[54]

Twelve more choristers were elected in January 1873, after open competition. 'Excellency of voice and a moderate knowledge of the rudiments of English and Latin' were the qualifications to be expected, and these boys lived at 1 Amen Court – later to become Stainer's house – until the new choir school was ready. By 1880 Stainer had a full complement of forty choristers.

5

A widening of the cathedral's musical activities

One of the important sides of Stainer's work at St Paul's, though seemingly forgotten now (it was hardly given a mention in his obituary notices), was the performance of special musical works in the cathedral on festival days. It is true that there had been the occasional performance of Handel's *Messiah*, the last time this occurred being after the organ from the Panopticon of Science and Art in Leicester Square had been installed in the cathedral, in 1861. And there had also been the annual Festival of the Sons of the Clergy which took place in May. But that was all. However, it was the wish of the chapter that the Patronal Festival, the Feast of the Conversion of St Paul, on 25 January, be suitably commemorated; this was done in 1871, but with no special music. For the 1873 festival Stainer suggested to the dean and chapter the singing of selections from Mendelssohn's oratorio *St Paul* and also, on some evening in Holy Week, Bach's *St Matthew Passion*. To this they gave their consent, 'the estimate of expenses to be approved by the Dean in conjunction with the Treasurer'.[1] W. A. Frost in his account states that Stainer had obtained permission to perform *St Paul*, but at his own expense; this hardly seems likely in view of the chapter minute.[2] How the choir reacted is not certain, but the chapter stated that all the assistant vicars-choral were 'bound to give attendance in the choir as a body on such special occasions as the Dean and Chapter may from time to time prescribe'.[3] This came following the elections of the new assistant vicars-choral. In 1878 steps were taken to increase their salary by £10 per annum, but Canon Gregory came to choir practice on 20 December to tell them that from then onwards there would be no payment for major extra events, Bach's Passion music and Spohr's *The Last Judgement* (performed in Advent) being part of their normal duties.

Mendelssohn's *St Paul*, Bach's *St Matthew Passion* and Spohr's *The Last Judgement* were the mainstay during Stainer's period at the cathedral, although movements from Bach's *Christmas Oratorio*, Handel's *Messiah* and Mozart's *Requiem* and parts from other Mendelssohn oratorios were often sung as anthems. Brahms' *A German Requiem* and Handel's *Messiah* were eventually to supersede Spohr's music in Advent and in time the performances of *St Paul* ceased to take place; but regular renderings of much of Bach's *St Matthew Passion* (in Holy Week) have continued for over a hundred years, with *Messiah* as the work sung in Advent.

The Corporation of the Sons of the Clergy was founded in London in 1655 by sons of clergymen, and had for its objects the assisting of necessitous clergymen, pensioning and aiding their widows and aged single daughters, and educating, apprenticing and providing outfits for their children'.[4] To gain funds for this institution it holds an annual festival consisting of a choral service with a sermon, followed by a dinner. Early records of the corporation were destroyed by fire in 1838 but it seems likely that the festivals have been held in St Paul's Cathedral from 1697. At first Purcell's *Te Deum* and *Jubilee for St Cecilia's Day* were sung, then Handel's service for the Peace of Utrecht (1713) was given, after which each was performed alternately. Later Handel's *Dettingen Te Deum* was performed until 1843 when, in deference to the wishes of Bishop Blomfield, then Bishop of London, the instrumental band was dispensed with. This service was then accompanied by the organ only, Boyce writing organ accompaniments to the Purcell setting of the *Te Deum* and *Jubilate*, and continued so until 1873 when Stainer revived the use of the orchestra. At some stage the festival was transferred to evensong, probably in 1873.

Under the 1872 arrangements, which had presumably been made before Stainer took up the post of organist, the festival was conducted by one of the assistant vicars-choral, Mr Winn, with Stainer playing the organ. Winn had for some years conducted the augmented choir used for this occasion, but this was the last time, it being thought that Stainer 'did not relish being conducted by one of his own choirmen. It was the last service of the old sort . . .' The responses were sung to the setting by Tallis, the canticles *Smart in B flat* and the two anthems were *Hosanna to the Son of David* by Gibbons and *Brother, thou art gone before us* by Goss. The first movement of this rather lengthy composition was later rearranged by Goss to the words *Lord, let me know mine end* and was subsequently included in the service repertoire. Stainer played Mendelssohn's *Prelude and Fugue in G* (dedicated to Attwood and St Paul's) and George Cooper played an arrangement of 'Worthy is the Lamb' from Handel's *Messiah.*

As time went on the music became more adventurous and interesting in character: in 1873 the *Hymn of Praise* by Mendelssohn was performed with orchestral accompaniment; in 1874 his setting of Psalm 42, *As the hart pants*; movements from Spohr's *The Last Judgement* in 1875; and a selection from Mendelssohn's *Elijah* in 1876. *Miriam's Song* by Schubert was sung in 1877, and Stainer's own work, *The Daughter of Jairus,* in 1879. *The Church Review* commented on the fact that the musical features of the service had been 'specially attractive since Dr Stainer succeeded Sir John Goss',[5] and for the same service another report states that the 'success of the whole service reflects great credit upon Dr Stainer both for his training of the choir and his able conducting'.[6] Spohr's cantata, *God, Thou art great,* was performed in 1878, evidently reaching the same high standard:

. . . the Choir showed the true characteristics of a highly trained body of vocalists – promptness, purity of tone, refinement as to general expression, and in nice gradations of power; all were here, and the result was, as might be expected, a service of almost unexampled excellence.[7]

A young and then unknown composer, Eaton Faning, subsequently Director of Music at Harrow, wrote the evening canticles for this service, again performed with an orchestra. It must have earned some popularity because it was performed again in 1882. Stainer was always ready to encourage young composers and was prepared to commission works wherever he could. In 1880, for instance, a setting was specially commissioned for the service – C. V. Stanford's *Magnificat and Nunc Dimittis* in A major. Stanford was twenty-seven at this time and had recently been appointed Organist of Trinity College, Cambridge. Stainer's handling of the music at this particular service is again highly praised:

The Stainer family, c1872. Stainer had married Eliza Randall in 1865 and they had seven children altogether, six of whom survived into adulthood

John Stainer in 1880, during his period as Organist of St Paul's Cathedral

Dr Stainer . . . is the right man in the right place, and judging by what he has accomplished since he was appointed to the post, may be relied upon for doing all that can fairly be expected at his hands. Himself a composer as well as an organist of distinction, he is thoroughly qualified to rule. Already he has effected much and the great improvement in the services, ordinary and extraordinary, in our Cathedral, has excited more and more attention.[8]

In 1881 the festival was described as 'a means of calling forth valuable additions to the musical repertoire of the English Church'.[9] Some of Goss's finest music had, indeed, been written for it. The 1881 festival was no exception and contained a setting of the evening canticles in E flat especially written for it by Joseph Barnby, a great friend of Stainer; and Ferdinand Hiller[10] wrote a setting of words contained in Psalm 125, *All they that trust in Thee, O Lord.* Another work specially written by Hiller was performed in 1883, *A Song of Victory.* In 1885 parts of Stainer's *St Mary Magdalen* were sung, the first time any of it had been performed in St Paul's Cathedral. He wrote his anthem *Lord, Thou art God* for the 1887 Jubilee Festival Service.

The music at this festival was always essentially music used within the liturgy of the Church, and it was often a source of inspiration to contemporary composers of church music. Although it did not draw the large numbers that came to the *St Matthew Passion*, it had a profound effect on the worshipper at that time. *The Musical Times* summed up its influence well: 'Those who remember the Cathedral services prior to 1873, both on St Paul's Day and other days alike, will best estimate the influence which good music, properly interpreted, is capable of asserting over an immense mass of people . . .'[11]

ORATORIOS IN THE CATHEDRAL

There had been some fear among the cathedral chapter regarding the performance of oratorios in St Paul's and it was made clear that the music formed part of the cathedral worship and was not just a concert. There was a division of opinion among the general public at the time: there were those who considered the cathedral debased by activities which should have been restricted to the concert hall, and those who thought an ecclesiastical building the ideal setting for the performance of a religious musical work.

Stainer's own view was that the performance of oratorios in church buildings was perfectly correct and retained much of what was lost in the concert hall performances. The oratorio, in its early growth was a 'valuable means of teaching sacred truths in sacred buildings – in churches'. It had moved to the concert hall because of the neglect of the Church, and Stainer considered that this should be remedied. Certainly St Paul's lent an aura of mystery, and the vast space of the dome gave a 'mellowness and tenderness to the tone of the stringed instruments which is never heard in a concert room'.[12]

As the years went by the number of performers sizeably increased, as did the number of listeners. There were four hundred players and singers and more than eight thousand people assembled to listen to Mendelssohn's *St Paul* in 1877, and later reports spoke of the cathedral being completely full and having as many listeners as for the Passion music, about ten thousand. This number seems to be slightly exaggerated. It is possible that such a large number might have been present at the charity children's services or at such national occasions as Wellington's funeral, but for these events elaborate staging and galleries were erected. Such stagings were not put up for any of the musical occasions, for this would have required the closing of the cathedral beforehand, a measure completely contrary to the dean's and Stainer's ideas.

For the performances of *St Paul* the solos were sung by members of the cathedral choir and the chorus work had the additional help of seventy boys and men from London churches. There was free admission, even though the costs were substantial, but there seems to have been an atmosphere of religious devotion that would have been less marked in a concert hall. For instance, in a report in the *Daily Chronicle* it was said of the performance in 1885 that, 'from first to last a more imposing and reverential musical service has probably never been given within the walls of a cathedral than that of yesterday afternoon'.[13] Again St Paul's was setting an example for other cathedrals to follow. With the reviving spirit of religious awareness came a new phase of musical dignity in worship, and the fitness of religious oratorios in church services became strikingly apparent.

In 1878, Spohr's *The Last Judgement* was first performed in the annual cycle of performances of oratorios. For this the cathedral choir was without any additional help and Stainer played the organ, there being no conductor or orchestra. In the performances of these oratorios Stainer was highly spoken of in his diverse roles as organiser, choir trainer and conductor; but it was in the Spohr that he came into his own as an organist. His 'execution of the rapid scale passages in the symphony to the second part was considered a marvel by all . . . Dr Stainer used to say that he began to practise the scale passages for it in the summer', wrote one of his own choirmen,[14] while *The Musical World* thought that the 'organ effects obtained by Dr Stainer were marvellously dramatic, especially in the symphony, ending in rolling thunder . . .'[15] Stainer's own talents as an executant were fully developed in the introductions 'and in other taxing portions of the score'.[16] *The Musical Times* considered that few of those present would forget Stainer's 'splendidly brilliant and well-judged rendering of the Symphony' to the second part: 'Our feeling at the close of this performance was that the Cathedral authorities, as well as those who usually attended St Paul's, might be not only satisfied but proud of both organ and organist.'[17] *The Last Judgement* continued to be performed in Advent for the rest of Stainer's tenure but was inevitably replaced afterwards when Stainer had left and as fashions changed.

BACH'S ST MATTHEW PASSION

Mendelssohn's influence was very strong in England in the latter half of the nineteenth century. Stainer was no exception in considering him among the best of church musicians and included much of his music in the cathedral service lists. J. S. Bach, however, was not an established favourite, and credit must go to Stainer for the introduction of the *St Matthew Passion* to so many people in such ideal surroundings.

As mentioned earlier, Stainer sang as a boy in the first performance in England of the Passion, given in the Hanover Rooms under the auspices of The Bach Society on 6 April 1854. Sterndale Bennett conducted, as he did in subsequent performances on 28 November 1854 and on 23 March 1858, the last occasion being in St Martin's Hall, Long Acre, London.[18] It was performed again soon afterwards at Windsor, at the desire of Prince Albert, the Prince Consort, and then not again for a further period of four years.[19] By the 1870s it was still only slightly known in London musical circles. Stainer had played the harmonium in performances at Westminster Abbey in April 1871 and March 1872, under the baton of Joseph Barnby. Barnby was founder of what was subsequently to become the Royal Choral Society, and was responsible for giving annual performances of Bach's *St John Passion* in St Anne's Church, Soho, once a great centre for the Anglo-Catholic type of worship with a similar reputation for the performances of Viennese masses in its services.

Following the success of the first experiment at the cathedral's Patronal Festival in January 1873, and having the dean and chapter's consent to perform suitable music in Holy Week (indeed they had minuted for this prior to Stainer's arrival), there was no reason why Stainer, with every confidence, should not embark on the first performance of the Passion music in the cathedral. It took place on 8 April 1873, Tuesday in Holy Week. The passion was preceded by the latter part of the commination office together with the *Miserere* (Psalm 51) sung to an arrangement by Stainer of the *Tonus Regalis.* The Passion music was not sung in its entirety but was abridged. The selection was made by Stainer and sung in an English translation, the whole lasting about two and three-quarter hours. This version[20] was subsequently published by Novello, and at the service in 1882 it was noted that something like a quarter of the congregation followed the music from this vocal score.[21] In Stainer's edition the opportunity was taken of modifying the words slightly. The text in the Novello complete edition was a literal translation from the German by Miss H. F. H. Johnston. Stainer pointed out, however, that several passages contained expressions which 'if not inconsistent with orthodox teaching (i.e. according to the views of an English Churchman) are, at least, misleading in their tendency', and other phrases were so ambiguous as to have little definite meaning.[22]

Stainer employed an orchestra of 47 people: violin I – 10; violin II –8; viola – 6; 'cello – 7; double bass – 7; flute – 4; oboe – 4; and continuo – 1. This was a combination which he thought 'as nearly as possible in these modern times, what the composer scored for'. (It seems certain that the cor anglais was used where Bach had prescribed the oboe di caccia.) What is more interesting than the details of Stainer's orchestra is his desire for authenticity in a period which many musicians today associate with the perpetration of musical liberties of every kind. Orchestra, choir and conductor were dressed in surplices and Stainer also wore his academic hood. There were about three hundred singers for the Passion (not quite so authentic), consisting of the cathedral boy choristers and the boys from Lincoln's Inn Chapel Choir and the Chapel Royal, together with the men from the cathedral choir and others from St Andrew's Church, Wells Street, Joseph Barnby's church, and from St George's Chapel, Windsor. The soprano and alto solos were sung by the cathedral choirboys with an additional seventy boys trained for the *ripieno* in the opening movement. Two detachments, mostly Christ's Hospital boys and numbering about four hundred in all, were located in each transept, each group with a trumpet, with the intention of encouraging the congregation to sing the chorales, but this apparently was not very effective. A similar arrangement was followed in early performances of the Royal Albert Hall Choral Society when Stainer accompanied on the organ. For those performances, *The Musical Times* commented that the 'audiences would join in the chorales and with no little spirit, being considerably aided in their efforts by the support of a trumpet played at each entrance to the amphitheatre stalls'.[23] Why the similar treatment was ineffective in the cathedral is not clear.

The performances of the Passion were given consistently good press reviews, and in 1878 *The Guardian* wrote that it would have been difficult to match the performance anywhere and was 'proof that Dr Stainer had raised the choir to its proper position as the chief Church musical corporation in the United Kingdom'.[24] The spirit of the remark is accepted but there were, of course, other singers taking part in addition to the cathedral choir.

All these special services and musical events were additional to the work entailed in the preparation and improvement of the normal service music, and the extra duty that Stainer put upon himself can be readily imagined. The Advent music came at the beginning of December, Mendelssohn's *St Paul* at the end of January, the *St Matthew Passion* in March/April and the Sons of the Clergy Festival in May. And under the new chapter the cathedral was thrown open to all kinds of other musical bodies as, for example, the Sion College Choral Union Festival, the London Church Choir Association and the London Gregorian Festival, in all of whose performances Stainer and his assistant, George Martin, took an active part. Thus the cathedral became known not only for the excellence of the service music but, in a much wider sense, as a promoter of the art.

THE SERVICE MUSIC IN THE CATHEDRAL

Although the ultimate responsibility for the day-to-day service music in the cathedral lay with the dean and chapter, in practice it fell to the succentor, Dr Sparrow Simpson, and Stainer to arrange the lists of music, sometimes referred to as 'the bills'. There were fifteen fully choral services each week, three on Sundays and two on each weekday. Only the men sang at the Thursday evensong, when the boys had a free afternoon for games.

As already mentioned, Stainer encouraged young composers to write music for the cathedral services and St Paul's became known as a centre of contemporary church music. But there was no particular emphasis on new music as Stainer's aim was to have a wide repertoire from all periods and to include, where appropriate, movements from oratorios. He made clear his views on the principle of selection at a lecture he gave to the Church Congress in Leeds in 1872. He thought that Gregorian music had its place in the repertoire as did the masses of Beethoven, Hummel, Mozart, Schubert and Weber. Within limits he would use music written in a strictly contrapuntal style but recognised the danger of losing the meaning of the text in order to make the music grammatical. As he put it, the pages of Handel's Passion music were found stained with the composer's tears but he doubted whether the contrapuntalist was moved similarly:

. . . the only anxiety you can trace on his face arises from his fears whether he can make his subject of so many notes or bars stand on its head, which he calls inversion; or whether he can stretch it out to twice its length, which he calls augmentation; or whether he can squeeze it into half its compass, which he calls diminution; whether worshippers will be edified or not by his music is none of his business; it is enough for him if it is ingenious.[25]

Stainer thought that the dramatic style of much of the post-Cromwellian period was often unsuitable although 'the genius of Henry Purcell could have made music in any style not only

74

palatable, but admirable'. Similarly, verse-anthems and chamber anthems were not particularly suitable for St Paul's; he thought it absurd 'to keep some three or four thousand people under the dome listening to a series of short movements for two or three voices, or to a long alto solo sung by men sitting in the Chancel'.[26] This was music written for use in the Chapels Royal or places of similar size. In cathedrals where there was the division of an organ screen, this kind of music could be effectively performed sometimes, but in St Paul's it was ineffective and hardly ever suitable. Having said this, as time went on, Stainer introduced more of Purcell's music and there was a fairer representation of anthems of Tudor composers.

He believed that the choice of music should be broad and eclectic – by 'broad' he meant that no school of music should be introduced to the exclusion of other schools; and by 'eclectic', that if he believed any composition capable of edifying worshippers, he would adopt it 'regardless of any suggestions thrown out by outsiders that the composer did not perhaps belong to the first rank'.[27] In Stainer's final year as organist, there were 26 anthems sung from the seventeenth century; 110 from the eighteenth century; and 365 from the nineteenth century, 170 of which were by composers still living. There was a preponderance of music by Mendelssohn, Gounod (including the *Messe Solennelle*), and to a lesser extent J. S. Bach, Handel and Spohr – admittedly a marked bias towards continental influence, the more so as the practice of singing detached movements from oratorios was more common than it is today. Compared with current cathedral lists, the amount of Tudor and even, perhaps, Restoration music was small, but the whole was not excessively out of proportion when compared with the repertoire of other similar establishments.

Stainer held the strong view that above all, there should be musical variety in worship, that it should include music of all styles and thereby exclude nobody; one should be able to say:

to the lover of Anglican music, come to our cathedral on such and such days; to the lover of Gregorian music, come on such other days; to those who can devoutly worship when listening to an oratorio (and who can not?) come at such times; to those who love congregational singing, come on Sundays and hear the roof echo again and again to the uplifted voice of the hearty congregation.

Cathedral music in England was still in a rather poor state even at the time when Stainer left St Paul's; he himself was progressive in his attitude to new music and, even though today one might not agree with the balance he struck between, say, movements from nineteenth-century oratorios and unaccompanied sixteenth- and seventeenth-century music, he successfully attempted a broadening of the range of music heard, both in period and style, during his time as cathedral organist. The widening of the repertoire was a further stage in his reforms and one which influenced other cathedral musicians at the time. But it was at St Paul's where his authority had the greatest and most immediate effect. As William Sinclair, Archdeacon of London, wrote in 1909, 'To Sir John Stainer, it is impossible to exaggerate the debt of St Paul's'.

THE ORGAN

We have until now been mainly concerned with Stainer's achievement in the improvement of the singing and the worship during his time at the cathedral. But his contemporaries were equally impressed by his organ playing and to this we must now turn. And this requires some account of the resources available to Stainer at St Paul's.

Sir Christopher Wren, in his plans for the cathedral, did not allow for the original organ screen which separated the choir from the rest of the building but wished to place the organ over the northern choir stalls, as in the old cathedral demolished in the Great Fire of 1666, in order that there might be an uninterrupted view from east to west. Towards the year 1860, when larger congregations were being drawn by the distinguished preaching of canons Dale and Melville, it was decided to remove the organ to the second arch on the north side of the stalls. In this buried position the lower part of the organ case and the choir organ could not be used. It then became only too apparent that the organ was inadequate to accompany the singing of the congregation seated under the dome and in 1860 a large four manual organ by Hill, until then standing in the Panopticon of Science and Art, Leicester Square, was purchased by the dean and chapter for £500 and placed in the south transept on a gallery with Ionic columns by Rondone. This instrument was subsequently sold in

1873 and removed to the Victoria Rooms, Clifton, Bristol, where parts of it were used in other instruments. The selling price of £650 was later 'appropriated towards the expense of the hanging of the peal of bells'.[28] The casework of the Smith choir organ provided the false case for the thirteen years it stood in the cathedral; the Byzantine case, which effectively adorned the Hill organ in its original home, was thought to be too secular and was not used. In 1870, the Cathedral Decorations Committee decided to rearrange the choir; the organ was to be placed in two parts at the west end of the choir. This was Sparrow Simpson's suggestion although he would have preferred its restoration with the choir screen 'but this was negatived on all hands'.[29]

W. L. Sumner considered the rebuilt organ both mechanically and tonally a revelation, containing 'beautifully balanced departments and individual stops of great charm'.[30] The swell organ has not been altered since and the great organ has received only minor extension.[31] The solo organ of six stops was considered to be very complete. 'Here the organ lost its Father Smith personality finally, and came into the Willis line; though the best of Smith's work was retained'.[32] Presumably the organ was not completely finished until the end of 1872 as Stainer writes of the incomplete organ on 14 October 1872:

I am at last settling down – but my organ at St Paul's is not yet quite finished. Lots of people came to hear the new Organist – when I had only about four stops to play on! I am ashamed to say I have been more amused than annoyed by their criticism. But I have *nearly* got one of the best organs in England. It will be quite splendid . . .[33]

This almost new organ gave daily service until 1897–1900 when it was again rebuilt and added to. In the summer of 1883 it was out of action for several weeks because of cleaning. A small moveable Willis organ, usually kept in the chancel, had been purchased in 1881 for £250 on the recommendation of Stainer[34] and was used during the times when the Grand organ was out of action, when it was placed immediately west of the choir stalls on the northern side. This organ is still in use at the present time.[35]

Because of the size of the building and the distance between the organ console and the choir stalls, and the console and the place under the dome where the augmented choirs were seated for the special occasions already described, some method of communication between these areas had to be devised. Today there is a telephone, but this was, of course, not available in Stainer's time although, as Bumpus recalls, they were not entirely cut off from each other:

There is electric communication between the organ loft and the engine room. The organist has the power of ringing a bell in the engine room and directing 'wind off' or 'wind on'; the bellows automatically answer the order by wiring the 'on' as it rises, and 'off' as it falls. There is also electric communication and a speaking tube between the organist and the singers in the stalls below, a simple and useful appendage to the organ loft which has prevented many a troublesome musical contretemps. On great days, when an orchestra of 50 performers and a special choir numbering more than 300 take part in the service, an electric communication is maintained between the left foot of the conductor and a moveable arm which beats time close to the music book of the player. When the selection from Mendelssohn's oratorio St Paul is performed on the Dedication Festival, or the great Passion music of Bach on Tuesday in Holy Week, precision and unity between organ, band and choir would be absolutely impossible but for this contrivance.[36]

STAINER AS AN ORGANIST

There are some cathedral organists who are also known as celebrated recitalists. Others are content to do their cathedral work and assist in local musical activities. A third group, once appointed, may play little and concentrate on choir training and conducting activities. In Stainer's time the recitalists of the day, Smart, Hollins and Best, did not hold cathedral appointments; on the other hand, apart from his activities with the Royal Albert Hall Choral Society where he acted as organ accompanist, there is no record of Stainer's touring the country giving organ recitals once he had been appointed to the cathedral. However, he did give the opening recital of the Willis organ in Canterbury Cathedral in 1886. It has already been shown that he was interested in recital work, but though he was willing to perform in the cathedral there were, to him, other more important activities that claimed his time.

There is only a limited evidence available about his organ playing from music; but his facility in extemporisation, or improvisation, has been written about so often that one assumes

that he was one of the best, if not the best, of his day. W. L.
Sumner, who claimed to know more about Stainer than any other
living person and had considered writing a monograph on him,
said that Stainer asserted that in his improvisation before evensong on Sunday afternoons he used every stop on the organ,
'there was then no heavy stuff in the quarter galleries'.[37] His
influence as an organist at St Paul's was vast: crowds came to
listen to him on Sunday afternoons.[38] Not surprisingly Sir Walter
Alcock, Organist of Salisbury Cathedral until his death in 1947,
spoke of Stainer being 'a genius at improvisation'.[39] In a letter to
The Times written at the time of the centenary of Stainer's birth,
Alcock commented that 'if those who so glibly dismiss it [his
music] as unworthy could have heard him extemporise, or have
listened to his magnificent organ accompaniment, they would at
least be compelled to acknowledge his fine musicianship'.[40] He
recalled Arthur Sullivan at a composition class at the National
Training School for Music when Alcock was a pupil there, saying
'I was at St Paul's yesterday, listening to Dr Stainer extemporising. My dear young friends, he is a genius, and I hope you will
miss no chance of hearing him.' Walter Alcock added that he had
never since heard a finer exponent of the art of improvisation, and
that 'his introductory voluntaries are an imperishable memory
for me'.[41] Canon Scott Holland mentioned his inspiring improvisations at the communion service each Sunday at St Paul's.[42]
J. H. Coward, a minor canon at St Paul's, remembered how great a
feature at St Paul's were Stainer's accompaniments to the psalms
and how much they were missed after he had left.[43] W. G.
McNaught described Stainer, as a young man, as having a
'remarkable facility in extemporising on the organ, in the manner
of Bach' and says that St Paul's Cathedral 'soon acquired a world-
wide reputation for the beauty and reverence of its service music,
and for Stainer's masterly organ playing'.[44] *The Musical
Standard* commenting on Stainer's extempore playing said that it
stood out as a bright example 'to show that really good
extemporaneous playing is not yet amongst us a thing of the
past'.[45] Parry talks of Stainer playing 'gloriously' at Magdalen
College Chapel[46] and comments particularly on his rendering of
the last of the set of six *Fugues on Bach* by Schumann, which
moved him to record in his diary that it was 'one of the finest
things I ever heard in my life'.[47] Canon Scott Holland also

recalled that Stainer's power of accompaniment was simply magical and 'his soul would pass out from him as he played, and possess the sounding spaces of the great cathedral with the movement of its inspiration'.[48] He went on to say that no one who had ever heard Stainer play at St Paul's could have the smallest doubt of his splendid power as an organist:

He had entire mastery over the instrument and expressed himself naturally and inevitably within the bounds imposed by the peculiar character of the organ. Though he was fully aware of the quasi-orchestral capacities of an organ, his use of it in this line was the nature of reproduction rather than imitation. Though his accompaniments were habitually reserved and self-controlled, he knew the value of a great rush of sound and used it unerringly. He was so thoroughly at home with the very spirit and idiom of an organ that he spoke in its language with faultless taste.[49]

Hadow rated him as 'undoubtedly the greatest English organist of his time',[50] and Bumpus recalled that Stainer was 'a brilliant instrumentalist, and as an organist he has few equals, and in some respects he is acknowledged by the highest authorities to be quite without a rival . . .'[51]

While we know that Stainer mainly played organ music from the standard repertoire of Bach to Mendelssohn, there is evidence from various press cuttings that, in common with other reputable organists of his day, he played organ arrangements of orchestral works. A contemporary account of Stainer's organ playing at the cathedral is found in a letter Bumpus wrote in defence of the cathedral's music. This reveals something of Stainer's detailed repertoire which, under his hands, was apparently spellbinding:

. . . magnificent renderings of such things as Bach's E flat (St Ann's) [sic] and D minor fugues, of Smart's grand solemn March in E flat, and Postlude in C, many of Handel's sublime choruses, Mendelssohn's organ sonatas, etc. Some of the introductory voluntaries are of inexpressible beauty, such as Mozart's Andante from the 5th quintet in E flat and Andante from quartet in D minor, Bach's 'My heart ever faithful', Smart's Andantes in F and A, and many of the pathetic airs from Handel's oratorios.[52]

Stainer's advice was often asked on the rebuilding of organs, especially those by Willis. He advised on the instruments in New College, Oxford, Plymouth Town Hall, Oxford Town Hall and

Doveridge Parish Church in Derbyshire, and he was a juror on organ building at the Paris Exhibition of 1878, for which services he was created a Chevalier of the French Legion of Honour. But his influence was limited. His ideas, it seems, never progressed beyond the traditional Willis lines, being too romantic with much orchestral work, too much diapason work, insufficient mixtures and mutations on manuals and pedals. As Dr Sumner commented, 'Stainer was too keen on organ arrangements to know the registration of the historic English and European repertory'.[53] In this respect Stainer was firmly of his time, for almost every organ of British design was built on similar lines at this period, just as it was the accepted custom to play organ arrangements. Stainer must not be thought of too badly because of this; in the late nineteenth and early twentieth centuries, organ recitals served as the main source of musical appreciation for people who could not attend orchestral concerts, both within and outside London, in the few places where concerts were available. And it would doubtless have been better to acquire a knowledge and appreciation of Wagner's Prelude to Act I of *The Mastersingers*, for example, from an organ arrangement than not at all.

Stainer's views on the position of the organ were made known in a private letter to F. G. Edwards. Writing from St Paul's in 1886 he said that generally an organ placed behind a congregation gives more support to their voices than when in front, but he thought that there were other important considerations. When a congregation can see a choir (whether surpliced or not) there is a natural tendency to listen rather than to take part; when the choir and organ are behind a congregation 'this temptation ceases to exist and the congregation feels compelled (I might almost say *driven*) to exert itself in the music'.[54] In St Paul's Cathedral, in hymn singing, he found that the sound of the choir and organ (in their normal position) passed up the dome and down again to the ears of the people sitting beween the centre and the back of the dome floor. This caused a certain amount of dragging but 'nevertheless we sometimes have some magnificent congregational singing in St Paul's, especially at our quasi-parochial Sunday evening services'.[55] The soloists at St Paul's preferred to be accompanied by an organ opposite to them rather than just over their head.[56]

Stainer's opinions were influenced partly by the fact that, in this instance, he was a strong supporter of Wesley's ideals contained in *A Few Words on Cathedral Music*; he would have agreed that the beauty of the choral service must necessarily render members of the congregation speechless and produce a spirit of rapt silent attention. He would have been a strong advocate of the organ gallery being positioned in the choir.

RESIGNATION AS CATHEDRAL ORGANIST

Quite early in his period at St Paul's Stainer had suffered under the initial strain of the work, and the worry of reforming the choir and restoring the music to a suitable standard led to a nervous breakdown after eighteen months in office. Stainer went to the Isle of Wight for a rest where 'someone saw him looking desperately ill and thought he would not get over this breakdown'.[57] Following this he seemed much better until an incident in September 1875, when he was playing a game of fives with Ouseley at Tenbury. A ball struck his good eye with 'such severity that the sight of it was for some time totally lost'.[58] It was hoped that he would completely recover the sight of the eye because the other had been lost in an accident as a child. He was away from the cathedral for over six months but 'thoroughly restored to health'[59] on his return. Even in illness his reading activity was diminished only slightly.

But though Stainer had successfully contended with these early troubles, his unremitting labours ultimately took their toll and in 1888, after sixteen years at the cathedral, he decided to resign. 'He is out of health, and as he pathetically expresses it, he is going to retire from his post of organist in time, he hopes, to save what little bit of eyesight is left to him.'[60] Tributes were many and all bore witness to Stainer's success in raising the standard of the musical services to the high level it had by now attained. To quote but one: 'The record of Dr Stainer's work at St Paul's is written in letters of gold on the memories of all those who contrast the Cathedral services as they are now with what they were twenty years ago. The progress is almost phenomenal.'[61]

Stainer communicated officially with the dean and chapter and, on 27 January 1888, they accepted his resignation to take effect from 25 June 1888. His sub organist for many years, Dr George Martin, was appointed his successor. In his letter of resignation

Stainer spoke of his 'deep sense of the kindness and consideration which I have received during my tenure of office and I feel thankful that I have had the privilege of devoting sixteen years of my life to the great work being done by St Paul's'.[62] He said that he would sever himself from the close ties with the cathedral with sincere regret, 'but the delicate state of my eyesight and the gradual falling off of my general health compel me to take the step'. In his reply Canon Gregory, on behalf of the dean and chapter,[63] said that they wished to record:

. . . their deep sense of the very distinguished services which he during sixteen years had rendered to the music of the Cathedral, to the beauty and dignity of Divine Service, and in numberless ways to all with whom he had been brought into contact during his tenure of the post . . .[64]

Stainer played his last service in the cathedral on the morning of 4 May and was given a testimonial with portraits and signatures of all the choir and a pair of beautiful ormolu and enamel candlesticks, an inkstand and a mirror with an elegant frame, all to match. The Sunday Evening Choir had previously given him a brass clock, a pair of candelabra and an inkstand.[65] Later, on 22 June, Stainer entertained the assistant vicars-choral to dinner at the Albion Tavern in the city and was further presented with a painting by one of the assistant vicars-choral, Mr de Lacy – 'Pool of the river Thames at evening', a view taken from Rotherhithe showing a distant view of the dome of St Paul's.[66] On 17 July 1888, he was knighted by Queen Victoria at Windsor Castle[67] in the same ceremony as Sir Charles Hallé, and on that evening was entertained to dinner at the Hotel Metropole. This was attended by a large number of guests distinguished in music, painting, science, literature and the law, and a great many important clerics.[68] Stainer spoke of his good fortune in the support he had had from the dean and chapter and from the assistant vicars-choral, and went on to say:

I have often thought that in the music in St Paul's when I was accompanying and listening to it myself, as it was sung by that admirable choir (for I feel I may compliment them now) there was something more than mere precision and correctness, and even than merely good style: there was something I know to be a fact, that the men who took part in that music entirely subordinated their own wills to the general effect and beauty of the music, and felt too that it was church music. It often impressed itself on me at the close of a beautiful anthem (or whatever it might be) so that I more often felt inclined to say 'Thank God' than to say 'Thank you, gentlemen of the choir.' And I am sure we all feel that that is what should be the case.[69]

Canon Gregory spoke on behalf of the dean and chapter and said that they proposed to found a scholarship as a testimonial to Sir John.[70] Sir Arthur Sullivan spoke of Stainer as one of his oldest friends and reminisced about their boyhood days. Some music was sung by a section of the cathedral choir under Mr Walker. It was a fitting and harmonious ending to what had been the most important period in Stainer's career and, perhaps, the happiest. As *The Guardian* recalled later:

There, as in Oxford, he worked wonders with his choir. Unlike the majority of church organists, he seems to have had a happy experience of ecclesiastical authority, for he often spoke of the effectual support in the work of reorganisation that he had received from the Chapter and the Vicars-Choral of the Cathedral.[71]

Eleven years later the dean and chapter, always ready to recall their gratitude to Stainer, entertained him to dinner in the Chapter House to celebrate the fiftieth anniversary of his admission as a chorister of the cathedral. Time had not weakened memories and Gregory, who by this time had become dean, gave an accurate résumé of all that Sir John had found on his appointment and the radical and salutary changes he had made by the time he retired. During his life's work Stainer left his mark most indelibly on St Paul's Cathedral music.

6

Professor of Music at Oxford and other appointments

Within a year of his departure from St Paul's Cathedral, John Stainer was elected Professor of Music at the University of Oxford in succession to his former master and friend, Frederick Ouseley. Their joint endeavours conferred on academic music created an aura of respectability that it had previously lacked, and the foundation of the faculty's present role can be traced back to them.

At the beginning of the nineteenth century there were in the whole of Great Britain only two chairs of music – those at the two then existing English universities, Oxford and Cambridge. But although there were professors of music at both Oxford (1626) and Cambridge (1684), neither provided any teaching of music and, as will presently be seen, their arrangements as to musical degrees were unsatisfactory. Apparently very few musicians took degrees in earlier times and it was estimated that at the beginning of the nineteenth century the number of Bachelors and Doctors of Music in this country numbered only between twenty and thirty.[1]

Although many eminent musicians occupied the chair of music at Oxford, up to the middle of the nineteenth century none took much interest in the post. At the opening of that century Dr William Crotch[2] had been professor for three years and he continued to hold the post until 1847. Henry Bishop, a prolific writer of now forgotten operas, ballets and other musical stage works, succeeded him. After his appointment, however, he appeared in Oxford even less frequently than Crotch and his achievements there were negligible.

STAINER'S APPOINTMENT TO THE OXFORD PROFESSORSHIP

In May 1889 a notice appeared in the *Oxford University Gazette* about the vacant professorship in music, requesting those who wished to become candidates 'to communicate their intention to the Registrar on or before Saturday, June 8, 1889'.[3] Just a few days prior to this announcement, T. L. Southgate, editor of *The Musical Standard*, had some pertinent words to say about the appointment. A summary is quoted at this point as it gives some indication of current feeling on the subject. Southgate considered that the salary of the professor should be raised from £130 per annum to a sum 'nearer the equivalent of that allotted to the occupants of other professorial chairs'. It was reasonable also that whoever was elected should be resident in Oxford during term time, not occupied in teaching, conducting or playing at concerts in London or 'at the other end of the Kingdom', and should not be closely connected with any other institution that might take him frequently away from Oxford. What was needed, Southgate continued, was a:

. . . thoughtful, experienced skilful teacher, a man who knows the art in all its phases, historically, acoustically, practically, a man who is devotee of no one school but has sympathies as wide as the art itself is boundless, a man of broad culture and reading, able to discourse and illustrate his teaching by practical example, and as ready in the class room and at the head of his orchestra as he is on the lecture platform and in his private study when examining the contrapuntal exercises of those who appear before him to have their merits assessed.

He continued to eliminate those whom he felt would not put their Oxford duties before their own previously acquired musical commitments. What was not wanted, he wrote, was 'some brilliant player or clever composer, or book maker, or magazine article writer . . . possibly grounding his claim for the office on past achievements, or regarding it as an additional honour to be attached to his name, rather than as a position of great responsibility entailing important duties on its occupant'. It was hoped that the electing body, consisting of nine heads of colleges and other professors, would seek advice from outside; a great change had come over public opinion 'as to the esteem in which music is now held, the demand that exists for reform and enlargement of the duties attached to the office and beyond it'. An ornamental professor was not wanted; the electorate, it was hoped, would 'make an appointment beneficial to the art, and worthy of the great teaching institution itself'.[4]

It was not surprising the Stainer should apply; his previous experience within the university and his academic standing nationally made him an obvious candidate. But there were two other advantages – that Stainer was a teacher in addition to being an academic musician, writing and editing text-books, primers and tutors, and also that he was already an Oxford resident. Lady Stainer's mother had continued to live in Oxford when the Stainers were in London and the family house in South Parks Road (the house is now demolished) became their home when they returned to Oxford in 1888.

It is most unlikely that Stainer should have returned to live in Oxford merely to wait for Ouseley's death so that he could snatch up the professorship as a resident again. Oxford was the Stainers' home and reasonably centrally situated for Sir John's work visiting the training colleges in his capacity as an Inspector for the Board of Education and for his multifarious activities in London. Clearly he had resigned his cathedral appointment not because the duties there were too absorbing (even though they must have been a great restraint because of the regularity of the services), but owing to the concern over his failing eyesight. And leaving London, even though he was only forty-eight years old, would give him more time for academic pursuits and reflection. However, although Stainer was of a retiring disposition he was also industrious, and having previously been so busy for so long it was to be expected that after a short break he would want to get himself fully back into action again. The condition of his eye seemed better so there would appear to have been no reason why he should not resume some work which, at the same time, would not preclude him from his other musical activities; additionally he would also be able to spend time on his foreign tours, a pleasure which both he and Lady Stainer could share.

In 1865, Ouseley wrote to Stainer, 'I have set my heart on resigning my Professorship in your favour, as soon as you are MA and MusDoc'.[5] He did not do so, and this kind of statement or some more recent recommendation from Ouseley was certainly no guarantee of appointment. We have no evidence that Stainer's relationship with Ouseley was as close as it had been, although when Stainer lectured on Ouseley's life and influence to The Musical Association,[6] he left no doubt of his discipleship and devotion to Ouseley.

It is reasonable to assume that canvassing for appointment was frowned upon, but Stainer may have been at least content to see himself favoured for such a position by *The Musical Times*. The editor pointed out the desirability of having a resident professor rather than one who came to Oxford once a term just to deliver his lectures and had little influence within the university. Prerequisites were administrative skill, aptitude for hard work and the ability to organise prevailing enthusiasm:

If such a man be appointed, it would not be rash to prophesy a brilliant future for the Oxford School of Music. The names of many eminent musicians are spoken of as candidates. There can be no doubt that if Sir John Stainer were appointed, his acceptance of the office would give the highest possible satisfaction in all quarters. He possesses all the qualifications necessary, and would command the confidence of musicians and of all interested in music throughout the world.[7]

Stainer did apply for the position, supplying a curriculum vitae with a broad statement of his aims and ambitions. One assumes that he was interviewed along with other candidates for the appointment in the normal way, but there is no surviving record of the other applicants. After his appointment he did make some attempts to find out what competition he had been up against, but the university authorities would not say 'who else was in for the job but it leaked out that the Board had 24 applications'.[8] Meanwhile, Stainer would have known that Hubert Parry had been urged to stand as a candidate and had had some influential support chiefly from Henry Pelham, a contemporary under-graduate friend of Parry's at Exeter College who later became president of Trinity College. This caused some uncertainty, for while Parry had a strong following it was not at first clear whether Stainer would accept the post if offered because of his fears (later resolved) for his sight. In April 1889, Parry wrote to Stainer urging him to accept 'as the only man who had a chance of doing any good' and saying that he would be delighted to be his choragus.[9] Stainer delayed for over a month before deciding; he thereby placed Parry in a difficult position with his supporters. Finally Parry decided to apply, making it clear at the same time, however, that if Stainer would accept 'he would welcome the appointment of one who was not only his senior and an old, dear and much respected friend, but a first-rate musician and already an Oxford resident'. By chance Stainer and Parry subsequently met on Gloucester railway station when 'Stainer told Parry that his eyes [sic] were much better and that he was quite willing to accept the professorship'. Parry decided, in those circumstances, not to stand, and their relationship continued to be close and harmonious. As Parry's biographer stated, 'Parry frequently stayed with Stainer at Oxford and never failed to speak of the kindliness and sympathy of his host . . .'[10]

On 12 May, W. H. Hadow recorded in his papers that it seemed pretty certain that Stainer was to be appointed professor. He continued: 'If so there is talk of his starting a Musical Conservatoire in Oxford, a thing which I have long wanted to see. And I have been offered a place on the Board of Studies provided that I will conform to popular prejudice by taking my Mus.Bac.'[11]

Walter Parratt, lecturing on Oxford music twenty years after Stainer's appointment, said that no worthier successor to Ouseley could have been found than Stainer, who 'was not only his [Ouseley's] friend but to some extent also his pupil, whose vivifying personality had done much for music in general and for church music in particular . . .'[12]

The *Oxford University Gazette* formally gave news of Stainer's appointment on 18 June 1889, he being elected as from that date. *The Musical Times* showed its delight with the decision and its high regard for Stainer as a person and as a musician:

> The University of Oxford has made a wise choice in selecting Sir John Stainer from among the many applicants to fill the Professorial chair of music. His appointment will give the greatest satisfaction to all who are interested in the progress of musical art in this country. For reasons which are needless to specify, the position is one which hitherto had not been so completely commanding as all would wish to see. It is, therefore, to be hoped that the University, in making its choice of a musical representative whose views of art are liberal and comprehensive, has been guided by sentiments fully in accordance with the spirit of the age . . .[13]

The editor went on to comment on Stainer's theoretical works, saying that these revealed the qualities which helped the electors to choose Stainer as professor, 'and they are also those which, being recognised by the world of music at large, will strengthen the applause which follows the delivering of the verdict'.[14]

Edward Chapman, MP, who remembered Stainer before he was appointed to St Paul's Cathedral, recalled that his return to Oxford was hailed with delight by everybody:

His ruddy, merry face has lost none of its brightness, nor his manner its freshness, while his interest in the progress of his art was as keen as ever. What I specially noticed in him as Professor was his unique power of welding men together and the total absence of professional jealousy. The petty quarrels of rival societies he would ignore, and no differences or difficulties between individuals could long survive an interview with him, disarming as he did by his acute yet genial and sensible manner the difficulties which rival interests brought up before him. Once he said to me in his laughing way, 'If certain officials cannot be brought into line and agree, I shall run them all round the Parks together in a wheelbarrow'.[15]

STAINER'S HOPES AND INTENTIONS

Stainer was a few months short of fifty when he assumed his duties as professor. Although he had not made his intention known at this stage, it is likely that a ten-year period of service would have been in his mind. He had, within this kind of time limit, to continue the work of Ouseley and to make his own mark on the faculty. Under Ouseley the standard of the degree had improved and it had become something worth having. The syllabus had become more liberal and imaginative and the examinations contained some scope for composition; eventually this was to play a larger part, replacing to a great extent the series of dry contrapuntal exercises which were required working. The remainder of this chapter will show how Stainer played his part in continuing the reforms that Ouseley had begun.

The Stainers in Oxford were friendly and hospitable to students. To the undergraduates Stainer attempted to give practical help in their academic work and also in their instrumental playing. He was responsible for improving relations between town and gown music makers. His great wish to see some kind of school of practical instruction in Oxford was never fulfilled, but he got as near as he could to this ideal in the establishment of classes in general musicianship. His endeavour to stimulate interest is shown in the wide range of his lecture topics. With the help of his musical colleagues he succeeded in encompassing a range of studies.

Towards the end of his time as professor, the issue of compulsory residence and the necessity of candidates taking an arts course prior to a music degree came up again. Stainer, as professor, took no active part in the campaigning although his views were clearly known to be opposed to these particular changes – the outline of events is revealed later. The clash of various personalities left their mark and Stainer, there can be little doubt, must have been grateful that his time as professor was coming to an end.

STAINER AS LECTURER

There is little surviving record of the content of Stainer's lectures as professor. Two were published at the time: the first, in 1889, on *The present state of music in England*, and the second in 1892 entitled *Music in relation to the Intellect and Emotions*. The musical illustrations used in five of the other lectures were also printed at the same time. E. H. Fellowes, recalling his association with the Professor of Music's Choir, the purpose of which was to sing the illustrations for Stainer's lectures, spoke highly of Stainer's knowledge and of his capacity to deal with unusual subjects in addition to being a fine musical scholar.[16] A contributor to an obituary article on Stainer spoke of the lectures as being:

. . . no mere pedantic monotonous mumblings, delivered to a handful of somnolently inclined listeners. On the contrary, they were most interesting and instructive. With their admirable musical illustrations, and delivered in his bright attractive manner, large audiences eagerly flocked to the Sheldonian Theatre – even deaf Dons were to be seen in the front row with their hands to their ears in order that not a word should be lost.[17]

When Stainer lectured on Purcell in Michaelmas term 1895, an indignant MA, 'even though in academical dress', complained of the difficulty in finding a seat and thought that a certain number of seats should be reserved for members of the university 'who have a right to be there . . . I venture to think that the spectacle of learned MA's being forced to crouch on the steps of the Vice Chancellor's throne is not edifying . . . .' The correspondent considered that the courtesy of the university in allowing non-members to attend was abused at this lecture.[18]

91

Certainly the range of subjects included an extraordinarily wide variety of interests including both special and general topics. The custom was for Stainer himself to deliver one lecture each term, usually in the Sheldonian Theatre, often with musical illustrations, and for the choragus[19] to give three public lectures each term, sometimes assisted by other musicians.

THE FACULTY OF MUSIC AS A TEACHING ESTABLISHMENT

One of Stainer's first aims was to try to establish a music school and have it regarded as a teaching establishment. Ouseley had tried to do the same, but the classes received little support and it really needed the presence in Oxford of the professor. The introduction of the classes in Michaelmas term 1889, received guarded support from *The Oxford Journal*:

Sir John Stainer has practically settled some, at least, of the reforms which he proposes to introduce upon assuming the Chair of Professor of Music at Oxford. The most important is the foundation of a teaching school in connection with the University. Oxford and Cambridge have frequently been twitted with the fact that they are at present merely examining bodies for degrees, and that the degree of Mus. Doc. is placed practically beyond the reach of young men of moderate means, owing to the regulation that the candidate must publicly have his degree 'exercise' performed before the University, at an expense to himself of quite £100. The reform of the system of conferring Degrees must be a matter of time, but the introduction by Sir John Stainer of the teaching element is a distinct step in the right direction. The classes will begin during the ensuing term . . . the whole being officially directed by Sir John Stainer, who as an Oxford resident is taking a great personal interest in the progress of music in the University.[20]

It has been argued that the revival of the school of practical musical instruction was due to an article in *The Musical Standard* by the editor, T. L. Southgate, but this is unlikely according to the unpublished notes of George Thewlis. Stainer and Southgate were personal friends and were to have much close contact in connection with the Toronto degrees affair, the Union of Graduates in Music and the State Registration of Teachers Act. It is more likely that they simply held identical views and Southgate's article on this subject was prompted by Ouseley's death and the ensuing vacancy. Southgate's main points were:

1 Instruction in the performance of music was required.
2 Technical skill and theoretical knowledge should be treated as of
   equal importance.
3 'Methodical and systemized higher instruction in the art' should
   come from the professor himself.
4 There was need for an 'official influence' on music coming directly
   from the professor and having an effect both on the university and on
   the town.

Surely it is legitimate to desire such an influence, asked
Southgate:

Properly exercised, it would be of inestimable benefit in instructing and
directing the tastes of the youthful members of the University at a period
of their lives when such orthodox directing is of incalculable importance
in moulding the future aims and tastes of those who naturally spread
themselves over the length and breadth of our land and eventually
become authorities to others . . .[21]

Although Southgate's ideal was not altogether realised, there is
no doubt, according to George Thewlis:

. . . that the best man in England at that time was appointed, and anyone
who studies the state of music in England at that time will realise the
tremendous pioneer work done by Stainer upon which subsequent
composers have built their edifice. It is impossible to overestimate the
value of Stainer's influence on the music of his time – not only in
Oxford, but upon the whole course of musical life in the country. His
knowledge was as great as his predecessor's, his method of imparting it
infinitely greater; and those who know him only as a composer know
him not at all.[22]

PRACTICAL MUSICAL INSTRUCTION

Stainer lost no time in arranging these classes, and in October
1889 he published details of them together with a list of the
lectures for the term. W. H. Hadow of Worcester College recalled
as early as 23 June 1889 that Stainer's first act as professor was
to appoint certain deputies as readers to teach in specific
branches. Hadow was offered 'Musical Form and Analysis', but
only three people came to the class.[23] The lectures and practical
courses were open to all members of the university, the only
requirement, apart from the payment of the fee, being that undergraduates needed prior permission from their college tutor to

study music. Hadow gave six lectures each term (fee one guinea), C. H. Lloyd lectured on 'Composition', the Rev Dr J. H. Mee on 'Counterpoint', Varley Roberts from Magdalen College on 'Harmony', F. J. Smith on 'Elementary Acoustics', James Taylor on 'The Technique of Pianoforte playing' and Francis C. Woods on 'Organ Playing' (this last course being the most expensive at two guineas per term). [24] In 1891 Woods was to give classes in 'Musical Dictation', 'with practical instruction in the art of writing down music when heard', [25] and in 1897 'cello instruction was introduced into the list [26] which had varied little since the introduction of these classes in 1889 apart from the additions here mentioned. Classes in 'The Production of the Speaking Voice' were also introduced in 1897. [27]

Stainer was commended for the practice of introducing lecturers in specialised fields to assist in a music department which had become very flourishing, as the following report indicates:

There seems, if one may judge from the University Gazette, to be an increasing number of these Professors who get lectures delivered for them. This is no doubt due to the fact that their subject covers more ground or a longer period than the Professors can be expected to deal with. The practice is one which may, with advantage, be extended even further, as it seems to be the only way at present in which the teaching power of the University can be systematised. It will be a great thing if Professors come to recognise that they have a certain special responsibility in their special subjects. The most lengthy list in this respect is that of the Professor of Music who is assisted by no less than eight lecturers in different departments. Besides the Science Professors, there are at least five others who are thus trying to do their duty . . . [28]

But Stainer's ideal was ahead of his time. His work was not, and it must have been a major disappointment for him to fail to establish a flourishing practical teaching centre at the university. To run side by side with the academic instruction he wished to see instrumental and vocal teaching such as was provided in the music colleges in London. His experience in each kind of establishment had confirmed the value of providing both forms of teaching within the university.

Stainer referred to the whole question in his (unpublished) university lecture given in Trinity term 1897. [29] He doubted whether the university was giving a thorough and complete musical education that would enable the students to qualify as professional musicians. He felt it was not a place adapted for this purpose, and he advocated 'the claims of a larger centre of civilisation where operatic and oratorio performances with symphonic concerts would be more easily within reach'.[30] His advice to a boy leaving school was, where possible, to devote two years to the study of music, either at home or abroad, before going to Oxford. He thought that the arts course, as well as a musical degree, was the ideal education for which to aim. Although Stainer had mentioned going abroad prior to university, he was not necessarily recommending musical study in a foreign country, which, though fashionable, was not in his view essential.[31]

After this lecture, delivered in June, he returned to the subject in the following month. A professor without a school was an anomaly and steps should be taken, he thought, to establish a University School of Music, to cost between £15,000 and £20,000 per annum and to include opera on the best scale.[32] But in his heart Stainer must have suspected that such an ambitious plan was really quite out of the question and anything less would fall short of his ideal. If London had not been so near, and had the students not been absent from Oxford for six months of each year, Stainer might have found his ideal easier of realisation. As it was, some students managed to precede or combine a university course with some time at either the Royal College of Music or the Royal Academy of Music. Charles Wood, for instance, planned to go up to Oxford from the Royal College of Music on money donated by some of the teaching staff of the college.[33] Percy Buck was awarded an organ scholarship at the Royal College in 1889, and after some time there left to become organ scholar of Worcester College, Oxford. John Borland, also awarded a college scholarship in 1889 (for horn playing),[34] took the BMus at Oxford in 1897. Students at Oxford today probably get their instrumental tuition in much the same way. It appears that the only instrumental instruction available outside the range contained in the official list recently outlined was from chapel organists. One may imagine the warm feelings Stainer might have had today to see resident string quartets at the universities.

STAINER'S ASSISTANCE TO DEGREE CANDIDATES

If Stainer was unsuccessful in establishing a flourishing comprehensive teaching establishment within the faculty of music, he did try to give what help he could to degree candidates. When he arrived in Oxford as professor he soon revealed that he would not be content only to give his statutory lectures and to examine candidates for musical degrees. Before the end of the month in which he was appointed he had given the list of musical works to be studied for the next Bachelor's examination, and in September he published a list of twenty books recommended for study in preparation for the examinations – on harmony, counterpoint, instrumentation, history and, additionally for the DMus, acoustics.

Although Stainer did not write any text-book for his students during his professorship (he did revise the *Dictionary of Musical Terms*), he was not idle in his writing, for he was engaged in preparing lectures and his work on Dufay. In addition he published, in 1892, a little booklet, *A few words to candidates for the degree of Mus. Bac. Oxon.*[35] It is impressive because of its friendly hints and absence of pompous academic language; Stainer set out to help prospective candidates and show the pitfalls. The standards were high and had to be maintained because 'if an adventurer gets through by sheer luck or a 'fluke', it certainly does not gratify an examiner to find that he has merely added one more to some advertising tutor's list of successes.'[36] Stainer considered the first requirement for progress in harmony was 'to be able to hear mentally what is seen with the eye'[37] and advised students, weak in this direction, to start by looking through a short hymn tune until the pupil could hear the parts. It was not necessary to study any particular text-book (although, as mentioned above, Stainer had given a list of recommended books three years earlier) and examinees were advised not to regard the examination paper as a series of traps for unsuspecting students!

When you sit down before your paper in the examination room, do not suspect the questions or problems to be a collection of insidious traps laid by the examiners with the malicious intention of securing your overthrow. Try to discover the opportunities they offer you of combining technical correctness with artistic skill.[38]

A comprehensive knowledge of the music of the great masters was necessary in harmony writing, and analysis of great works helped not only with the study of form but in harmony also. Stainer considered a careful study of Bach's chorales to be most helpful.

Throughout his life as a professional musician, Stainer abhorred bogus degrees and diplomas, and he was careful to maintain certain standards in examinations. Unmusical candidates should not become Bachelors of Music, nor should those who, though musical, had not taken the trouble to become technically proficient:

This leads me to speak of two very different classes of men, both of whom may fail to pass our course. The one consists of persevering plodders who are absolutely devoid of musical gifts; the other, of more or less gifted men who affect to despise the technical side of their art. It may be true that inspiration cannot be created by plodding, but it is also equally true that even genius cannot dispense with technical study. Neither of these two classes of men should be surprised if they find a Degree unobtainable. The latter, however, have a better chance of success in the long run than the former. Music seems to be an art which offers a peculiar temptation to many who are by nature very poorly equipped for its mastery. To be 'fond of music' is frequently accepted as synonymous with 'having a gift for music' and the miscalculation of their own powers is not discovered by such persons until their eyes are rudely opened by the adverse judgement of qualified examiners.[39]

Stainer considered Mendelssohn's oratorio *St Paul* to be a valuable study of questions of form, but he warned against copying or any sort of malpractice in the presentation of the exercise where students were placed on trust. All academic exercises were examined most carefully by the professor, 'chord by chord, and sentence by sentence, keeping an analysis of every movement'. They went next to the choragus for further detailed inspection. Then they were forwarded to a third examiner, who eventually returned them to the professor. Only then were the papers returned to the candidates. Stainer commented, 'It seems to me that the only persons who get any profit out of this process are the postal authorities.'[40]

Stainer made very clear his views on the relative importance of mere grammatical correctness and musical quality:

I hope no candidates are so silly as to suppose that an otherwise good Exercise is ever rejected because it may happen to contain a few consecutive fifths or eighths; if an Exercise is rejected, it has more serious faults than this. I am quite aware that many people think the only requisite qualification for a musical Professor in a University is that he should be endowed with a sort of canine scent for tracking consecutives. We are not so narrow-minded. On the other hand, let no candidate imagine that any Exercise can claim acceptance because it contains no grammatical errors. If it is poor weak stuff it will be rejected as such.[41]

And he advised that the viva voce part of the First examination should not be regarded as something to be dreaded but 'should be looked upon as merely a pleasant ten minutes' talk with an examiner'.[42] This twenty-eight page booklet was intended to put the examination into perspective and to be a genuine help to candidates; Stainer hoped it would not be regarded as a publicity stunt as he made clear in his final paragraph – a typical gesture:

In conclusion, I should like to say that these remarks have not been published for the purpose of attracting men to present themselves here for musical degrees; I have neither reason nor wish to advertise our wares; moreover, if the number of our candidates should be reduced, I should be a gainer in every way. But as men do continue to come up, it is certainly desirable that they should be made fully aware of the conditions under which the examinations are carried on; and if the hints I have given should in any way help to economise the time and ensure the success of my younger brethren, it will give me genuine pleasure. J. S.[43]

Stainer always chaired the examining board with the choragus (Parry) and one other examiner; the third examiner was often a musician resident within the university or a music graduate of it. Within the university were Dr Varley Roberts (Magdalen College), the Rev Dr J. H. Mee, Dr F. Iliffe and Dr T. W. Dodds; but Philip Armes, Organist of Durham Cathedral, Haydn Keeton, Organist of Peterborough Cathedral and Sir Frederick Bridge, Organist of Westminster Abbey also helped.

Hadow thought little of the examination. He was one of ten candidates and recalled:

I have a meaner opinion than ever of the musical degree. The three papers were (1) Harmony in five parts, (2) Counterpoint in five parts and (3) Musical History. I went in on almost no preparation. I have never had a harmony lesson in my life. I haven't written a counterpoint exercise since last year (when I did have 3 lessons) and never one in as many as five parts. For Musical History I trusted to desultory reading. And now I am told I did the best work sent in . . .[44]

The recipient of this letter was Hadow's mother, to whom he wrote weekly for over fifty years. It must be remembered that Hadow was something of a musical prodigy possessing an acute mind. He was deeply familiar with music and at this time had already established himself in Oxford as a composer, apparently writing in the style of Brahms. In the letter to his mother he may well have been putting on a tone of bravado. In the 1889 examinations for BMus, the first of Stainer's professorship, seven candidates passed and seven failed and there were no passes in DMus in October 1889. In appointing him to lecture, Stainer saw in Hadow the kind of man who could contribute something distinctive to Oxford music. In those days Hadow was a young and energetic fellow of Worcester College and Stainer evidently found him reliable; he was appointed for this reason rather than for being a dry academic.

Stainer had known Hadow for some time. After Hadow had applied for membership to The Musical Association in 1884 (at the age of twenty-five), he introduced himself to Stainer who 'at once took my arm − ''come along'', he said, ''I've been wanting to make your acquaintance . . .'' Nothing could exceed his kindness, and when we parted I felt prouder than I have for a long time . . .' [45] And later that year, Hadow wrote to his mother that he did not wish for applause, simply to be recognised by other musicians as a comrade: 'Stainer and Lloyd have done more to hearten me than anything'.[46]

Their good relationship evidently continued. Hadow was 'startled to know that Stainer referred to ''Mr Hadow'' in a lecture',[47] and that Stainer once 'stopped in the middle to recommend my Sonata Form book. That gives it a cachet of respectability which, I fear, it rather needed'.[48] On one occasion when Hadow was trying to organise some public lectures of music for the next term, especially one on Parry's *Symphony*, he wrote that 'Stainer couldn't undertake it so then I asked him to let me write to Sir George Grove. ''No!'' he said, ''Grove is too much of an amateur!'' Then he asked me to do it. This I take to be one of the greatest compliments that have yet fallen to my lot. I am not sure whether I have the courage to rush in where Grove is forbidden to tread . . .'[49] When Hadow's *The National Element in the Music of Haydn* got the best reception any lecture of his had obtained, he recalls that 'Stainer waited outside the Sheldonian to discuss and congratulate'.[50] And on another occasion Stainer wrote to Hadow, 'What an admirable lecture you gave us on the 'Eroica'! I enjoyed it much. Will you give us another lecture next term? (I shall lecture on the oratorio, *St Paul* on Feb. 28) Please do.'[51]

DEGREE EXAMINATIONS

The basic structure of the Bachelor's examinations in Stainer's time remained the same in that harmony exercises in four parts worked to a figured bass were set as before together with questions concerned with species counterpoint. In Ouseley's time questions which dealt with a basic knowledge of rudimentary terms ('Define Plagal, Diatonic Harmony, inverted pedal', etc) were included in both the First and Second examinations. The Second examination during the Stainer period included a separate paper on fugue. In the 1895 paper the candidate was given three hours to write a fugue in four parts on one of two given fugue subjects. Stainer also included a question on modulation, in which an opening was given and certain keys specified for modulation. The whole level of the examinations in the 1890s was more musical, especially in the free harmony questions. The general impression left is that Ouseley's was more a 'text-book' examination, but that Stainer's, within the limits of the examination system, was a more effective test of written musicianship.

In the history paper Stainer appears to have tested knowledge in a more specialised way. For instance, Ouseley (in 1885) asked seventeen questions which were very detailed but superficial. The first question, for example, asked for the dates of birth and death of Handel, J. S. Bach, Haydn, Mozart, Weber, Spohr, Mendelssohn, Meyerbeer, Auber, Rossini, Crotch and Balfe; and question seven asked for instances of 'great composers for the lute' and for a description of the instrument. Ten years later Stainer set six questions, all compulsory, which demanded a wide knowledge of history and music of a particular period.

The five papers set for the Doctorate in Music were very similar in both Ouseley's and Stainer's period. Stainer asked for

100

eight-part harmony whereas Ouseley demanded six parts; and Stainer asked only two questions on species counterpoint whereas Ouseley required three to be answered. The structure, nevertheless, was much the same with little in the way of questions on acoustics (although there was a paper in 1893); and the papers more scientific in content were totally excluded.

SET WORKS FOR STUDY IN THE DEGREE EXAMINATIONS

Stainer may have favoured the early Romantic composers in his choice of music at St Paul's Cathedral, but the range of musical works he set that were to be studied for the BMus examinations was very wide. Included over Stainer's ten-year term were the following works (listed chronologically in respect of the various examination sittings): J. S. Bach, *St Matthew Passion*; Schumann, *Manfred* Overture; Schubert, *Symphony in C (no 9?)*; J. S. Bach, Cantata, *'Ich hatte viel Bekümmerniss*; Beethoven, *Symphony no 9*; J. S. Bach, *Magnificat*; Brahms, *Academic Festival Overture*; Weber, *Der Freischütz*; J. S. Bach, *St John Passion*; Schumann, *Symphony no 4 in D*; Mendelssohn, *Athalie*; Beethoven, *Violin Concerto*; Beethoven, *Mass in C*; Mendelssohn, *Violin Concerto*; Beethoven, *Symphony no 3*; Mendelssohn, *Lobgesang*; Mendelssohn, *St Paul*; Schubert, *'Unfinished' Symphony no 8*; J. S. Bach, *Mass in B minor*; Beethoven, Overture, *Leonora no 3*; J. S. Bach, *St Matthew Passion* (for the second time), Schumann, *Piano Concerto*; Beethoven, *Fidelio*; Brahms, *Variations on a theme of Haydn*; Beethoven, *Mass in C* (for the second time), Schumann, *Symphony no 3*; Brahms, *Schicksalslied*; Beethoven, *Symphony no 8*; J. S. Bach, *Christmas Oratorio* and Schumann, *Piano Concerto* (for the second time). The breadth of Stainer's approach is evident. At that time some works would have been heard only infrequently by concert audiences. Opera was enjoyed by relatively few, and it would seem an adventurous innovation to include operatic works for analytical study.

The principal differences between degrees at Oxford and London, where Stainer also advised and examined, were twofold. Firstly, the autocratic will of the professor prevailed at Oxford, whereas at London there was no professor and the degree was in the hands of at least four examiners: in the 1880s, Stainer and three scientists, viz Pole and the two lecturers in experimental philosophy. Secondly, the greatest difference was the heavy emphasis London University placed on a scientific knowledge and the complete lack of it at Oxford. Apart from this there was little to choose between the two examinations, and it is clear that Stainer used his experience gained at London to bring more of an element of free composition to the Oxford examination when he assumed the professorship.

Whereas a superficial knowledge of musical history was sufficient in Ouseley's time at Oxford, it was no longer so in the Stainer period. In short, Stainer replaced the earlier theoretical questions and contrapuntal workings with exercises which displayed more adequately a candidate's musicianship – as far as it could be done under examination conditions – and in this respect brought it nearer to the London degree.

MUSICAL EXERCISES

The public performance of the exercise for the Bachelor's examination was no longer required after 1878, and the regulations for the performance of the Doctorate exercise were relaxed in 1890 so that 'minimum orchestral and vocal forces' might be used.[52] But while performance of the Doctorate exercise was obligatory, Stainer was determined to improve the standards. The following paragraph from *The Musical Times* suggests that during Ouseley's later years the performance had sometimes been perfunctory:

The 'Testamur' will not however be given if the performance should (owing to carelessness or inaccuracy) be calculated to bring discredit to the Faculty. The regulation concerning the number and constitution of the Band, and that of withholding the 'Testamur' in the event of an insufficient performance, will greatly help to augment the value of the degree.[53]

In May 1891, not without some opposition from within the university, the fee for the Doctorate examination was raised from £10 to £25, bringing it into line with the fees charged for other doctorates in the university and thereby, in a small measure, raising the status of the degree within the university. The imposition of the performance of the degree exercise had that year been withdrawn and consequently the overall expenses, even with the revised examination fee, were less than before. Some idea of the cost involved is given in the detailed expenses of Dr Edward Hodges when he successfully applied for his Doctorate in Cambridge in 1825. The total expenses came to £206 13s 8d of which £83 6s 0d were expenses involved in the performance of the musical exercise.[54] The last public performance of the musical exercise for the Doctor's degree took place in the Sheldonian Theatre in February 1892 when Frederick Greenish successfully performed his sacred cantata *The Adoration*.[55]

GENERAL EDUCATIONAL ATTAINMENT FOR MUSICIANS

In the 1890s the general educational standard required of candidates for the Bachelor of Music degree came in for further discussion. The first of two main proposals for reform was aimed at reducing what was held to be the unnecessarily high standard in the arts tests. In addition to the established musical tests – which were to be unchanged – candidates were to pass Responsions and work papers calling for translation from two languages. This would help those who found mathematics stubbornly difficult, and those whose earlier classical education had suffered because of the amount of work demanded by their instrumental study. But the second main proposal for reform, in 1898, was concerned to raise the cultural standard of music undergraduates by enforcing a compulsory three years' study for an arts degree prior to the taking of the Bachelor of Music degree.

This second proposal was strongly urged on the grounds that the status of the musician would be raised to that of graduates in other faculties (though it must here be noted that music was never regarded as an established faculty 'with a proper salaried staff and fully equipped premises' until 1944, largely owing to the work of Sir Hugh Allen).[56] The case against the proposed change was that, although things had improved, there was still no satisfactory and systematic teaching of music. Professional musicians, it was argued, could not spare three years from their other duties. In short, the proposed regulations, if passed, would pretty well limit a degree in music to 'amateurs of wealth and leisure'.[57]

Stainer and Sir Frederick Bridge were against enforced residence. And so was Ebenezer Prout, notwithstanding the gain that would have accrued to him, for Dublin (where he was Professor of Music) welcomed external candidates. Parry, Hadow, Parratt and Stanford were in favour. Both Hadow and Parry, we know, thought the Oxford music degrees were granted too easily and the residence qualification could do nothing but help to improve standards. And, as Parry pointed out, external degrees in music could be gained from three universities at that time: London, Durham and Dublin. Ultimately Bridge presented to the Hebdomadal Council a memorial against the proposal signed by seventy graduates of Oxford holding both degrees in arts and music, and it was subsequently announced that:

The Hebdomadal Council of the University of Oxford has rejected the scheme of compulsory residence at the University on the part of those desirous of taking degrees in music. Thus the present conditions, which have existed for four hundred years, remain unaltered.[58]

Thus Stainer had his way. In fact he maintained the position he had adopted in 1870. He wished to uphold a high standard for the BMus degree but he did not want unnecessary restrictions put in the way of candidates. Before entering college or university, music students were compelled to spend much time on instrumental study, and as a result their general education suffered. At university level, too, candidates for music degrees were either still deeply engaged in instrumental study, or were parish church organists, assistant organists in cathedrals, or schoolmasters. The Oxford degree would have been out of reach of such candidates had the residence plan been put into effect. They would have lost the opportunity of obtaining the degree, and the university, in turn, would have lost many good candidates who would have been forced to look to the other universities where external candidates for degrees in music were accommodated.

Parry subsequently wrote to Hadow regretting the decisions of the council. He continued:

I am always trying to bring the tests and questions up to date as much as possible, and we will go on doing that. But you will never prevent 'scugs' and mechanic and plodding duffers getting degrees as long as exams and techniques are the only tests required.[59]

Music in Oxford was passing through a very anxious time, and though Stainer's popularity had never diminished, he may have felt disheartened at so much internal argument. His efforts to gain support for a teaching establishment within the university music department had come to nothing. As will be seen, he was strongly of the opinion that a professor should not stay in office for longer than ten years; at that time he was himself in his tenth year. It is not, therefore, surprising to find Stainer expressing the wish to resign office before he was sixty years of age.

RESIGNATION

Stainer's resignation was considered by the Board of Electors to the Professorship and accepted in June 1899. There is no mention of it in the *Oxford University Gazette* and the notice of the vacancy was not announced until later.[60] It would be quite unlike Stainer to resign following a disagreement, and, as far as can be discovered, it was not necessarily the last controversy over music within the university – the question of residence – that prompted his resignation. Before he tendered his resignation he had attempted to make some changes in the conditions of the appointment. A statute had been passed making the appointment of choragus subject to the discretion of the professor (thereby regularising what had been generally accepted by custom for some years), and abolishing the office of coryphaeus, the elaborate duties of which, as described in the statutes, had never been performed, and the stipend of which was nothing. Stainer suggested that in future the professorship should be tenable for ten years only. This was accepted by the Hebdomadal Council and a statute to carry it into effect was promulgated on 16 June. Out of a congregation of 460 members (resident Masters of Arts) 26 voted, raising the comment from *The Musical Times*, 'How deeply Oxford must be interested in the welfare of the Faculty of Music'.[61] If Stainer was miserable at the voting support, he must have been more so when the result was thirteen votes for the proposal and the same number against it, the motion therefore being lost. Although opinions may have been divided on the subject, observed the editor of *The Musical Times*, the result was unfortunate. He continued:

It is most important that examinations should not get into a groove, and that the type of 'exercise' should move with perpetual progress of the art of music. But the best of Dons are liable to become crystallized in old age, and Oxford, had this proposal been carried, would probably have been able to find a brilliant succession of learned lecturers and experienced examiners to represent the art.[62]

Notice of the forthcoming election to the professorship was published on 24 October 1899. Hadow wrote as soon as he knew of Stainer's resignation that he wanted to support Parry,[63] and subsequently considered Parry's appointment the 'best thing that could possibly happen'.[64] Fortunately we are left in no doubt as to whom Stainer wanted as successor, as Parry wrote in his diary at the time, 'Back to Stainers. Stainer took me up to his room and stood over me like a jailer till I submitted to writing offering myself as a candidate for the Professorship.'[65] So Sir Hubert Parry, Director of the Royal College of Music, became the newly elected Professor of Music. He was to lecture once a term 'on the theory and history of music'[66] and was able to select his own choragus who would assist him in preparing illustrations for his lectures, just as Parry had done ten years earlier for Stainer.

Parry paid a most graceful tribute to Stainer in his inaugural lecture in Oxford Town Hall on 7 March, describing him as our 'much-beloved Sir John Stainer' and the most valuable professor of music that Oxford had ever possessed. *The Musical Times* report continued:

He [Parry] could gladly run on for the whole of the allotted time for his lecture in singing Sir John's praises, but he thought that would be superfluous in Oxford. None, said the lecturer, but those whose inner vision was constitutionally oblique could fail to appreciate the large-hearted generosity, the frank sincerity, open-mindedness, wide range of interests, shrewdness of judgement, vivacity of mind and intelligence, the constancy in labouring to accomplish perfectly whatever came to him to do, his loyalty to friends as well as to ideals, all of which combined to make a unique professor, in whose footsteps he would endeavour to follow . . .[67]

Parry's tribute was generous and a fitting end to Stainer's work in Oxford.

One might speculate as to why Stainer resigned the professorship at this time. It would seem likely, however, that this had been his intention for some time, or was indeed the realisation of a decision he had made when appointed, to stay for a term of ten years. In letters to Edwards he had often said that younger men should be given a chance to show their worth, be given a 'leg up into the stirrup!', as he put it.[68] Crotch, Bishop and Ouseley had all died in office, but Stainer had lived in Oxford and had taken his duties more seriously than any of his predecessors. At sixty he doubtless felt he could permit himself more relaxation while keeping himself active in a more limited way, inspecting and writing. Whatever the reason – and the loss of Stainer's private diaries makes certainty impossible – it is clear from what follows that he wished to adopt a more private and relaxed style of life.

HM INSPECTOR OF MUSIC IN TRAINING COLLEGES

The president of the council of the Board of Education appointed Stainer Inspector of Music in the Training Colleges and Elementary Schools of the Kingdom in succession to John Hullah, his duties to commence at the beginning of 1883. The appointment was welcomed by *The Musical Times* because of Stainer's high academic qualifications, he being one of the few graduates in both arts and music. 'He thus represents a new and pleasing feature in the musical profession – the raising of the status of the professor'.[69] In addition Stainer also had a 'reputation for liberal mindedness' and would obviously prove adaptable in the changing circumstances of education.

When Stainer began his work in 1883, one of his first acts was to appoint W. G. McNaught to act with W. A. Barrett as assistant inspectors. The three men worked well together and between them, as will be seen, paid hundreds of visits to training colleges. In 1891 Barrett died and was not replaced. There were certain economic difficulties at the time and this may have been a determining factor, but what is certain is the fact that there was too much work for two men, both of whom bore an unduly great burden. From 1894 Stainer took over the practical work and McNaught looked at the written exercises. This system operated for the rest of Stainer's period with the board, except for a time in 1896 when Stainer was ill and Frederick Bridge acted for him. McNaught[70] was an expert in the practical side of school music. He had made his way in the teaching profession in most unfavourable circumstances, having little equipment and being obliged to teach at one time very large groups of children of different ages. He had exemplary teaching qualities and Stainer was a superb practical musician; between them they formed an outstanding team. Stainer was prepared to seek McNaught's advice on a whole range of topics, as is acknowledged in the reports, since his own experience in the classroom was negligible in comparison.

In 1870 elementary education had become compulsory in England and Wales for all children up to the age of twelve years. One system of payment to schools from the National Exchequer was to reward each institution according to the diligence of the pupils in the various subjects taught. In music schoolchildren were tested at prescribed stages, and if they could sing something that they had prepared by rote, the school was awarded sixpence. If they reached a more advanced stage, singing from notation, and certain other tests, the school was awarded one shilling per pupil. This was the basis of what was known as the 'grants' system, and while it meant an almost slavish adherence to a routine pattern of learning, it did ensure that all able pupils had some knowledge of music before they left school. The system was abolished in 1900 and this was welcomed by some as an opportunity to widen the curriculum of the music class. Others were more cautious and felt that this could be the beginning of musical illiteracy. With no incentive, such a thing as the music lesson could become worthless or cease to exist altogether. However, the Stainer period was the one during which the grants system operated, and although it ceased in 1900 it is unlikely that Stainer had a hand in the change.

Stainer's duties were concerned mainly with the training of music teachers in training colleges. When he began visiting colleges in 1883 there were forty-three of them. As time went on, and certainly once he had finished at St Paul's, he spent longer on these visits. Initially his task was to examine students to see if they were fit to go into schools to teach, but he was also responsible for advising colleges on curriculum and training. In 1883 he visited thirty-five colleges with one or both of the assistant inspectors; the remaining eight colleges were visited by his assistants.[71] In that year he visited a number of colleges in London and also in Liverpool, Warrington, Lincoln, Derby, Saltley, Cheltenham, Bristol, Glasgow, Chester, Culham and Winchester. All this work was, of course, in addition to his full-time cathedral post. And if he took holidays after the major

Church festivals of Christmas and Easter and in August, it was also the time when the colleges would be closed. He could not, therefore, have arranged his work so that the visits were made during his free time from St Paul's. Such was the load with which Stainer encumbered himself. And yet he continued his inspectorate work up to the time of his death, including the whole period of his Oxford professorship.

The inspection of the work done in colleges and of students might well have absorbed about ten to fifteen weeks annually, and Stainer seems to have been too conscientious to hurry over or attempt to abbreviate the reports that had to be written afterwards. In addition, at certain times in the year he was engaged in marking students' papers, and he speaks of being out of action for the 'Christmas papers' in 1883[72] when he had been advised to rest because clearly the pressure of work had been taking its toll. During the 1888 period, the year he left St Paul's (in May), he presumably had more time available for visiting colleges and did, in fact, visit all forty-three, examining 1,266 students. The extent of the travelling and the difficulties encountered generally in train travel at that time may be imagined from the list of colleges he visited. Apart from a number in London, he went to Chichester, Brighton, Winchester, Salisbury, Truro, Exeter, Fishponds (Bristol), Swansea, Carmarthen, Saltley, Derby, Edgehill (Liverpool), Mount Pleasant (Liverpool), Cheltenham (Masters and Mistresses), Culham, Oxford, Bishops Stortford, Saffron Walden, Norwich, Peterborough, Lincoln, York, Durham (Masters and Mistresses), Darlington, Ripon, Chester, Caernarvon, Bangor and Warrington.[73] The geographical distribution[74] suggests that Stainer planned his travels as a number of separate 'grand tours' in order to be able to accommodate all his visits.

It is clear that Stainer's influence in the field of elementary education was quite considerable. Although the work was tiring, Stainer derived a good deal of pleasure from his college visits. In most of his annual tours he visited nearly all the colleges and each year examined approximately 1,000 students, in some years considerably more. From his annual reports it is evident that his work did not consist only of examining students, he also listened to college musical performances. He referred to these in, for instance, his 1891 report in which he commented on hearing a group of songs sung from memory and to the singing in one college choir of a complete cantata from memory. The standard of both the choral and instrumental performances in the colleges and schools continued to improve over the period of his inspectorate.[75]

Stainer's duties were concerned primarily with the work of the student teachers, but he realised that any improvements made in schools would eventually bring better equipped students to the colleges, enabling him ultimately to raise the level of the teachers' examination. The grants system, although criticised as mechanical and displaying little in the way of musical initiative and inventiveness, helped Stainer in this way: he wished to see his candidates better equipped in the basic skills of music, that is, having the ability to read music and some, albeit elementary, instrumental ability. The grants system tested sight-reading, and the music lessons — and without this fund-raising system there may have been fewer — no doubt stimulated an interest in instrumental work. At this point it might be remembered that while some schools had pianos and harmoniums many did not, so any kind of instrumental ability was both useful and welcome and a facility at the keyboard was not always so important.

The school music lesson in the latter part of the last century was virtually a singing lesson. All aspects of musicianship could be taught through song: sound aural awareness, a knowledge of the rudiments of music, an appreciation of music and an ability to sing in parts were all important. And a singing lesson also gave students some ideas on choir training and management. Stainer, therefore, emphasised the importance of singing in training colleges and did what he could to encourage this, at the same time urging the use of only the better kind of song.

Apart from the annual reports Stainer made to the board, he left very little which might give some idea of the routine work he had to do. He did, however, mention to Edwards after his appointment as assistant inspector in 1901, 'I have always found it very interesting, but after eighteen years at it, the labour begins to tell on me'.[76] An account by Sir Frederick Bridge of what really was entailed in the work illuminates Stainer's characteristic tendency to self-effacing understatement.

110

I have never done much work as a travelling examiner, such employment for me being very fatiguing. On one occasion when Sir John Stainer was incapacitated through illness, I accompanied the late Dr McNaught for a week on one of those whirlwind examination tours in which his soul delighted. The genial doctor was Sir John's assistant, but I believe Sir John's physical make-up could not support the fierce bouts of 'inspecting' that seemed to be the breath of life to McNaught. My week with him is a nightmare, in which processions of candidates come and go endlessly; in which we seem always to be boarding trains by the smallest margin of safety; in which night brings no rest, for we have to sit far into the small hours making up returns and preparing for the morrow; and generally the whole thing proceeds at breathless speed and the problem emerges in all its stupendous proportions. I remember telling my companion that it really had been the hardest week's work I had ever done, and I would not undertake his job for £5,000 a year.[77]

The reports that Stainer submitted to the Board of Education indicate the broadening of the whole philosophy of the place of music in education, and Stainer's influence was extremely valuable in many areas of musical education in this country. His appointment came when compulsory elementary education was in a period of consolidation, and his own influential position in the musical world as a scholar, teacher and executant no doubt helped him in his efforts to establish sound departments of music within the colleges. The benefits in the wider field of musical appreciation that pupils enjoyed at this time was due largely to Stainer's efforts. His advice on matters of policy benefitted countless numbers of children in an indefinable way, and to an extent impossible to evaluate. His influence here lived long after him and is another illustration of the immeasurable value of a firm foundation on which others can build.

MISCELLANEOUS ACTIVITIES

All through his professional life Stainer carried out numerous musical and educational duties parallel to his main work in Oxford and St Paul's. When he went to the cathedral, the dean and chapter had hoped that Stainer would accept no other appointment, and this had originally been a condition of engagement.[78] But it soon became apparent that Stainer could give much to London musical life, and that this, in turn, would reflect on the cathedral.

In the early days of his work there, his main activities outside the cathedral were restricted to the National Training School for Music where, in November 1875, he became one of the five principal professors and eventually succeeded Arthur Sullivan as Principal. Early in 1882 it was decided to close the school to make way for the formation of the Royal College of Music. Here Stainer served on the college council and the executive committee, a small sub-committee from the council mainly dealing with financial matters of the college, and he continued to work in both capacities until his death. Early on he was appointed one of the five principal examiners to the college, and he did this particular work until he left London in 1888. Stainer also served on a joint committee from the Royal College and the Royal Academy to establish The Associated Board of the Royal Schools of Music in 1889, following the example set by Trinity College of Music, London, in 1879. The purpose of these two bodies was to examine young musicians at local level in singing, instruments and theory.

Stainer (along with William Pole) was the first examiner for the University of London music degrees from 1879 until his appointment as professor at Oxford. He was largely responsible for the musical content of the syllabus which, in many ways, closely resembled that of Oxford except for the very strong scientific bias. By the time Stainer relinquished his examinership in 1889 the degrees had become firmly established and respected for their completeness. He was also one of the first examiners for musical degrees in the University of Durham, with Professor Philip Armes, Organist of Durham Cathedral. He examined for four years from 1890 but it is unlikely that he had any hand in the degree-making policy.

Stainer and Pole were founder members of The Musical Association in 1874. When Pole went to Oxford in 1867 to be examined for his DMus, he and Stainer agreed that there ought to be a musical society on the same lines as other learned bodies, namely an organisation for encouraging and collection of information or papers on special subjects connected with music. In addition to his Inaugural Address to the 21st Session, Stainer read papers on the following topics:

On the principles of musical notation	1874–5
The principle of musical criticism	1880–1
The character and influence of the late Sir Frederick Ouseley	1889–90
A fifteenth century ms book of vocal music in the Bodleian Library	1895–6
On the musical introduction found in certain metrical psalters	1900–1

In his Presidential Address (1894–5), he called for the support of the rising generation of young musicians and thought that it would be a scandal if no such body existed 'for interchange of thought amongst cultured musicians'.[79] He recalled that papers read to the association since its formation had contributed valuably to musical literature, and this statement is borne out when one looks at the wide range of lecture topics. Stainer was president of the Musical Association for twelve years and on his death was succeeded by Sir Hubert Parry, thereby maintaining the link between the Oxford professorship and the presidency of The Musical Association. The prestige of the association grew both in Great Britain and abroad during Stainer's term of office and by the turn of the century membership for the first time exceeded two hundred.[80] The initial drive was Stainer's and that the association continued to flourish was to a great extent due to his own loyalty and foresight.

Stainer was well aware of the fact that Ouseley and he were at one time the only graduates in music who also held the degree of Master of Arts. He was proud of his academic achievements and, following controversies with one Thomas Fowle[81] and Trinity University, Toronto, regarding bogus musical degrees, he helped to establish The Union of Graduates in Music in 1893 for the purpose of protecting British degrees in music and the university graduates. The university honours that came Stainer's way were an honorary fellowship of Magdalen College, Oxford, in November 1892 (the first musician ever to be so honoured) and the presentation of a MusDoc (1885) and DCL (1895) honoris causa, both from the University of Durham.

Stainer attended meetings to discuss the state of cathedral and church music at the end of the nineteenth century, which led eventually to the formation of the Church Music Society. He examined for The College of Organists from 1871–3, served on its council and subsequently served as vice president and, in

1889, president. Stainer did much in the way of adjudicating for church organist posts and advised on cathedral appointments. He was also one of three advisers to the Archbishop of Canterbury on Lambeth musical degrees, from 1891. Earlier on in his London days he had examined for musical degrees in the University of Cambridge, had taught at the Guildhall School of Music and the Crystal Palace School of Music and done some reviewing work for *The Manchester Guardian.* He conducted the London Male Voice Club from 1873–87, and during that time also acted as accompanist for the Royal Albert Hall Choral Society. He served as president of the Incorporated Society of Musicians, of the Plain Song and Mediaeval Music Society and of the London Gregorian Association. He was Master of the Worshipful Company of Musicians on two occasions, and in 1887 he was elected to the Athenaeum.

RETIREMENT AND DEATH

Following his retirement, John Stainer continued to live in Oxford, in the family home. He had many contacts in the area, being responsible at various times for conducting choirs comprising a mixture of university members and people from the town. Since his return to Oxford he had also been sidesman and later churchwarden at the Church of St Cross in Holywell and he maintained his links there.[82] His work as HM Inspector of Music also continued with no hint of a relaxation in the number of visits to colleges.

Stainer did, however, wish 'to sink into private life as soon as I have produced a few things long ago promised to friends . . .'[83] He had been asked to agree to be featured in the main biographical article which at that time *The Musical Times* frequently included, but he refused 'while in the flesh'.[84] There is evidence of F. G. Edwards approaching him on a number of occasions, the second time probably in October 1898 when Stainer was not quite as adamant as he was to become in the following months. Writing, again to Edwards, he says:

I must think over the matter of the biographical notice. My life has been so varied and cast in so many spheres of work that its story would almost make a book. At one time I began to collect notes for an autobiography but my scheme was nipped in the bud by pressing work. I intended to include a lot of illustrations of ceremonies, places, with a few *funny* sketches illustrating true stories. Your article would just spoil my autobiography – unless you became my Boswell (!) and carried it on.[85]

A reluctance to be drawn into public life any more also became evident when Parry and Stanford spoke to the Church Congress in 1899. When it was considered that some criticism of their remarks might be in order, Stainer refused to have any part in it as he knew that even were he to write anonymously his hand would be detected. On this occasion he recalled that the paper *Truth* had advised him to compose more and talk less and he now confided to Edwards that this would be good advice to 'my two friends'.[86]

Although Stainer refused to be written about he was always ready with his pen to help with articles; in the short period of his retirement he produced articles on the founding of The Musical Association, the history of St Michael's College, Tenbury (giving him an opportunity to spend a few days there with his eldest son, J. F. R. Stainer), and The Bach Society performance of the *St Matthew Passion*, an article on Croft and comments on a variety of people such as Pole, Dykes, Gauntlett and those associated with his research on Dufay. But clearly he was becoming tired and with only isolated exceptions refused to take on more work. One of these was to give a lecture to The Musical Association in November 1900, with the title, *On the musical introduction found in certain metrical psalters.*[87]

Stainer completed work on a set of organ pieces, telling Edwards something about their composition together with a few words, in his humorous way, on the lack of English music in organ recital programmes:

If you are reviewing my second set of Organ pieces – 'miserere mei'. The slow movements are on the type of the extempore voluntaries I used so often to play before service at St Paul's. I think the Pastoral on two octaves of the scale an original idea. The fugal treatment of the chorale in no. 11 is full of contrapuntal devices, some of which are hardly visible to the naked eye.

You might suggest that English composers ought to appear more often in programmes of organ recitals. I often read them and find *very often* a whole programme without a single English name. Audiences are partly to blame; a foreigner always gets careful attention; an Englishman is discounted before heard.

He went on to suggest some foreign names for English musicians such as Chevalier Dupont (Sir Frederick Bridge), Henri Adroit (Henry Smart), Walter von Papagei (Walter Parratt − Parrot), Georg von Mauerschwalbe (George Martin), Kohlerücken-Kleidermache (Coleridge (Coal-ridge)−Taylor), Hans von Farbenbeizer (John Stainer), M. Galetas (Garrett) and Chevalier De La Riposte (Hubert Parry).[88]

Within the space of barely a month Arthur Sullivan (22 November 1900) and William Pole (30 December 1900) died. Stainer was gratified with the great tributes that Sullivan received and made no secret of his distaste for the article on Sullivan in *The Guardian* with its criticism of his music, commenting, 'Apparently everything which is melodious ceases to be serious.'[89]

Stainer's last public honour was to be made Master of the Worshipful Company of Musicians, for a second period, in November 1900. In that year he and Lady Stainer made their plans for a long holiday early in the following year. They left England at the end of January 1901 for an extended tour of the south of France and Italy. Not only was it a well-earned rest, but also preparation for the future which would have included, immediately on his return to England, the spring examination of training college students. It was during this holiday that he had the opportunity to play the organ again − for matins in the English Church in Florence, in the absence of the regular organist who was ill. It was one of the few occasions (some reports say the only time) that Stainer played the organ for a service following his departure from St Paul's Cathedral.[90] On 31 March (Palm Sunday) he and Lady Stainer were at Verona on their way to Venice, staying at the Hotel des Londres. Stainer 'was in the best of health and spirits during his wanderings in the sunny south, journeying here and there, writing the usual cheery letters to his friends, and making plans for the future'.[91] He had visited the ancient amphitheatre in Verona on this particular morning and after lunch Stainer slept in his room while Lady Stainer went to church. When she returned she found Stainer 'in a shivering condition and suffering severe pains in his chest'.[92] It was a heart attack, from which he died that afternoon.

His body was brought back to England for burial in the cemetery attached to Holywell Church. The funeral, which took place on 6 April (Easter Eve), was attended by a large and distinguished gathering, including numerous representatives of bodies with which Stainer had had some connection in his public life. So large was the number coming from London that special carriages were attached to the 1.45 express from Paddington. The choir of Magdalen College, under Dr Varley Roberts, sang Croft's *Burial Sentences* and Spohr's *Blest are the departed*, but none of Stainer's music was given, not even the *Sevenfold Amen* which has since retained its popularity much as *The Crucifixion* has done. There was some criticism of this omission at the time. Parry and Hadow went to the funeral together, Parry describing it as 'a very large gathering of friends and a very quiet and unpretentious service, just as he would have liked. I met the Stainer boys after, and they asked me to go with them round to the house. Saw Lady Stainer and the girls. They bear up very bravely. But it was harrowing to see them'.[93]

In a tribute to Stainer, Canon Newbolt, preaching in St Paul's Cathedral on Easter Day, spoke of the equality of all men in the eyes of God, the greatest and wisest, the ignorant and foolish, and remarked that 'God's house is not the place for panegyric'. But music, almost more than any other gift, confers immortality, and it was for his music that Stainer would be remembered:

Certainly, we shall feel he is more among the living than the dead when we say Amen! to our Eucharist in the sevenfold cadences of the harmonies which he taught us. Certainly he will continue to be near us at our Easter festival in the stately music in which he had taught us to realise the mystery of the Resurrection. He will be with us every Lent as we approach God in the plaintive tones of the Miserere which he has adapted for our use . . .[94]

The obituary notices in the national press manifest the warmth in which Stainer was regarded generally. Subsequently, memorials were placed in Holywell Church, St Michael's College, Tenbury, St Paul's Cathedral and in Magdalen College antechapel. The Holywell memorial, a stained-glass window placed at the east end of the south aisle, depicting the Adoration of the Lamb of God by a group of angels, some playing instruments of music, others singing, was given by Lady Stainer and commemorated one year after his death. The second, at Tenbury, was a memorial brass placed in 1906 by Stainer's eldest son, J. F. R. Stainer; it shows Stainer kneeling in prayer with words

117

engraved from George Herbert's poem 'Employment' (The Temple):

Lord place me in Thy consort; give one strain
  To my poore reed.

These words were a favourite prayer of Sir John; he would have liked them to have been inscribed on his tombstone, but there were certain difficulties that prevented this.[95]

In 1905, a monument was placed on the west wall of the ante-chapel of Magdalen College, Oxford. It was a gift from Lady Stainer and consists of a mural tablet of brass, framed in alabaster, after a design by G. F. Bodley, the Latin inscription being the composition of the president, Mr T. Herbert Warren.[96] The main memorial was the one in St Paul's Cathedral, placed on the eastern wall on the aisle of the north transept, designed by Mr H. A. Pegram. Sir George Martin, Stainer's successor at St Paul's, had recommended *I saw the Lord* as his finest anthem and Pegram used this theme in his monument. The memorial was unveiled on 16 December 1903, Canon Scott Holland making a generous tribute to Stainer. His *God so loved the world* was sung and also the *Sevenfold Amen* after the final Blessing.[97] The translation of the Magdalen College memorial reads as follows (there is a slight error in that Stainer was sixty when he died – his sixty-first birthday would have fallen on 6 June 1901):

In the pious memory of John Stainer, Master of Arts, Doctor of Music of this College and organist of St Paul's Cathedral in London, Professor of Music in the University of Oxford, a genial, well-known, good-natured and learned man who never practised his art (surely divinely-inspired) except in a religious way, whether he was composing melodies or playing the organ. He fell asleep in Christ at Verona on 31 March 1901, aged 61. The love of his wife set up this monument.

7

Stainer's music

George Thewlis wrote of Stainer, 'And those who knew him only as a composer knew him not at all.'[1] The improvements he effected as an educator and in the field of church music have been lasting ones. His musical compositions, however, were not great, and it is unjust to assess Stainer's worth by remembering him only as a composer. They served an immediate need, and while a few are still worth keeping in cathedral and parish church music lists, most are not. In making an assessment an attempt has been made to avoid extreme views like those of Erik Routley, who rarely has anything good to say of his music, the most flattering being, 'Stainer at least once reached the top flight in his chant in E minor';[2] or of writers such as Bumpus, who seemed to consider that Stainer could do no wrong:

. . . during his tenure at St Paul's Stainer continued to pour forth service after service and anthem after anthem, in all of which beauty of melody, great individuality of form and originality of harmony, scientific skill and expressive effect were blended in the happiest and most judicious manner. When all is so fine it would be invidious to single out any one composition for special remark, but it is impossible to resist pointing out the Morning Service in E flat, the Communion Service in A and D, the Evening Service in E major, and the anthems 'I desired wisdom', 'O clap your hands' and 'I saw the Lord' as being among the highest flights of his inventive genius.[3]

Hadow wrote that Stainer's 'compositions are marked by wide sympathy, notable skill and eclectic knowledge',[4] but did not regard him as a great composer. Stainer did not think of himself as a great composer either; in a list of achievements he would have placed his own compositions low down. Fellowes recalled the time, on his last visit to Stainer before the latter's death, when 'he suddenly stopped me in the Magdalen walks and said he wanted me to know that he regretted ever having published most of his compositions; that he knew well they were ''rubbish'' and feared

119

Part of the manuscript score, in Stainer's own hand, of the 'Double Chant in E flat' c1890

that when he was gone his reputation might suffer because of their inferiority'.[5] He was urged to write anthems by 'parson after parson' who received them as being just what was wanted; he was then a poor man 'and gave way to the demand . . .'[6] The authenticity of this statement is not in doubt and, indeed, the prophecy was fulfilled. Yet in one sense Stainer's self-condemnatory remarks could be regarded as the regrets of a tired man. What is more relevant to a reassessment is that Stainer, writing to order, never judged himself to be a great composer. Thus it is hardly fair to judge him on what he himself would have considered his least distinguished work. As Sir Richard Terry has observed: 'Stainer's very kindliness has proved (more or less) his undoing. He could never say "No" to the clergyman who asked him for a nice little anthem for our Harvest Festival; not too difficult for our choir, don't you know.'[7] Terry pointed out that nearly all European virtuosi (pianists, violinists, etc) had indulged at some time or other in musical compositions:

Few of them can be taken seriously in that connection. Fewer still have shown any wide range of musicianship apart from their instrument and fewest of all is the number who have given evidence of general culture. We judge them, however, on their 'strong suit' – their virtuosity – and hold the memory of that in honour. Stainer was a virtuoso with a wider range of culture than we are entitled to expect from virtuosi. Surely it is time we judged him on that score and did justice (however tardy) to the musicianship of an outstanding Englishman who, as a virtuoso, upheld the honour of his country amongst that brilliant school of continental organists who flourished in his day.[8]

Nevertheless, despite Terry's plea for fairness and apart from periodic outbursts of praise and reassessment (such as Sir Walter

Alcock's on the centenary of Stainer's birth), it is only now that he is being treated more sympathetically. Stainer himself, delivering his first lecture as Professor of Music to the University of Oxford said: 'I believe posterity will have a kind word to say for these hard workers of the present generation who have means of raising the music of this country to a higher level than it has reached since the Restoration.'[9] It is clear that Stainer was too optimistic; his reputation stands or falls for most people by *The Crucifixion*. Regrettably, his professorial lectures were never available in book form (only two were published); had they been, some have thought, 'he then would not go down to posterity mainly as the composer of *The Crucifixion* but as one of the greatest musical scholars of the time'.[10]

Arthur Hutchings comments that had Stainer been born a Parisian or Viennese 'his facile melodic gift and command of harmony could have made him a witty rival to Offenbach, Johann Strauss . . .'[11] Do not underestimate Stainer, Hutchings warns us. But he goes on to assert that most of the church music ought to be pulped, 'and if Stainer goes, then let most choir music by his contemporaries and inferiors precede it. Not much is worth saving before the best of Stanford's'.[12] Most commentators will agree that all Victorian composers of English church music produced shoddy anthems which, in better days, would not have been published.

At the beginning of Stainer's professional career, the upheaval caused by the Oxford Movement led to a new awareness of the value of ritual and music in church services. There was a demand for church music that would suit the new times, not only for complete settings of the Holy Communion service (the Benedictus and Agnus Dei were generally omitted before then), but also for a new style of music. It was a kind of spring-clean in which the earlier styles were looked at again to see how they could be improved. There is no doubt that Parry and Stanford in this 'New Renaissance' gained something from Stainer's music, just as Stainer himself had done from the music of Goss and the compositions of earlier periods. Having been associated so closely with church music of most periods during his life, Stainer was in a more fortunate position than most to introduce a new type of music. As his obituary article in *The Guardian* was to comment:

It was Stainer with his complete knowledge of the old, and wide sympathy for the new, who was able to do what others had not done. He gave musical expression to the popular appeal of the movement in the Church. Just at the moment when churches all over the country were wanting great ornateness and less stiffness in their services, Stainer was ready to supply the sort of music that was possible for them to use: and at the same time to set before them at St Paul's an ideal of a Cathedral service that was popular and dignified and, in the true sense, artistic. It is surely no mean achievement to have succeeded in this. [13]

But the appeal of that kind of elaborate music, while popular up to the beginning of this century, has now almost vanished. Comparing the English music in use at St Paul's almost a hundred years ago with the average cathedral list of today, one finds that only Stanford and S. S. Wesley are still represented by most of their compositions. A little remains of Attwood, Sterndale Bennett, Crotch, Goss, Ouseley, Steggall and Walmisley. Of Stainer's contemporaries Steggall stands alone with his anthem *Remember now Thy Creator*, used sometimes on Advent Sunday. Stainer himself is remembered with *I saw the Lord* and, to a lesser degree, with a part of *Awake, awake; put on thy strength O Zion – How beautiful upon the mountains.* Compared with other schools of church music, the Victorian period is sparsely represented in the lists. Stainer gets little enough representation, and most of the church composers in this period get none.

In the attempts by composers to write music in the new style, dignity of style was lost in the poorer church anthem; and with this there was also lost the dignity of words because of the sentimental type of melody often associated with the text, and the thoughtless repetition of phrases and the lush harmonies. Nevertheless, the composers of this period had a sincere approach and were writing more up-to-date music than many of the English cathedral composers in the previous century. Whatever their deficiencies, Victorian composers avoided the dullness of eighteenth-century church music, especially in the settings to the church offices; Long is fairer in his conclusions than some of his detailed writings would suggest likely:

. . . in spite of frivolous melodies, juicy harmonies, jog-trot rhythms and lamentable taste, in spite of second-hand quasi-operatic style, brass band type accompaniments and a strong whiff of parlour balladry, this music usually avoided the most heinous fault of all – that sheer stultifying dullness, which so often blighted eighteenth century church music . . .[14]

Dealing with what he labels 'Victoriana' in particular, Long admits that some of the music has stood the test of time:

Barnby, Stainer and Sullivan, whatever their weaknesses, must have had some outstanding qualities or inner strengths not shared by their contemporaries which have enabled them to survive a whole century of regular use and which have confounded their critics. There may be some substance in this: undoubtedly all three were far more talented and technically skilled than most of their contemporaries; Stainer occasionally shows glimpses of true greatness . . .[15]

It must be remembered that church music, in particular, can be judged only by its fitness to the service. This does not mean that church music can be acceptable with lower musical standards, but simply that it needs some kind of ecclesiastical environment to give an added effect in performance; it needs to be judged with due concern for its practical context. As C. H. Phillips says, 'The Litany looks bald to a degree in the music copy. Sung in procession with cross and candle in the half-light of some Cathedral, it comes to a new life.'[16]

Although Stainer engaged in so many musical activities, he was essentially a church musician. The Oxford Movement brought about changes in emphasis in the manner of worship, which, among other things, directly affected the music. The Restoration provided us with a new style of music, and this was the foundation on which composers up to the mid-nineteenth century built. Church choirs, moved from the west end gallery position to the chancel, were required to contribute more to the service, either by leading the congregation in its singing, or by playing their own part in singing more sections of the service and in anthems. But, at first, few anthems were being written – practically none during the early days of the Oxford Movement up to 1853, and not many more during the next decade.[17] The collection of anthems in Boyce's *Cathedral Music* was both cumbersome to use because of its size and expensive to buy; Arnold's collection was even bigger. But, as Long points out, even if these collections had been easily available for parish choirs, the music was too complex for them to sing:

The specialized technique required for singing freely-barred and cross-accented renaissance music was a lost art and, in any case, far beyond their capabilities while most baroque and Restoration works were much too lengthy and demanded first-rate solo singers.[18]

Although the musical repertory was enlarged by the introduction of excerpts from oratorios as anthems, the demand was not fully met until the 1880s. Whether in more normal circumstances Stainer would have written as many anthems as he did is doubtful. As the chief church musician in the country he evidently felt his responsibility and made his contribution; but he was aware of his limitations. The need for new church music was evident, and he, like many of his fellow cathedral organists, helped to provide an extensive repertoire. From this period – between Goss and Stanford – relatively little remains in use; but what is now regarded as dispensable served an important role in bringing order and high standards to Anglican worship as we now know it.

ANTHEMS

All Stainer's anthems can be attributed to one of three periods. The first, prior to his appointment at the cathedral, saw the publication of eight anthems, either separately or in Ouseley's *Special Anthems for Certain Seasons* (1866), five of which were subsequently included in the cathedral service lists; in the second, the years at St Paul's, he published fourteen anthems eight of which he included in the lists; and after he resigned from the cathedral he published thirteen anthems.

The first period shows Stainer at his best. He wrote *I saw the Lord* while Organist at St Michael's College, Tenbury. While still Organist of Magdalen College, Oxford, he wrote *Awake, awake; put on thy strength*, *Drop down, ye heavens* and *Lead, kindly light*. All these, or sections of them, are fine anthems. There was some good fugal writing in *The righteous live for evermore* and *They were lovely and pleasant in their lives*, although in their entirety these do not come up to the standard of the four mentioned earlier. In the middle period, the better anthems are *I desired wisdom, Let the peace of God* and *Lord, Thou art God. They have taken away my Lord* is also worthy of mention, although it is not quite of the standard of the others. In the final period Stainer succeeded best in his smaller anthems such as *Behold, God is my helper* and *Blessed is the man*. Of his larger anthems in this period, *O bountiful Jesu* measures up well to Stainer's earlier works, though it is restrained in design and similar in style to the smaller anthems. During this period Stainer also republished three of the anthems written prior to 1872, *Drop down, ye heavens, The Lord is in His holy temple* and *They were lovely and pleasant in their lives* (Novello Octave Anthems, published about 1900), all of which had been included in Ouseley's *Special Anthems for Certain Seasons*. The curious fact is that in the last twelve years of his life Stainer wrote almost as many anthems as he had done during the sixteen years spent at St Paul's. Perhaps some had been promised earlier and only when he returned to Oxford would he have found the necessary time for composition. From correspondence of this period we know that he refused commissions on the grounds of pressure of work. None of his compositions during this period bears any inscription or dedication, and this suggests that he wrote either because he wanted to or his publishers wanted him to. There is, however, little firm evidence for either possibility except that we know that two compositions were included in *The Musical Times* supplement series. Why he wrote the rest must remain a matter of conjecture.

Working under pressure or strictly to order did not bring out the best in Stainer. Following the better anthems of the first period, *I desired wisdom* came after a period of convalescence following the breakdown and eye injury he suffered in 1875, and *They have taken away my Lord*, the opening of which displays a tenderness most appropriate to the text, came following the death of one of the Stainer children. In a letter to J. S. Egerton, Mrs Stainer tells how their two-year-old son, Harry, had died in the early hours of 30 December 1874 as a result of scarlet fever. That evening 'my husband sat up late and the thoughts of a joyful resurrection suggested what you now see on paper. I naturally think it very lovely, but it has touched others very remarkably, and one or two letters from America we have which shows what singular influences it has had'.[19]

Commenting on Ouseley's music, Stainer observed that the flair he showed in his improvisations seemed to be lost when he attempted formal written composition. The same could be said of

Stainer. A common criticism is that while he had some good ideas and often began an anthem well, the effort could not be sustained. He is best described as a miniaturist; his hymns, chants and smaller anthems succeed whereas the larger anthems generally do not. He is also criticised, often unfairly, for excessive use of the German sixth and dominant seventh chords, static harmony, immovable bass line with melody restricted to the treble part, and regular four-bar phrase lengths which created a general lack of movement. Although he used texts which indicated a wide knowledge of the Bible, he was sometimes unable to match his music to the level of the scriptural text.

Stainer was, no doubt, aware of certain weaknesses in his church music, although this must have been through self-examination rather than press reviews and other criticism, which were almost always full of praise. He spoke at his first professorial lecture on differences between church music and other types of composition. One of the requirements that stifled creativity in church compositions was prescribed length since services and anthems could not be allowed to last longer than a certain time.

Our Church composers are compelled, therefore, to get the largest amount of musical and religious effect from the smallest quantity of music, and some of our best services and anthems may be better described as running comments on the character of the words, than as artistically constructed movements . . .[20]

The criticisms of some of his anthems are unjust. Far from being weak in melodic content his better anthems show how capable he was of writing soundly constructed and expressive melodies which possessed adequate movement yet were not fussy. There is also movement within the parts of his homophonic writing and the bass line contains as much interest as the others. As a contrapuntist Stainer must be recognised as outstanding, restoring to church music the life and vigour that seemed to have been lost in the works of his contemporaries. A fine example of his fugal writing can be seen in *How beautiful upon the mountains*, a section of a larger anthem previously mentioned. It is compact and the short lively subject develops as the anthem proceeds. Here is the opening section:

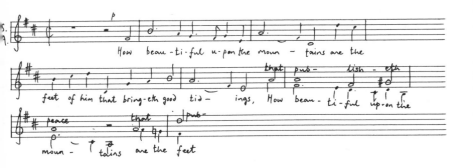

As for Stainer's use of words, while most composers looked only to the psalms as texts for their church anthems, Stainer went much further afield and selected the more unusual texts – from Isaiah, Ecclesiasticus, Wisdom, Ezekiel, Zechariah, Baruch, Job, St Paul and the Book of Revelation. But he was not always able to do them justice, and there are instances where the meaning of the text becomes obscure. In listing the various characteristics of Victorian church music, Long observes that the text becomes subservient to the 'tuneful' melody falling into a balanced series of two- and four-bar phrases. Treated thus 'the words counted for little and were crammed in, spaced out, or repeated as much as was necessary to carry the tune'. Many instances similar to the following can be found:

> Oh for a man-, Oh for a man-
> Oh for a mansion in the sky

Although such extreme examples of verbal infelicity cannot be attributed to Stainer, he is sometimes guilty to a lesser degree. For example, in *God so loved the world* from *The Crucifixion* the meaning is obscured in the passage 'that whoso believeth' by repetition of part of the text and by a musical break where the words need to continue immediately to make sense. Much the same applied in his anthem *Lead, kindly light*. The metre here is difficult and no hymn-tune writer was able to make much sense of the text before Sir William Harris in *Alberta*.

It is clear that Stainer still had in mind the acoustical properties of St Paul's Cathedral when he wrote the anthem *I saw the Lord*. Indeed, he had only recently left there. The opening is a powerful one with chords on full organ and voices in unison heard in antiphony, the whole moving through a variety of keys – seven in the space of only the first twenty bars. Up to the entry of the verse

'O Trinity!', the anthem is scored for double choir combining simple chordal writing in the one with four-part counterpoint in the other. The middle section, beginning with the words 'And the posts of the door mov'd' is both dramatically and effectively worked out. In seventeen bars Stainer builds up to a climax; and this undoubtedly is his realisation of an effect created in St Paul's Cathedral.

Stainer creates a tension in this short section which contrasts well with the subsequent tender passage 'O Trinity! O Unity!', a passage which he uses again later in combination with the material earlier associated with the Sanctus idea.

The final Amen is also linked with the Sanctus theme, and this final section might easily be attributed to C. V. Stanford or Charles Wood writing some seventy years later.

The opening of the anthem reflects the influence of S. S. Wesley, though here it is on a slighter scale than most of Wesley's full-scale anthems. The four sections are well balanced in tonal design, mood and subject material, and it is difficult to accept the criticism of some writers that the early promise of the grand opening is not fulfilled. There is a hint of Victorian sentiment in the final phrases of 'O Trinity!', but the whole effectiveness of the music is undeniable. The anthem had wide appeal and in the last two decades of the nineteenth century was sung in almost all cathedrals and parish churches on Trinity Sunday. It has maintained some degree of its popularity.

Stainer's anthems often include extended fugal passages, but *Lead, kindly light* provides instances of many short contrapuntal sections. The opening melody of the anthem is typical of this particular period and shows a certain charm which matches the emotional appeal of the text; and the less extended passage at the conclusion of the section does much the same.

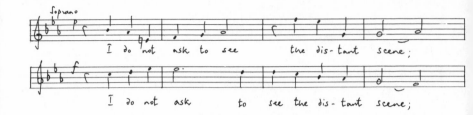

In this anthem, dating back to Stainer's Magdalen days, one can observe the style of this period, yet it does not conceal the better elements of harmonic writing. The work is divided into three balanced sections, corresponding to Newman's verses, and although there is too much repetition of the text, Stainer on the whole captures the atmosphere of the words, a result to which the frequent modulation contributes.

The whole pattern and mood of worship has changed so much since Stainer's time that now most of his church anthems seem irrelevant to present forms of church service. In his day, however, he was an important contributor to church music, and the style of his music was clearly acceptable at that time to clergymen, choirs and congregations. No matter what may be thought of his music today, it cannot alter the fact that it was, in its own time, not merely acceptable but highly esteemed; nor can modern estimates of his music diminish Stainer's importance as a composer who exerted a wide and beneficent influence on church worship.

SERVICE MUSIC

Stainer's contribution to service music for the church was an effective one. In addition to various settings for parish use, a Holy Communion service in A major and one expressly dedicated to St Paul's Cathedral choir, in C (six voices), he wrote three complete sets of services for the Holy Communion office and morning and evening services. All of these had frequent use in the cathedral and elsewhere and, for the most part, were concise settings.

The service in E flat, no 1, especially the evening canticles, retained a place in the cathedral repertoire for longer than any other of Stainer's services, and up to about ten years ago the evening canticles were sung regularly in St Paul's Cathedral. A survey conducted by the Church Music Society showed that in 1898 thirty cathedral establishments included this service in their lists, but the number fell to fourteen in 1938 and to eight in 1958. The 1958 figures are those for evening canticles only. The evening service was written in 1870 and the remainder of the set came four years later. In 1899 Stainer added two sets of the Benedictus and Agnus Dei which completed the communion service. One set was for festival use, the other for parish choirs. At the time the communion service was written it was not the custom to sing settings to the Benedictus and Agnus Dei. The morning service was a very popular setting; in the year beginning June 1877, it was sung in St Paul's more than any other, twenty times in all.

The second service, in D and A major, was often performed at St Paul's, especially at festivals such as Easter Day. The evening service was written for the Festival of the Sons of the Clergy in 1873; an orchestral score was available in addition to the usual organ accompaniment. It is not quite as concisely written as the E flat service; there is more repetition of the text and the whole effect is grander. In 1898 twenty-two cathedrals included the service in their repertoire, but by 1938 this number was down to nine and in 1958 to one.

The third set was in the key of B flat. The evening canticles of this service were written in 1877 for the Fifth Annual Festival of the London Church Choir Association, held at St Paul's. The remaining parts of the setting followed between 1883 and 1885, and by the latter date they were in use at the cathedral. It was in the repertoire of nineteen cathedrals in 1898, six in 1938 and one in 1958.

The evening service in E flat was the most popular, perhaps because of its conciseness. But it is the evening service in B flat that is the most successful in construction. The *Magnificat* is larger in scale and includes a balanced measure of both homophonic and contrapuntal writing. There is repetition in the opening material, and it is this that gives a unity and coherence to the *Magnificat* as a whole. But what is particularly remarkable is the latter half of the Gloria, where Stainer treats us to a fugue, broad and forceful, demanding much of the singers in control, volume and vocal range. At the final 'As it was in the beginning' the trebles are required to sing a high B flat, and this needs neither St Paul's nor the thousand singers of the first perform-ance to make it on its own a thrilling sound; but before then the

131

altos, just after their entry in the fugue, sing high D, rising above the trebles. The effect – one to be experienced only in actual performance – is electrifying.

These three services formed a significant contribution to English cathedral music in the nineteenth century. Their success lay chiefly in their suitability for liturgical use; all three show Stainer's understanding of the liturgy, especially in the service of Holy Communion, and his interpretation of the text is always most appropriate. It was not the usual practice for the various movements in the services to employ the same thematic material. There is however, a strong sense of unity in the longer movements themselves. It is unfortunate that these services should suffer almost total neglect and scarcely find a place in cathedral lists at the present time.

HYMN TUNES

The study of hymnody is a subject in itself. Suffice it to say that prior to *Hymns Ancient and Modern* there were many hymn books published – in 1872 probably about two hundred. There were too many bad hymns and tunes, and the editorial and musical boards of *Hymns Ancient and Modern* set out to make a general improvement. For the first edition, published in 1861, Dr W. H. Monk, Organist and Director of Music at King's College, London, was appointed music editor assisted by Ouseley. For the most part the tunes were old, but Ouseley contributed five new ones, Dykes seven and Monk seventeen. A supplement was added in 1868; the music of the added hymns was more adventurous and half the tunes were printed for the first time. Dykes provided the largest number, eleven, but there were also contributions from Barnby, Elvey, Henry Smart and Stainer. 'It was in this edition that the felicity shown by the compilers in matching hymns and tunes first became really manifest.'[21] In 1870, Stainer was appointed to assist the Tunes Committee and he was in constant touch with Sir Henry Baker, first chairman of the board (serving until his death in 1877), to whom he wrote at some stage, 'My entire work hitherto has been work of protest. Tune after tune has reached me with which I feel thoroughly ashamed to have anything to do.'[22] The revised book first appeared in 1875 with 473 hymns and following that a supplement was issued in 1889, edited by Charles Steggall. By this time Stainer had ceased to act in his former capacity, although he was still contributing to the book. Not that this hymn book was the only one to accept his contributions – there were about forty other publications and choral associations for whom Stainer wrote, including The Baptist Church Hymnal, The Church Missionary Hymn Book, The Congregational Church Hymnal, A Flower Service for Children, New College Hymnal, Hymns in time of War, Rugby School Hymn Book, The Sarum Hymnal, The Westminster Abbey Hymn Book and Holy Gladness, to mention but a few.

In 1900 Stainer collected his tunes into one volume, 157 in all. This was not his total output, as an additional ten were traced later by his son, J. F. R. Stainer, who thought that some may have been omitted intentionally. In the Preface to the collected edition Stainer stressed the importance of the relationship between hymn and tune, and the fact that one ought not to divorce one from the other in judging them. He said that he would be criticised for having written so many tunes but:

I must plead in excuse that, almost without exception, they have been written at the request of musical and clerical editors and personal friends. If those who thus prompted me to compose hymn tunes were leading me into an evil course, I can only say they have added the still greater unkindness of condoning my offence by taking the tunes into constant use. [23]

This collected edition was reviewed in *The Guardian* by W. H. Hadow, though he felt loath to do so 'since it is in direct antagonism to Stainer and to lay hands on him would make me feel a sort of parricide. But the book was put in my way – I did not seek it – and I cannot say things unless I believe them to be true. I do think that his view on the subject is fundamentally wrong . . .' [24] Hadow had first asked if someone else could review the book. As it turned out the review brought 'a kind note from Stainer', [25] but Hadow wished that Stainer's name could be kept out of any controversy.

Curiously, though perhaps not entirely unexpectedly, it was a generous tribute to Dykes that annoyed Hadow. Stainer must have known what effect it would have, yet he wrote:

It is impossible to speak of Dr Dykes without enthusiasm; he devoted his musical genius (for genius he certainly had) entirely to the service of the Church, with splendid results with which we are happily so familiar . . . It requires some courage at the present moment to announce oneself as a disciple of Dykes, because modern hymn tunes are likely to have to pass through the fire of severe criticism. They are, it is said, 'sentimental' and 'weak'; these epithets are mild and polite compared to many others hurled against them. No doubt many tunes that are over-sweet may, after twenty-five years' use, begin to cloy. But it must not be forgotten that the critics of hymn tunes nearly always fall into the insidious snare of judging of the old by the best specimens, and of the modern by the worst.[26]

Stainer made the point that the old tunes that people were urged to imitate 'are held up as proof of the general merit of the heap of worthless rubbish from which they have been extracted'. He also said that the true estimate of a tune cannot be found by principles of abstract criticism or by any strictly musical merit. 'There is something, indefinable and intangible, which can render a hymn tune, not only a winning musical melody but also a most powerful evangeliser.'[27]

Hadow took issue with Stainer for extolling the type of hymn tune commonly associated with Dykes:

. . . our contention against many of the tunes which we would wish to see eliminated is not that they are simple, but that they lack simplicity; not that they are artless, but that their art is elaborately bad; that they seek the honeyed cadence and the perfumed phrase; that they touch the surface of emotion, but can never sound its depth.[28]

Contrary to what Stainer thought, the choice, Hadow said, was not between sentimentalism and 'a cold respectability', as Stainer himself had put it; it was merely a matter of seeking higher standards, and it should be easy enough to make people familiar with the good as well as the inferior:

In its choice we would advocate the widest freedom which is compatible with the maintenance of a due standard; the Chorale, the Plainsong, the Genevan Psalm, the successive periods of English composition should all be represented in so far as they are worthy. But at whatever cost, and with whatever regret, we would urge the exclusion of all for which this standard is too high. Special expressions of personal feelings are not always suited to congregational use and cannot always be uttered by a congregation without insincerity. The weak or imperfect phrase may sometimes carry a true thought, but there is no need that we should borrow it if we have the same thing said more finely elsewhere. On all grounds, both of loyalty to our Church, and of respect for the purity of her service, let us take the best and let the second-best go.[29]

It has already been stated that Stainer admitted he had been constantly urged to write tunes for all kinds of bodies and hymn-book compilers. Some of the tunes, like the ones of processional use, came to fill a new need in liturgical practice, such as processing around the church singing hymns on festive occasions; the first fourteen hymns in his book are of this kind. Hadow particularly recommended the first of these, *Deum Videbunt* to Dean Plumptre's words 'Rejoice, ye pure in heart'; but the tune has not withstood the test of time or, perhaps, it was composed too late for one edition and for some reason it was not included after Stainer's death, even though *Hymns Ancient and Modern* has the hymn itself. Yet Stainer did not expect that many of his tunes would last. In the concluding paragraph of the Preface he wrote:

Bearing in mind the small proportion of tunes which survive any particular period, I cannot hope that many of this collection are destined to enjoy a long existence; but I can honestly say that if any single one of my tunes should for a few centuries float along the ever-gathering stream of sacred song, even unlabelled with my name, I shall not have lived in vain. [30]

Of the 157 hymns tunes in the collected edition about twelve are in general use, two of them from *The Crucifixion*. In the 1940 edition of *Hymns Ancient and Modern* there were thirty of Stainer's tunes; in the *Hymns Ancient and Modern Revised*, issued in 1950, there were fifteen. It is interesting to note that of the twelve mentioned above only one (and that more of a hymn-anthem, *Day of Wrath*, written in 1894) was written after 1889, and if one omits the hymns from *The Crucifixion*, all were written by 1874 with the single exception of *Love Divine*. It is a further indication of much of Stainer's better writing coming early in his career. The twelve hymns mentioned are:

Gracious Spirit, Holy Ghost	Charity (1868)
The Saints of God!	Rest (1873)
Hail gladdening light	Sebaste (1874)
Holy Father, cheer our way	Vesper (1874)
Lord Jesus, think on me	St Paul's (1874)
My God, I love Thee, not because	St Francis Xavier (1874)
Jesu, gentlest Saviour	Eucharisticus (1874)
There's a friend for little children	In Memoriam (1875)
All for Jesus!	All for Jesus (1887)

Cross of Jesus	Cross of Jesus (1887)
Love divine, all loves excelling	Love Divine (1889)
Day of Wrath	Day of Wrath (1894)[31]

It is difficult to imagine tunes such as *St Francis Xavier, Charity, Love Divine, St Paul's, Cross of Jesus* and *All for Jesus* ever losing their place in hymnals. Not only do these tunes suitably express the nature of the words of the hymn, the mood created by them enhances the whole hymn.

Compared with his contemporaries, Stainer has not fared too badly as a hymn writer, and he would, no doubt, have been gratified that so many of his tunes have remained in constant use. In the collection of his hymn tunes there are other tunes that, had the time been different, would have survived also. It is often a matter of chance whether a hymn tune becomes popular or not, yet one has to admit that Stainer produced some bad ones. *Rex Regnum* reaches a low standard of musicianship and *Gloaming* is as bad as its title suggests. *Homeland* could well be confused with an aria from a Sullivan operetta and *Love is of God*, written in 1900, seems a copy of Dykes' *Strength and Stay*, written much earlier.

The more successful writers of hymn tunes contemporary with Stainer were Henry Smart, H. J. Gauntlett, J. B. Dykes, S. S. Wesley, C. V. Stanford and Basil Harwood. Gauntlett is said to have written as many as 10,000 hymn tunes but he, like Smart and Dykes, is now remembered for little else. Stainer was contributing to music in many other ways. But what he did for hymnody can be fairly described as a significant contribution to this branch of music as well.

OTHER CHURCH MUSIC

For parish and congregational use Stainer made a useful contribution to the Novello series, including his morning and evening canticles arranged to Gregorian tones, in four sets. *The Story of the Cross* (1893) was suitable for Holy Week and consisted of a series of hymn-like sequences interspersed with brief interludes on the organ giving opportunity for meditation. The Rev H. R. Bramley, Dean of Magdalen College, Oxford, assisted Stainer in compiling *Christmas Carols New and Old*, with new and traditional carols. It was a very popular edition and is still published. One of Stainer's most frequently sung compositions is the *Sevenfold Amen*; sung well, its twelve bars encompass great beauty. It was composed with St Paul's Cathedral in mind, to be sung at the end of the Prayer of Consecration in the Holy Communion service. Heard in that building the intermingling of sounds and the eventual resolving creates a most appropriate effect to the conclusion of the prayer.

Stainer also arranged the *Dresden Amen* in five parts, and edited Daniel Purcell's Service in E minor from existing part-books in Magdalen College Library, Oxford. The SATB arrangement with organ accompaniment of Schubert's *The Lord is my Shepherd* was also Stainer's and sung extensively.

In 1873, at the request of the dean and chapter of St Paul's, Stainer prepared a complete choir book of the various liturgical offices containing the whole of the traditional music of the priest's part together with the '*Confiteor* and *Pater Noster* newly and beautifully harmonized, and a very lovely Sevenfold Amen of his own composition'.[32] *The Cathedral Prayer Book* sprang from this choir book. This later work, edited by Stainer and William Russell, one of the cathedral clerics, filled the need for a book containing all the various offices of the Anglican church in one volume. An appendix included, among other things, Stainer's arrangement of the *Ambrosian Te Deum* of Merbecke, the organ accompaniment to the Athanasian Creed, parts of the Holy Communion service of John Merbecke and the setting by Stainer of *Miserere* (Psalm 51), the one customarily sung before the performance of the *St Matthew Passion* in the cathedral. It also contained pointing of the psalms and canticles together with chants, Stainer commenting that this system of singing the psalms (Anglican chant) 'appears to be considered more satisfactory than any other that has been tried'. In the Preface Stainer gave some advice, which contains much good sense, on how the psalms should be sung to a natural speech rhythm.

In arrangements of Merbecke's setting of the Holy Communion service and various other plainsong settings, Stainer has been criticised because the harmonic style of the accompaniment is so alien to the plainsong, with use of the dominant seventh and diminished seventh chords. Stainer did take the trouble, however, to help the organist who was unable to supply a plainsong accompaniment himself, and his arrangement was doubtless superior to anything that the average organist could achieve. In these settings he did achieve a natural speech rhythm, and, as Sir Richard Terry observed, Stainer still stands as the editor who came nearer to Merbecke's *rhythm* than any of his contemporaries.[33] Long accuses Stainer of misunderstanding the original Merbecke: 'Typical of these is the barbarous travesty which appeared in Stainer's Cathedral Prayer Book (1891) divided into bars and harmonized in four parts!'[34] But Long is confused here; there are no bar lines in the vocal part, nor is that in four-part harmony. It is true that the accompaniment is written in four parts with irregular bars, but as a footnote to the *Ambrosian Te Deum* (after Merbecke) Stainer writes: 'In singing this Te Deum, no accent should be made on the first note of each bar, and the rhythm should not be rigidly observed. It will thus in time be found to assume the form of a free chant-service.'[35] So Stainer was nearer to modern thinking here than people would give him credit for.

Stainer wrote a number of Anglican chants in single, double, triple and quadruple form. They were written with specific psalms in mind or for the Gloria of a particular psalm. This practice is particularly evident in the Westminster Abbey Chant Book to which Stainer made a special contribution; it is for this psalter that Stainer also wrote the triple-form chants for occasional use. His chants show a sensitive feeling for the mood of the psalm. The single chants, in particular, and one or two of the double chants are still used today.

SECULAR VOCAL MUSIC

Apart from vocal exercises and various exercises for use in school, Stainer has left little outside of church music. A number of madrigals were published following his death and it seems likely that these were early products for The Magdalen Vagabonds. In 1892 he published *Seven Songs*, dedicated to his two daughters, Cecie and Ellie, with both German and English texts and attractive piano accompaniments. He wrote the music and words for a few songs for school use including *Six Action Songs for Boys*, requiring singing and the movement of various parts of the body and face.

ORGAN MUSIC

Stainer, in conjunction with F. Cunningham Woods, edited *The Village Organist* series. These volumes, which contained material specially composed for the series together with arrangements of orchestral and chamber music, were widely used at the time and, indeed, continue to be so today. In all, forty-eight volumes were published at 1s (5p) each. They were intended for small organs but this resulted in no restriction in the wide variety of pieces. Each volume consisted of an assortment of pieces and there were eight containing music for special occasions. In volume one Stainer included a short piece of his own, *A Song of Praise*, and in another the *Procession to Calvary* from *The Crucifixion*. In the main, the series consisted of short organ pieces or arrangements of vocal music, mostly from the classical period, but Stainer also sought new works from contemporaries such as George Martin, J. F. Barnett, Henry Smart, Arthur Sullivan, E. H. Thorne, S. Coleridge-Taylor, G. A. Macfarren, T. L. Southgate, Hubert Parry, Joseph Barnby, Alfred Hollins, J. E. West and others. The series has influenced and helped generations of organists and its value is well worth emphasising here.

It is curious that Stainer wrote so little for the organ as a solo instrument. Apart from a single contribution to *The Village Organist* series and *Jubilant March* there is nothing other than the two sets of *Six Pieces*, and these were late works. There was a great demand for new English music to be written; organs were becoming an essential in churches. There was a great deal of interest in the instrument and many people wanted to make a serious, if not professional, study of it. Of course, Stainer made a valuable contribution to organists in editing *The Village Organist* volumes in that none of the music in the series had previously been published. Apart from the *Organ Primer* nothing of Stainer's organ music survives in print.

In his organ music the influence of Mendelssohn appears quite prominent, but in general it is fair to say that Stainer evolved his own harmonic style, though he did lean to some extent on the early Romantic composers. The organ music is acceptable without being distinctive in any way. As already mentioned, it is strange that Stainer wrote so little for the instrument that he knew so well; perhaps he felt that he had little to say and that what strengths he had in composition might be better used in his service music and church anthems than anything else.

8

Larger-scale choral works

The revival of the English oratorio was chiefly due to Parry, Stanford, Mackenzie and Elgar. The writers of the previous decade, Sullivan, Macfarren, Barnby and Stainer, are now remembered for other contributions they made to English musical life and not for their oratorios. Stainer is, of course, remembered for *The Cruxifixion*, but he described this as 'A Meditation' and it can hardly be classed as a full-scale choral work. His exercise for DMus (1865) had one performance only, and that not in its entirety, and was never published. In addition, little is known about the instrumentation of this oratorio, *Gideon*, and although it received a good deal of local publicity in Oxford at the time, one suspects the popularity may have been due more to regard for the composer than to the work. It need hardly detain us here.

THE DAUGHTER OF JAIRUS

The Daughter of Jairus, first published in 1878, was written for the Worcester Triennial Festival of that year and first performed on 14 September 1878. Because of difficulties with the dean and chapter of Worcester it was performed at the closing service and not at a concert; this was criticised at the time because the work was thought sufficiently important to be played as part of one of the musical concerts.[1] It was received and reviewed most favourably. *The Times* commented that some of the movements exhibited very high merit,[2] and *The Musical Times* said that the work had made its mark and that 'it will be most cordially welcomed . . . not only on account of its worth but as an earnest of what may be expected from so accomplished a composer in the future'.[3] Stainer himself selected the text with assistance from H. Joyce. It is scored for SATB chorus, soprano, tenor and bass soloists with orchestral accompaniment. William Hodge, an acquaintance of Stainer, arranged the orchestral parts for harmonium or piano accompaniment.[4] There are nine choral movements preceded by an introduction and the work lasts for about an hour in performance. Stainer's popular hymn tune *Love Divine* came later, in 1889. However, he used the same words of Charles Wesley here in this cantata with great effect, set for two solo voices, soprano and tenor. He changes tempo and style for the middle section, and the short movement, one of the most attractive in the work, is both graceful and full of charm. It was published separately, along with *Sweet tender flower*, and became popular with church choirs.

There were many performances of this work in churches and concert halls subsequent to the Worcester Festival performance. *The Musical Times* reported various performances in America, India and Australia, and one performance, in 1898, in the Moravian Church of St John, Antigua, in addition to many in this country. From press accounts it appears to have been overtaken in popularity by *The Crucifixion* when that appeared in 1887, and after Stainer's death it seems to have been practically forgotten. It achieved very great popularity, far more than *St Mary Magdalen*, mostly because, it may be, of its conciseness and a stronger continuity between the movements. The cantata had fairly regular performances for a period of twenty years – no mean achievement for Stainer, especially when one considers how popular *The Crucifixion* was for much of this time.

ST MARY MAGDALEN

This oratorio consists of twenty movements divided into three sections: (i) The Magdalen in the House of Simon, (ii) The Magdalen by the Cross, and (iii) The Magdalen at the Sepulchre; and it lasts, in all, for about two hours. The text, as for *The Crucifixion*, was compiled and written by W. J. Sparrow Simpson. It is scored for soprano, contralto, tenor and bass soloists, with the solo bass aiso acting as narrator, and SATB chorus with orchestral accompaniment. The work was commissioned for the Gloucester Triennial Festival of 1883 and repeated at Hereford in 1891. Stainer's friend, C. H. Lloyd, had been organist at Gloucester Cathedral up to September 1882 and presumably wished to conduct or have a new work of Stainer's at the festival. This was not to be, however. Oddly enough, through Stainer's influence, Lloyd became organist at Christ Church, Oxford, before the 1883 festival took place. Stainer conducted the first performance, on 5 September 1883.

The work was described by *The Times* as his most successful so far[5] and by *The Musical Standard* as 'the most important novelty of the meeting . . . so well considered and original a composition has not emanated from the pen of an English musician of late years'.[6] *The Daily Telegraph* disagreed with those and the other complimentary reports, saying that the work deserved a place amongst the works that went very near but did not reach eminence, and at one point stated:

While I find distinct reason for censure in the frequent changes that give many numbers the aspects of shreds and patches the music moreover assumes too much of the result of mistaking effeminacy and sickliness for depth and real feeling. When all this is noted much remains to praise, melodic charm, musicianly skill, the reticence of true and judicious art, and an almost entire absence of the bombast under which incompetence now tries to hide itself . . .[7]

This review was by far the most critical of the work.

The orchestral prelude makes use of the *leitmotiv*, and, one suspects, partly because of this, the various press reports note a strong similarity in the style to that of Wagner, J. S. Bach, Schumann, Spohr and Gounod which seems to show not a little imagination on the part of the reviewers. The general style of Schumann's writing is apparent in the prelude but the style may fairly be said to be Stainer's own. Apart from the use of this *motiv* idea, it is difficult to see how it can be related to Wagner. The orchestral prelude uses it at the beginning and it reappears at various stages in the cantata, mostly in fragmentary form as shown in the following musical examples.

This cantata, while containing some fine writing, seems generally less effective than *The Daughter of Jairus*, and also, though not totally in a musical sense, than *The Crucifixion*. It seems to lack continuity and the number of *recit* passages is out of proportion to the work as a whole. With such a promising beginning generally one might have expected this work to survive; yet although it was repeated at the festival later, it failed to hold the respect of the general musical public. According to the news columns of *The Musical Times*, it had numerous provincial performances and two in Capetown Cathedral but never achieved the popularity of his other works on a similar scale.[8] Stainer was again asked to write a work for the 1898 festival but was unable to accept the invitation.

THE CRUCIFIXION

The Crucifixion was the last of Stainer's larger choral works. It is the least significant musically, it demanded less of the singers, employed organ accompaniment only and had a libretto which, in certain parts, was impoverished. Yet in England it is still among the most frequently performed pieces of Passion music, if not indeed of sacred works generally. Its popularity remains almost undiminished, and there is no other work of a like kind which has withstood the passage of time as it has.

The work was dedicated to Stainer's friend and pupil, William Hodge, and the choir of Marylebone Church in London. When first performed it was as part of a series of Lenten services in which there were prayers and an address. Stainer intended it to be used in this sort of setting and not in the concert hall; this is not altogether surprising as he thought the proper context for all sacred oratorios was a place of worship. *The Crucifixion* was modelled on Bach's Passion music but, of course, on a far more modest scale. It was intended for use by parish church choirs, and should therefore be not too demanding yet serve a need for a devotional aid during Passiontide. Although the idea may have been suggested to him by clergymen, it was apparently not written as a commission but was an original conception. Stainer restored the Passion music here to the place and role for which it was intended, telling the Passion story in simple terms in the vernacular and using two soloists and men's voices to sing the narrative and Christ's utterances.

It was performed on 24 February 1887, in Marylebone Parish Church with Stainer conducting and Hodge playing the organ. Apart from some reference to the libretto, selected and written by W. J. Sparrow Simpson – son of Dr Sparrow Simpson, the cathedral succentor – there was no hint of adverse criticism. At

146

the time it was described as simple in structure and form, with a 'happy union of artistic feeling with simplicity'.[9] One reviewer wrote that 'studied simplicity characterises the entire work . . . Dr Stainer's music is scholarly without ''smelling of the lamp'' and he depends for his effect upon melody of a refined, devotional and appropriate type, rather than elaborateness of structure or varied forms of treatment.'[10] Another said that Stainer had 'carefully avoided any pedantic display of musicianship. To a church composer the temptation to introduce at least one fugue must have been great, but it has been successfully resisted.' This reviewer commented that the organ 'is treated in so masterly a fashion that the absence of the orchestra is hardly perceived . . .'[11] *The Musical Times* said that Stainer had 'contrived to impart a flavour of high class musicianship to almost every number' and predicted that the work would be in 'extensive demand – structurally, technically and artistically, it is precisely suited to its purpose'.[12] *The Citizen* went as far as to say that Stainer had enriched the world with many fine compositions, 'but perhaps for no other does the world owe him so great a debt as for this'.[13]

Recent critics have not been so kind, however. Fellowes, while admitting that it meets a 'demand for the simpler kind of Passiontide music as nothing else does', asserts that no musician can find a word of praise for it. 'It suffers primarily from the extreme poverty, not to say triviality, of the musical ideas dealing with a subject which should make the highest demand for dignity of treatment.'[14] Long asserts that Stainer wished he had never published the work, but gives no evidence for his assertion. It would seem reasonably certain that he assumed this from Fellowes' article, quoted earlier. But Fellowes does not say exactly this; he says that Stainer wanted him to know that 'he regretted ever having published most of his compositions. I didn't like to follow this up nor to ask him if it applied also to *The Crucifixion*; but quite probably it did.'[15]

Little comment was made at the time about the libretto; one paper said that although 'perhaps not absolutely perfect from a literary point of view, it is an agreeable change for the trash which has done duty for the words of some recent oratorios'.[16] Long says that Stainer had a libretto 'which for sheer banality and naïveté would be difficult to beat. Sparrow Simpson's appalling doggerel set to Stainer's squalid music is a monument to the inane.'[17] Erik

Routley thought much the same: 'it was the libretto that killed the work';[18] and Fellowes said that 'Stainer was particularly unfortunate in his librettist'.[19] What Stainer thought we do not know except that he referred to the hymns in *The Crucifixion* as 'beautiful'.[20]

In fact, we know very little about the collaboration that took place between composer and librettist. Certainly Stainer and Sparrow Simpson's father, who was also librarian at St Paul's in addition to being succentor, had a great admiration for each other and were personal friends. Sparrow Simpson, the son, was approached by Stainer and the request to write a libretto 'was eagerly seized upon'.[21] When this happened, it is difficult to say. William John Sparrow Simpson, born in June 1859 and educated at St Paul's School and the University of Cambridge, graduated in 1882 with first-class honours in the Theological Tripos and an Honourable Mention in Hebrew. After ordination he went as a curate to Christ Church, Albany Street, little more than a mile from Marylebone Parish Church, and remained there until 1888. One can assume, perhaps, that Sparrow Simpson wrote the libretto shortly after his appointment to Christ Church. In 1888 he became vicar of St Mark's Church, Regent's Park, and from 1904 until his death in 1952, at the age of ninety-two, was chaplain to St Mary's Hospital, Ilford. He was an effective preacher and a scholar of some repute; but to most, he will be remembered only for what is surely his least successful writing, the libretto to *The Crucifixion.*

Stainer was well acquainted with Bach's Passion music and probably with a number of the earlier works of a similar kind. He followed the lines of earlier Passion music but kept his work to about one hour in length. Unlike other music in this category, however, *The Crucifixion* is a meditation and not a historical treatment. It lacks the fugal treatment often associated with Stainer's works, and relies to some extent on modulation. Its popularity derives chiefly from its brevity, its simplicity, its tunefulness, its rather superficial sentimentality and from its having been written to be within the capabilities of parish choirs.

The work itself is scored for two solo voices, tenor and bass, and SATB chorus, with hymns to be sung by the choir and congregation. It has been described as a cantata and as an oratorio, but, in fact, Stainer described it as 'A Meditation on the Sacred

An orchestra of eminent musicians brought together to perform Haydn's 'Toy' Symphony at a charity concert arranged by the Countess of Folkestone (seated, middle) at St James's Hall, London, on 14 May 1880. Stainer is standing, second row on left; Arthur Sullivan is seated on floor, centre left

Stainer while Professor of Music at Oxford, as seen by the cartoonist Spy in *Vanity Fair*, 29 August 1891

Passion of the Holy Redeemer'. It consists of twenty sections, including five hymns. There is an almost equal amount of solo and chorus work and there are short solo passages intended for members of the choir to sing. Certain sections are given to the tenor and bass chorus voices alone, divided into four parts; otherwise the chorus work is SATB. There are no interlinking themes between the movements or motifs associated with any particular character or action. The key scheme is varied but without any special significance.

A feature of *The Crucifixion* is the evocation of mood at different stages in the Passion story. C. H. Phillips describes the more fiery dramatic passages as 'blood-curdling'; this is evident in places such as 'And they laid their hands' and 'There was darkness over all the land' (though whether it comes off depends greatly on the capabilities of the organ), in certain sections of *Fling wide the gates!* and in *From the throne of his Cross* at the passage 'They shouted against me'. But it does contain more seemly moments, and here Stainer is successful in creating a more appropriate atmosphere. In a similar way the organ introduction is carefully designed to establish the tone of meditation for the whole work, as is the tenor solo that immediately follows.

The opening prelude to the *Procession to Calvary* presents all the thematic material subsequently to be used by the chorus, and the theme at 'fling wide the gates! for the Saviour waits' imparts some degree of unity to the movement because it repeats in the manner of a rondo; but the words 'fling wide the gates!' are allowed to recur too often. The principal theme returns at the end in a different mood following the tenor solo at 'How sweet is the grace'. The themes are shared between the solo voice and organ parts.

King ever glorious, a solo for tenor, has a majestic beginning whose theme recurs during the aria and in a more extended form at the end. Yet the movement suffers from its libretto in, for example, 'The dews of death are gath'ring round Thee' and 'Here is abasement'. Inevitably these passages spoil the effect created by the better ones. This movement is also an example of Stainer's use of chromaticism which is a feature in the work as a whole.

One of the weaker movements, if not the weakest, is the duet for tenor and bass, *So Thou liftest Thy divine petition.* The libretto is poor but the music is devoid of strength and character; there are too many moments of insipid writing which can make it totally distasteful. Take, for example, the passages:

> Oh! t'was love, in love's divinest feature,
> Passing o'er that dark and murd'rous blot.

and

> Yes! and still Thy patient Heart is yearning
> With a love that mortal scarce can bear;
> Thou in Pity, deep, divine, and burning,
> Liftest e'en for me, Thy mighty prayer.

and

> So Thou pleadest, Yea, he knew not,
> for My sake, forgive.

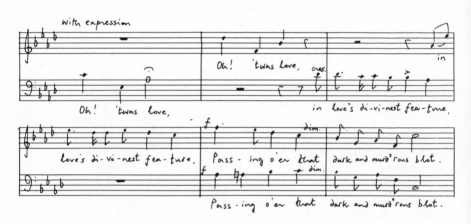

The final chorus suffers in much the same way, although there are some better sections which help the movement as a whole. For instance, the simplicity of the recurring theme 'Is it nothing to you?', mostly sung in unison, is a considerable improvement on the rather crude beginning and places like 'Crucify!' and the repetitive 'O come unto me' in the final section.

These two movements are extreme examples, however, and there is much else that is fine in the work. The chorus writing for tenors and basses is good, an especially moving passage, in its context, being 'My God, Why hast Thou forsaken Me?' The unaccompanied quartet and chorus *God so loved the world* is an effective piece of writing for voices and as an anthem warrants a place in every cathedral music list. Should the time come when *The Crucifixion* is totally forgotten, this very affecting movement would still justify being sung as an anthem during the Lenten period.

The hymns are also a strong feature of the work; *Cross of Jesus, Holy Jesu, by Thy passion* and *All for Jesus* are especially fine, melodious and dignified and contain good part writing. Indeed, *Cross of Jesus* is one of the finest hymns ever written.

As Scholes points out, Stainer, along with Monk and Dykes, is responsible for some of the best and worst hymn tunes of the period. In *The Crucifixion* we undoubtedly have the better ones, with only *Jesus, the Crucified* 'depending overmuch on sweetness of harmony'.[22] To compare the latter part of this with *Cross of Jesus* is to make the disparity obvious.

One of the attractions of *The Crucifixion* is that it is for organ accompaniment alone and with a well-trained choir needs no conductor, except, perhaps, in the unaccompanied chorus *God so loved the world*. The organ part is well within the reach of a competent player, and the work can be accompanied effectively on a small organ, though Stainer does give some indications of registration outside its resources, for example 'Tuba' in *Fling wide the gates!* Indeed, the use of pedal reeds at 'There was darkness over all the land' would make the passage sound more effective, even though it is not expressly marked. There is something in the aura of *The Crucifixion* which makes it seem more in place in a village church than in a town parish church or a cathedral. Yet, perhaps more than others, this work needs a beautiful performance from accomplished singers to draw out its beauty; thus, ironically, the parish choir, for whom it was intended, is only rarely able to do it justice. The cruder the performance the more crude sound the weaker sections; in a refined performance these movements sound far better.[23]

The score of *The Crucifixion* has sold in its thousands and the work is performed all over the English-speaking world, including an annual performance in Marylebone Parish Church, where it was first performed. It is sad, however, to recall that *The Crucifixion*'s only popular rival in Passiontide music has been Maunder's *From Olivet to Calvary*, which Scholes succinctly describes as still aiding 'the devotions of undemanding congregations in less sophisticated areas'.[24] The controversy over Stainer's *The Crucifixion* will go on, very likely, for many years and the work will continue to evoke hostility and admiration alike. What is equally certain is that the Lenten performances will also continue in the teeth of all criticism.

9

Miscellaneous works

Stainer wrote widely on educational topics, encompassing church music, organ and harmony work for students in the colleges of music and the basic rudiments and classroom skills required by trainee teachers, as well as for university undergraduates. Most of his books, and especially those in the Novello *Music Primers and Educational Series*, enjoyed great success for many years and some are still in use now. Stainer's contribution to the mass of published educational works in the latter half of the last century is considerable.

In 1871 Stainer published *A Theory of Harmony*, a work developed from notes used by him in his lectures and classes at Oxford during his first period there. By the time of the fifth edition in 1876, Stainer had changed the title to *A Treatise on Harmony and the Classification of Chords* but the work remained basically the same. It was a comprehensive study of harmony, covering every aspect of the subject and profusely illustrated with examples from the music of famous composers. For instance, in the chapter dealing with major chords on the dominant, Stainer illustrated his points with twenty-five musical examples, only once using an example of his own. Stainer provided sixty exercises for harmonisation and there were questions on the rudiments and on the principles of harmony. The book preceded those of Ebenezer Prout (1889) and Stewart Macpherson (1894).

The *Dictionary of Musical Terms* was jointly edited with the collaboration of W. A. Barrett. It was first published in 1876 and by the time of the third edition had sold 24,000 copies. On the death of Barrett, Stainer undertook the revision of the work himself, for it was constantly being brought up to date. Of the English dictionaries of the time this one had the widest impact and, with its 9,000 entries, was the most comprehensive. When the compressed edition was first published in the Novello *Music Primer* series (1880), *The Musical Times* described it as 'the best shilling's worth in all musical literature'. It contained not only musical terms but, with the exception of the lives of composers, touched on every other aspect of music and was extensively illustrated with pictures, sketches and musical examples. It was extraordinarily comprehensive. There were, for example, twelve pages on fugue, and in all there were seventy-three examples of music by J. S. Bach, Eberlin, Graun, Haydn, Mozart, Beethoven, Handel, Benevoli, Leuthard, Mattheson, Mendelssohn, Kirnberger, Cherubini and others. Matters of practical interest to the musician were also included – for example, interesting and useful sections on copyright and licensing. There can be little doubt that the *Dictionary* soon became, and remained for may years, an indispensable work of reference for musicians. T. Wotton's *Dictionary of Foreign Musical Terms* (1907) was the next English publication of this kind but it was more restricted as its title implied. Stainer and Barrett's work did not have a real successor until the *Oxford Companion to Music* (1938) edited by Percy A. Scholes.

Novello began publishing its *Music Primers and Educational Series* in 1877. Stainer was the first editor and later Hubert Parry joined him as co-editor. At this time the series, covering as it did such a comprehensive range of topics, constituted the most important and valuable body of material for the teaching of music. Stainer contributed four books: *The Organ* (1877), *Choral Society Vocalisation* (1877), *Composition* (1877) and *Harmony* (1878). The *Dictionary of Musical Terms* was also issued (in 1880) in an abridged form as one of the primers; and following Stainer's death one of his published Oxford lectures, *Music in relation to the Intellect and Emotions* (1892), was issued in 1911 as another of the series. Of the first four mentioned here, it was estimated that nearly 320,000 copies had been sold by the time of Stainer's death.

The Organ originally cost two shillings and at the time of its reissue in 1886 had sold 46,000 copies. In 1901 F. Flaxington Harker revised the tutor and it was published in New York by Schirmer. It is still published and has not been displaced by the more recent tutors of W. G. Alcock (1913), P. C. Buck (1912), Eaglefield Hull (1912) and H. F. Ellingford (1922). In 1853 W. T. Best had issued his *Modern School for the Organ* and followed this in 1870 with *The Art of Organ Playing*. Other main tutors

157

at this time were W. J. Westbrook's *Practical Organ Tutor* (1872), F. Archer's *The Organ* (1875) and Steggall's editions of Julius Andre's *Organ Book* and Adolf Hesse's *Organ Book* (c1870). Stainer's tutor consisted of four sections, 102 pages in all. There was a description of the history of the organ and an explanation of its construction with good illustrations. A description was also given of the various organ stops and their uses together with practical notes on body position, the principles of pedalling, and the use of foot, ankle and heel. There were ample exercises, and chorales and pieces to be used for practice.

The arrival of this tutor was very timely; many new organs were being built both in churches and town halls, and the churches were encouraging an increased use of the organ in their services. Recitalists such as W. T. Best, Henry Smart, George Cooper and Stainer himself were creating a great and new interest in the instrument by their own performances. The influence of organ builders was by no means negligible; great impact was made by men such as 'Father' Henry Willis, J. W. Walker, W. Hill, T. C. Lewis, Bishop, Gray and Davison, Bevington and also Schulze via the English firms of Binns, Abbott & Smith and Foster & Andrews. Some idea of the contemporary interest may also be gathered from the increase in the number of candidates presenting themselves for the examinations of the Royal College of Organists in the last quarter of the century. Stainer's tutor immediately became the most used book of its kind, catching the imagination of the player as perhaps no other did. Its strength is good pedagogy supported by exercises graduated in difficulty and designed to develop all the essential skills. Stainer always regarded himself as a teacher as well as a performer, and this may be seen from the textual content of the tutor. Stainer also published a *Tutor for the American Organ* (1883).

The *Composition Primer* was Stainer's third contribution to the Novello series, and this also appeared in 1877. It consisted of 140 pages and nine chapters, with analyses of eight movements from Beethoven's piano sonatas. He assumed a knowledge of harmony but the early stages were quite elementary and served as a good basis for more advanced study. Again it was conspicuous for the many examples of music given in the text. His *Harmony Primer*, published in 1878, was a simplified version of *A Theory of Harmony*. It was the most popular harmony book in the latter part of the century; by the time Stainer died in 1901, 186,000 copies had been sold and it is still in use.

In 1875 Stainer had contributed to two publications on the Bible[1] and the substance of his *The Music of the Bible* came from these articles. He attempted to make the work as comprehensive as possible, and, rather than merely give an account of old instruments, he associated them with the passages in which they appeared. *The Musical Times* commented that Stainer had 'accumulated a large mass of reliable information upon a subject of the deepest interest and has thrown additional light upon much of this evidence by giving us the result of his own practical experience'.[2] Stainer acknowledged help from his friend Ernest Budge, oriental scholar of Christ's College, Cambridge, on all philological questions; apart from this, the book is his own work. Although it was subsequently revised and published again in 1914, nothing has superseded it, though the standard Bible commentaries do, of course, deal with musical subjects.

Stainer's lectures to The Musical Association appeared in the annual *Proceedings.* Two of his professorial lectures to the University of Oxford were subsequently published, *Music in relation to the Intellect and the Emotions* in a much expanded form. His talks to the Church Congress were also published. His first lecture to The Musical Association, *On the principles of Musical Notation*, took place in 1875 and dealt with the advantages and disadvantages of the various types of notation. In 1880 he spoke again to the association on *The Principles of Musical Criticism.* Here he did not discuss performances or performers but concentrated on the question of what constituted good music and on what a critic should found his opinions.

In his first lecture to the University of Oxford as professor, in 1889, Stainer took as his theme *The present state of music in England.* He began with a generous tribute to his predecessor, Ouseley, and proceeded to show that England was no longer 'a land without music'. His lecture displayed a wide and deep knowledge of music of all periods and countries. He held the view that the premature death of Purcell and the advent of Handel 'were equally conducive to crushing the singularly rich development of early English music', and that the excessive worship of Handel had had a most injurious effect on English music. In this lecture he expressed his support of the music of Mendelssohn,

Wagner and Arthur Sullivan and gave a brief historical survey of music in England with comments on what had been done and what Stainer himself hoped for the future both from the professional and the amateur. Clearly he was confident; his talk displayed sincerity and conviction. His whole message was that constructive things were being done to restore our musical heritage so that we could stand, without any sense of inferiority, by the side of our more musically cultured European neighbours. His second published lecture to the university, given in 1892, was entitled *Music in relation to the Intellect and the Emotions*, and in 1895 he lectured to the Incorporated Society of Musicians on *Does Music train the Mind?*; in each lecture he gave his view on the intellectual and emotional approach to music, referring to concert-going and musical appreciation generally.

Stainer addressed the Church Congress on three occasions: in 1872 (Leeds) with *Church Music*; in 1874 (Brighton) with *On the Progressive Character of Church Music*; and in 1894 (Exeter) with *Music considered in its effect upon, and connexion with, the Worship of the Church*. Here he displayed his wide knowledge of church and cathedral music, its status and impact on society. Sing church music of all periods was his message, but only the best within each period. He maintained that there was no room for shoddy and undistinguished church music and clearly had a high regard for the Gregorian plainchant. His second lecture was illustrated with the church music of Tye, Palestrina, Leo, Mozart, Crotch, Goss, Gounod and Sullivan. In his last lecture he had good advice for parochial clergymen and musicians when he spoke mainly of music at the parish church level, where congregations were increasingly to demand a full share in the musical parts of services. He urged a spirit of tolerance between clergy, organists and congregations, and his views and advice are still very relevant today. Stainer's solutions were constructive ones and showed an understanding of human personality.

RESEARCH ON EARLY BODLEIAN MUSIC

Ernest Walker remarked in 1907 that 'fortunately Stainer's reputation depends not on his music but on his services to scholarship. Musicians today have no use for *The Crucifixion* (1887), but *Dufay and his Contemporaries* (1898) and the volumes of *Early Bodleian Music* (1901) are still known and valued by historians'.[3]

A glance at the topics Stainer chose for his professional lectures gives an indication of his wide musical interests, as do the set works prescribed for study for the Oxford and London University degrees. Moreover, music from all periods was included in the repertoire at St Paul's Cathedral. But it was in 1895 that Stainer became deeply interested in the music of Dufay and his contemporaries. In the summer of that year, E. W. B. Nicholson,[4] Librarian of the Bodleian Library, Oxford and himself a keen amateur musician, suggested that Stainer should undertake the publication of facsimiles of early Bodleian manuscript music. Charles Stainer, the fifth of Stainer's children and at that time aged twenty-four, examined various documents at the direction of Nicholson, and it subsequently became clear that the Bodleian Library held manuscripts of early music hitherto almost unexplored. Among Nicholson's suggestions to Charles Stainer was the examination of Ms Canonici misc 213, which Nicholson admitted inspecting in 1887, 'but knowing nothing then as to the rarity of fifteenth century continental secular music, had made no note of it, and had forgotten its existence'.[5] It was this manuscript to which John Stainer was initially attracted, and although at that period he frequently claimed to be too busy to undertake any new work, he began this with great fervour, assisted by his two children, John and Cecie, and in the ensuing six years delivered a lecture to The Musical Association in November 1895, *A Fifteenth Century Ms Book of Vocal Music in the Bodleian Library, Oxford*, and two lectures to the University of Oxford, *The secular compositions of Dufay* (November 1896) and his penultimate lecture in March 1899, *Madrigalian composers of the Gallo-Belgian School.* There were, in addition, his published works *Dufay and his contemporaries* (1898) and *Early Bodleian Music* (1901).

When Stainer examined the manuscript he found it contained a large proportion of secular songs in French and Italian, mostly composed by Dufay and Binchois. There were thirty-eight French songs of Dufay alone, in three or four parts (which J. F. R. Stainer transcribed for subsequent publication), besides Italian songs and sacred music. Stainer's research led him to regard Dufay as the greatest master of his age, but his interest was not limited to

Dufay alone. In addition to Binchois, mentioned above, Stainer also researched into contemporary composers including Brasart, Cinconia de Leodio, Tapissier, Carmen and Cesaris. The Bodleian manuscript consists of 280 folios of vocal music, written on five-lined staves throughout, and contains over 300 pieces of vocal music (mostly in three parts). The notation is the white or open-headed notation which began to come into use in the early part of the fifteenth century. There are seven pages of music written in the old black notation, some of which may come from the fourteenth century.[6]

Dufay and his contemporaries contains fifty compositions, ranging from about 1400 to 1440, transcribed from the Ms Canonici misc 213. Following E. W. B. Nicholson's introduction, J. F. R. and C. Stainer contributed one chapter containing a biographical account of Dufay and his contemporaries and another outlining the system of mensurable music. Sir John's own contribution was a chapter giving some critical and general remarks on the musical examples. In some eighteen pages he comments on the tritone, mutation, musica ficta, modulation (Dufay's modulations in particular), survival of earlier systems of methods of composition in these secular works, use of discords, cadences and key signatures, together with a note on the compass of the voice and instrumental parts. The fifty transcriptions that follow, mostly in three parts, are written using the treble and bass clefs in the majority of cases, together with an arrangement of the voices for keyboard use.[7] There is also a glossary and an index to the whole contents of the Ms Canonici, misc 213. The range of manuscript compositions in *Early Bodleian Music* is wider, originating from the period of about 1185 to about 1505. Stainer contributed an introduction of some eight pages, incomplete at his death, in which he again dealt with such topics as musica ficta, compass of voice parts, instrumental accompaniment, use of consecutive fifths, influence of church music on secular music and aspects of modulation. One hundred and two transcriptions by J. F. R. and C. Stainer followed. Stainer's work is still published and is still of service to scholars of this period.

Stainer's lecture to The Musical Association in November 1895 took place before the published works on the subject appeared. He described his interest in the subject and how he became aware of the existence of the Bodleian manuscript. Copies of the musical illustrations played at the lecture were distributed to those present and the aim of Stainer was to create an interest in Dufay and to let some of his newly found music be heard, almost certainly for the first occasion in contemporary times. In the discussion that followed the lecture, Hubert Parry said how privileged he felt to hear 'such a revelation as that brought forward by Sir John' doubting whether that 'important member of the Netherlands School' had ever before had a chance of being adequately represented. The debt to Stainer was enormous because his research opened up a period of musical history which before then had been only inadequately explored. Dufay's name was known, but people really knew very little about him, his place in musical history and his music. The collecting together of the manuscripts was a piece of valuable scholarship. Parry made this point at the end of his vote of thanks: 'Sir John is undoubtedly doing a service of the greatest importance to the history of our art by this very interesting revelation of Dufay's work.'[8] As for Stainer's university lectures on the subject, we know nothing except that printed musical illustrations were available for the lecture on 'Madrigalian composers'. Knowing the importance that Stainer attached to musical performances within a lecture, and being aware that some were given at his lecture to The Musical Association, one may safely assume that performances of Dufay's music were given at that particular university lecture.

Stainer's interest in the subject is known to musicians of today because of his two major publications. Strictly speaking, however, they were the work of his eldest son and daughter. Yet there can hardly be any question of the fact that he gave valuable advice and offered suggestions to his two children on their chapters and closely supervised the work generally. The responsibility for the editing of the transcriptions must be regarded as Stainer's. And it is on them that Stainer's reputation as an important contributor to musical scholarship stands.

LIBRARY

Stainer's own library was extensive both in number and range; at the time of his death it was estimated to contain up to 3,000 books, about twice the number listed in the *Catalogue* privately printed in 1891, which contained only his collection of English song books. He was very proud of the library and regarded it as his great hobby. In the Preface to the *Catalogue* he wrote: 'I can only hope that this collection will be still thought worthy of their [his children's] care in the not far distant time when it will have the additional value of being a memorial to bygone days.'[9] Although it is believed that the greater part of the library is intact, it is difficult to say how far this is so. It was sold in 1932 for £520, a bargain price even in those days, to Walter Harding, a well-known English collector of books at that time resident in America. A further part of the library was sold in 1934 and it is likely that it was also acquired by Harding, though it has not been possible to confirm this. In any event, Harding, who died in December 1973, bequeathed his collection to the Bodleian Library, Oxford.[10]

The *Catalogue* gives some idea of Stainer as an antiquarian and scholar, as a man rather like his father. It also shows his wide range of interests in vocal music of all types. Other portions of the library contained books on the history of music, dancing, campanology, theology and English literature, including books by Chaucer (1542), Byron, Lamb, Kipling, J. M. Barrie, Thackeray, Shakespeare, Crabbe and Trollope to mention only a few. The part sold in 1934 contained the *Praecordiale Devotorum* (1489), which was the oldest printed book in the collection. The majority of the collection of song books were from the nineteenth century, but the earliest ones, listed here in the order they appeared in the *Catalogue*, were:

Ayres and Dialogues for one, two and three voices by Henry Lawes, three books dated respectively 1653, 1655 and 1658.
Cheerful Ayres and Ballads by J. Wilson: Oxford, W. Hall, 1660. Three volumes of which two volumes had pages missing.
Deliciae Musicae, a collection of the newest and best songs sung at Court. Four books in one volume, two books in the second, 1696.
The Gentleman's Journal, Letter to a gentleman in the Country. Consisting of News, History, Philosophy, Poetry, Musick, Translations, etc. Complete set of the monthly numbers from January 169½ (sic) to November 1694.
Harmonia Sacra or Divine Hymns and Dialogues. Two volumes and one supplement, 1693, 1700 and 1703.

Loyal Songs, a collection of 180 Loyal Songs, all written since 1678. 4th edition, 1694.

Canzonets or little short songs to three voices by Thomas Morley, 1593, Cantus part only. Also the *First booke of Balletts to five voyces*, 1593, Cantus only.

Muses, Farewel to Popery and Slavery or a Collection of Miscellany Poems, Satyrs, Songs, etc. made by the most eminent wits of the nation, as the Shams, Intreagues, and Plots of Priests and Jesuits gave occasion, 1689.

Pill to purge State Melancholy, or a Collection of excellent New Ballads, two volumes, 1715 and 1718.

Political Merriment; or Truths told to some Tune, two parts, 1714.

Rump or an exact Collection of the Choycest Poems and Songs, two parts, 1662.

The Dancing Master, 7th edition, 1686.

Dutch Songs, 't Nieuw Groot Hoorn's Lied-Boekje, nd (c1630).

Nouvelles Parodies Bachiques, mêlées de Vaudevilles ou Rondes de Table, Paris, 1702.

A contemporary account describes Stainer's study and its library; though it gives only a general impression of the place, it does give some idea of how valuable the library was:

The library in which Dr Stainer reads and writes is the room of a student; three sides of it are devoted to books, many of which are of exceptional interest and value. Indeed, it would be difficult to find a finer collection of those quaint and choice volumes, the old English song and ballad books published at the close of the last and commencement of the present century, the contents of which are not less interesting to the musician than the printing and illustrations are to the bibliophile. On other shelves you may find a comprehensive series of the Volkslieder of different nations, not only Teutonic but Slavonic also. There are too, many works on bells and bell-ringing, besides hundreds of standard books on music and general subjects.[11]

Lady Stainer presumably retained the library in their Oxford home until she died in 1916 when it passed to the eldest son, J. F. R. Stainer. He died in 1939 but had begun to dispose of the collection in 1932. The following extract indicates Walter Harding's interest in the library and knowledge of it:

In May of 1932 I received by airmail a catalogue of the sale of the library of Sir John Stainer whose collection of song books was the most extensive ever formed privately in England. For many years I had dreamed of equalling it or of acquiring it . . . The Stainer collection was being offered en bloc at what was described as a modest reserve price. I took my luck in my hands and cabled Pickering and Chatto to buy and they replied that they would go to £2,000 but no more. Two days later the collection had been bought for me by Pickering for £520, and, of course, on credit. Even in those days the collection was worth double the reserve price – probably more. After I had received it, a comparison with my collection showed that many of the important items were of different editions. My collection was larger in all the sections that developed from song-books, such as the vocal scores of 18 c. comic operas, etc. and the works of individual composers. The Stainer collection had a few music sheets or librettos and a few poetical miscellanies or ballad operas. Mine had more song-books but his was very much stronger in the earlier song-books, especially those with music of the 17 c. Incidentally, as the pound was devalued shortly after, I obtained the Stainer collection for even less than the bargain price it fetched in the rooms.[12]

On Harding's death at the age of ninety, security men were apparently sent to guard the collection, displayed on home-made book shelves and stored in boxes on the floor of Harding's home in Chicago's West Side. He had gone into debt in order to purchase Stainer's library but at his death his whole collection was estimated to be worth over £250,000 and was 'one of the finest in Chicago and perhaps in the mid-West'.[13]

An undated portrait of Stainer

A well-earned rest: Stainer on holiday after his resignation from the Oxford Chair of Music

10

Conclusions

A leading article in *The Times* two days after the centenary of Stainer's birth, under 'Entertainments', admitted that the centenary of a man's birth was likely to fall when his public reputation had faded but commented that there were many who remembered Stainer 'with a glow of personal affection'[1] and felt hurt at the low esteem in which he was held by many younger musicians. 'He is decried by superior musicians for the one work which the multitude treasures, and his life of devotion to music, especially church music, is remembered only by those who were his friends.' Certainly, at the time of his death his reputation was such that it would have been thought impossible that most of his life's work should suffer eradication. Indeed the obituary notice in *The Morning Leader* remarked that: 'When the history of music in England during the last half of the nineteenth century is written, the name of Sir John Stainer will doubtless stand for all that is highest in endeavour in the musical profession.'[2] *The Pilot* wrote that there was:

. . . scarcely anyone with whom he came in contact in the course of his long career who cannot recall some occasion on which his advice, given with the kindliness and modesty that ever characterised him, was not of infinite value and help. The good that he did will be a greater claim to his posthumous fame than his actual achievements as a musician, considerable though these were. No nobler model of an upright and honourable life could be held up to the rising generation of musicians, and it will be a bad day for English music if his memory should ever be forgotten . . .[3]

Perhaps somewhat apprehensive of future neglect, George Thewlis wrote in his unpublished notes of Oxford life: 'Those who knew him personally knew his worth, but in the bustle and turmoil of modern life memory is short and it is only just that he should be given his due before he is forgotten.'[4] Canon Scott

169

Holland, writing Stainer's obituary notice in *The Guardian*, commented that twelve years away from St Paul's Cathedral, according to him, in 'comparative retirement', had erased the 'idea of his personality from many people's minds' but hoped that Stainer's:

... great services to the cause of music in England may be neither underrated nor forgotten. He has helped to re-create and develop and elevate the general interest in music: and, as far as he has departed from the traditional type of Church music, his successful response to the demands of the changeful age in which he lived must give him a high place in that great line of which England has reason to be proud.[5]

The Morning Post commented that with the death of Stainer England had lost one of its ablest exponents of church music, one who 'never debased his art and always maintained its purity'. It continued: 'He occupied a position among Church musicians few men have equalled, and his loss will be felt not only by a wide circle of musicians and friends, but by every one who has the welfare of British music at heart'.[6] And later Bumpus was to comment that there were few men 'whose influence on the music of this country has been so great and salutary'.[7]

All such tributes speak highly of Stainer's great contribution to the musical life of the country, but it is an appreciation of John Stainer that appeared in the *Oxford Magazine*[8] that he would have valued most himself. It refers to his work in the context of change and the somewhat uneasy acceptance of new values both in the Church and with regard to music generally. It was not easy to estimate the loss which English music had sustained in Stainer's death, the notice began, and it continued:

For nearly half a century he was in a great measure its guiding and directing influence; he was one of the few men to whom all schools and all parties looked with unvarying affection and respect; his leadership, accepted from the first without controversy, was followed throughout his life without deviation . . . He will be remembered for his personal relation to the development of music in this country. Brought up in an atmosphere of close artistic conservatism he was nevertheless one of the most generous and broad-minded of judges, glad to recognise good work in whatever direction it appeared, and always ready to give full consideration to new methods and new ideals. Living as he did through a period of considerable artistic change – when he began his career

Schumann was regarded as a heretic and Wagner as a madman – he gave cordial welcome to every sign of progress, and set the standard of a criticism at once more liberal and more enlightened than any that this country had known before.[9]

Stainer's contribution to the reform of cathedral music alone should give him long-lasting recognition. However, the wonder of Stainer is that his was not a contribution in a single field but in many. Versatility has its disadvantages: the wider the range of a man's interests, the less the depth and quality he tends to exhibit in each. But here one has a man who could claim eminence in many areas of musical life. As Sir Richard Terry wrote in 1932: '. . . he has left behind him a record of which any musician might be proud and which none of his highbrow critics have (so far) come within a hundred miles of.'[10] Terry illustrates his versatility by reference to his varied employments: (i) as an organist he was among the best executants in the country and in the art of improvisation he was probably the best; (ii) as a choirmaster he raised St Paul's Cathedral music to a level of perfection which earned the cathedral the reputation of possessing the most impressive Sunday morning choral communion service (as Gounod concurred) in Europe; (iii) as Professor of Music at Oxford he raised the standard of musical degrees 'to a point at which they became the tests of scholarship as opposed to mere exercises in organ-loft counterpoint and musical arithmetic';[11] and (iv) as HM Inspector of Training Colleges he showed student teachers how to look at music from an artistic standpoint rather than become absorbed in academic theoretical studies which would have little relevance to their work as teachers.

The range of his professional interests becomes even more striking when one compares him with his predecessors at St Paul's and Oxford or in his training college work. Attwood and Goss, his immediate predecessors at the cathedral, restricted themselves to their duties there and to composition. When Professor of Music at Oxford both Crotch and Ouseley were chiefly engaged in other more arduous activities elsewhere and were certainly not absorbed in Oxford music to the extent that Stainer was. Hullah confined himself to his work connected with musical education in schools. And it is worth reiterating that, in addition to the many activities on a lesser scale already outlined, Stainer, for the last eighteen years of his life, held two major appointments at any one time; his work in the inspection of training colleges was far from negligible.

The following extract shows Stainer in yet another light, in connection with opera:

He was a remarkably broad-minded musician, especially so for a church organist, though it must be confessed that the ideas of the church organist are not nearly as much limited by the organ-pew as they used to be. He had sufficient breadth of view to appreciate Wagner at a time when to do so was by no means to go with the stream. The writer remembers meeting him at a Bayreuth Festival in 1889, when he expressed his admiration for 'Parsifal' while not unnaturally deprecating any suggestion that such a work should ever appear on the English stage – at least under present-day conditions. He was then on his way to Regensburg in order, as he said, to hear what was described to him as the only cathedral service in Europe equal to that of St Paul's. From Wagner to Palestrina may seem a far cry, but a musician as open-minded as Sir John Stainer could find no difficulty in detecting genius, however and whenever manifested. [12]

COMPOSITION AND STYLE

A general survey has been given of Stainer's music and no special claim is made that he was an eminent composer. Whatever the reactions to his music in his time, he realised that most of it would not last; it was written to serve a need and he made no pretensions to being a great composer. But there were others who thought that he was, and he was constantly being encouraged to write more by his publishers and his clergyman acquaintances. He does not appear to have been the kind of man who would succumb to flattery; indeed, the very reverse. The testimonies of obituary reviews and from friends indicate a degree of humility which marks itself out for special respect. His own spiritual beliefs helped his church music to be truly religious, but in all his work he was not attempting to ape others but to create his own style, even though it may not be easily apparent. Although there is little in the way of evidence for this, it is believed that composition did not come easily to him but only after much thought. If there is an evident affinity with any composer it is with Bach, especially in his fugal writing, rather than with Mendelssohn as some would suggest.

On the question of a new style, it is interesting to read Stainer's thoughts on a piece of music he had recently heard (especially as his own music produces much the same kind of reaction today). Writing to J. F. Bridge[13] on his appointment to Manchester Cathedral in 1869, he comments on Sullivan's *The Prodigal Son*, performed at the Worcester Triennial Festival that year:

. . . the instrumentation throughout is *charming* − but as a whole the work lacks 'bottom' − you understand me. Melodies are graceful but not always original. It will keep afloat until the publishers have made a good thing of it, then −! It is as good as the Woman of Samaria by Sterndale Bennett and very much in the same sugar candy style.

I do wish dear Sullivan would put his thumb to his nose − to the public and critics − and write for the *future*. The later works of Mendn. & Beethoven, and all the work of poor neglected Schubert and tardily acknowledged Schumann − all point to the future of music. Sullivan ought (I feel that he is a great man and could do so) to begin where they left off − regardless of encores and bank notes. This is private − burn it.

St Paul's Cathedral during Stainer's tenure became known as a centre for contemporary church music. It has been seen that he welcomed, sometimes perhaps too freely, compositions from his contemporaries and younger men. He encouraged a new style of church music that was more in keeping with the changing liturgy. Yet, as already mentioned, he evidently did not himself find the actual task of composition easy. For instance, writing to his wife he commented:

I have sent off the proofs (*all*) of the small Dictionary and have made *several attempts* at an Anthem for Gloucester but *all* are complete failures. I cannot get a happy selection of words and am quite desperate. Of course, the more I worry myself the less able I am to collect my musical ideas. I really do not know what to do. I was trying to begin a fourth or fifth attempt when the man commenced an afternoon's work at *rolling the gravel!* − so I must turn to other work.[14]

Stainer also found difficulty with the structure of compositions for liturgical use. As he pointed out, the criticism of English church music from those foreigners not accustomed to Anglican services was that thematic development was missing in the various 'movements' from a service. Stainer's answer to this was simple:

It has to be explained to them that the duration of the movements is practically controlled by a strict limit. Should any composer attempt to develop the separate divisions of the Te Deum, for example, he would call up such a protest from the congregation and no doubt from clerical authorities also, that his elaborate work would be sentenced to perpetual imprisonment in the cathedral archives. [15]

He returned to his attack on the unsuitability of 'excessive employment of contrapuntal devices' in church music of a previous era, but saw new dangers in his own period. That he should have been aware of such dangers may well confound his critics:

In these days there is no danger of fanciful counterpoint getting the supremacy, but there is a cause for fear lest a too plentiful use of that descriptive and sentimental colouring which we derive from the modern 'romantic style' should tempt our church composers into a striving after picturesque and dramatic effects not consistent with the dignity or repose of worship. [16]

Stainer's particular strength in church composition would seem to me to be the fact that he could capture the atmosphere of the liturgy. He was aided in this by the use of various harmonic and stylistic devices, mainly in the use of counterpoint and form, but in the main it is an indefinable process just as, although all may be perfect examples of four-part harmony, some hymn tunes are good and others are not. A good example can be seen in the *Sevenfold Amen*; Thomas Armstrong echoes my thoughts:

It is no matter of mere chance that a musician as fastidious as Ernest Walker should admit to finding one of his first great musical thrills in Stainer's Sevenfold Amen, for although on paper the chords look simple and even commonplace, the effect of performance is out of all proportion to one's expectations. This is, in fact, one of the signs of good music – to sound better than it looks: and the quality is by no means a common one since we all know plenty of pretentious music that looks good to the eye and sounds awful when you try to perform it . . . Whatever you may say about Stainer's music, it was real and not sham, and this is why it was so effective and so widely performed even when it was perhaps not very good. [17]

Armstrong continues to speak about hearing the *Amen* in the cathedral:

While the organist was extemporising at the end of the Amen, the great bell of St. Paul's struck 12 noon, and filled the Cathedral with its reverberations, not obliterating the strains of the organ, but gathering them up into a wonderful complex of deep harmony. If only a composer could create at will such a sound as this! But it comes only by a sort of magic, and when it happens it fills one's whole being and seems to envelop all one's senses and aspirations. This is the real power of sound itself which sets up in the human mind and heart all sorts of echoes and overtones that are beyond analysis or comprehension. Intellect has little to do with it. Knowledge about music contributes nothing. But an instinct for sound and a realisation of its possibilities are the composer's principal asset; and the secret of Stainer's Amen is that he knew exactly how the Cathedral itself would respond to chords laid out in a particular way . . .[18]

Because Stainer's music is so rarely performed during cathedral or church services, it is unlikely that there will ever be a revival of his compositions. *The Crucifixion* will remain in the repertoire of Passiontide music, and some of his hymn tunes also. But his work has been too much discredited by those critics who do not appear to know his music or by those who should know better. For instance, in their anthology of church music, G. H. Knight and W. L. Reed, after admitting certain contrapuntal interest in *How beautiful upon the mountains*, write:

It cannot be denied that for Stainer, as for most of his contemporaries, the simple and sweet melody was of chief, and the words only of secondary importance. These could be repeated at will in order to fit into the melodic scheme, often with absurd results. For this reason it seems unlikely that the major portion of Stainer's church music will ever be restored to use.[19]

Such generalisations, often without foundation, have done Stainer's reputation much harm. That his service music and anthems are neglected in cathedrals whose boast is a catholic repertoire representing all schools and periods, seems little short of a grave error of musical judgment.

There is, perhaps, some small consolation for the neglect of Stainer's works in the fact that most of his English contemporaries who are featured in the St Paul's Cathedral music lists during Stainer's period as organist have suffered a similar fate. Those fitting into this category are: Baden Powell, Barnby, Benedict, W. S. Bennett, Bridge, Calkin, Elvey, Garrett, Goss,

175

E. J. Hopkins, Lloyd, Macfarren, Martin, Oakeley, Ouseley, Prout, G. Smart, Stainer, Steggall, Sullivan and Tours (excluding S. S. Wesley and Walmisley who are not regarded as strict contemporaries). Represented in the current lists are: at London – W. S. Bennett, Goss, Ouseley, Stainer and Steggall; at Canterbury – Goss and Stainer and at York – W. S. Bennett, Goss, Ouseley and services by Elvey, Garrett, Ouseley and G. Smart.

Although one may be critical of much of Stainer's music, one must surely acknowledge the undoubted merit of his three major services – in E flat, A and D, and in B flat – the *Sevenfold Amen* and anthems such as *I saw the Lord, I desired wisdom, Lead, kindly light, How beautiful upon the mountains* and parts of others previously cited. Stainer is one of the best representatives of his period and, as George Guest points out:

> . . . there were some works of genuine merit in this period, for no aesthetic period is wholly bad; but it has not proved easy for the layman to distinguish them from the less good. The pendulum of critical approval and disapproval has swung more extremely than usual and we are only now coming towards a historical and objective appraisal of a period of cathedral and church music which for many is too near their own time to view with dispassion.[20]

One cannot help wondering why only the layman was signalled out for disapproval.

PERSONALITY

Though Stainer came from a humble home, the members of his family had a great interest in music. Stainer's mother was a stabilising influence on the home and, it would seem, gave the family the sense of security that his more erratic father was unable to provide. But for a man in his position John Stainer's father had unusual qualities; he not only raised the quality of daily life materially, but he encouraged John in various musical pursuits and gave him an insight into literature and the pleasure to be obtained from collecting books. His father was thus responsible for the wide cultural background which enabled Stainer to become one of the most educated musicians of his day, a bibliographer, a linguist of some ability, especially in French, and an expert on bells, eventually giving valuable advice when some new bells were being cast for St Paul's Cathedral.[21]

It is not surprising that Stainer encouraged younger musicians. He himself had been greatly helped by others, and a man of his largeness of heart would wish to repay the debt to the next generation. He owed much, of course, to his parents, but also to Ouseley, Pole and Canon Liddon, and to a lesser extent to Goss, George Cooper, Dean Bulley and Steggall. Pole influenced Stainer at various times during his life, from the occasion when Stainer sang the then unpublished music of Bach and Mozart at Pole's home to their working together at The Musical Association and the University of London. Canon Liddon was obviously a great influence at Oxford and most likely continued to encourage Stainer during the early days in the uphill struggle with the music at St Paul's. Liddon, by all accounts, was saintly and sincere, the sort of person that a man with Stainer's character would look up to. The influence of Goss is an expected one; he was a kindly man and could not fail to impress a young musical chorister at the cathedral. It is, however, to Ouseley that the greatest credit must go. A priest and an aristocratic intellectual figure, Ouseley first became known to Stainer in his annual instrumental examinations as a chorister. His meeting with Ouseley and the subsequent appointment at St Michael's College, Tenbury, have already been described, and it is from the Tenbury days that, despite the difference in their ages, Ouseley and Stainer became close and firm friends. Ouseley was professor at Oxford when Stainer was examined for his BMus, and there is little doubt that Ouseley was responsible for Stainer's various university appointments when Stainer was still organist at Magdalen College Chapel. Stainer modelled himself on Ouseley and compared even their physical similarities.[22] Ouseley officiated at the marriage of the Stainers and evidently became a family friend. Stainer spoke of Ouseley at his first lecture as professor in 1889:

He will be remembered by those who knew him as a consistent Christian, a sound Churchman, and a warm-hearted amiable gentleman. I personally owe much to him; when I was a mere child, he gave me valuable advice and warm encouragement; and in later years when our intercourse ripened into close friendship, I gained much alike from his erudition and his noble example.[23]

Such was Stainer's background, but what of him as a man? Reports concur on his impressive personality – genial and charming, kindly and tactful. As *The Pilot* put it:

No man was freer from pettinesses and narrownesses which are so often found in the professional musician; whether dealing with his own art, with philosophy, theology or literature, his point of view was always evenly balanced and broad-minded. It was this faculty, the result of wide study and deep human sympathy, that made Sir John a power in the musical world whose loss is almost irreparable. In any delicate matter, where it was difficult to decide between conflicting interests or to keep the peace between over-excited and highly-strung temperaments, it was Stainer to whom everyone looked as the wise counsellor whose advice was sure to be right in the long run. [24]

We have already seen how he was received at the performance of his DMus exercise in Oxford and, on other occasions during his first Oxford period, how his academic robes were given to him from a subscription list in Magdalen College and how singers adored him. A contemporary wrote of him:

Of Sir John Stainer in private life, it may be said that no one more readily secured the regard and esteem of his fellows. Endowed with a ready sense of humour, a good conversationalist, and having himself the gentleness and delicacy that distinguish his music, he was an always interesting and attractive character, upon whom the least responsive looked with approval, and whom the sympathetic loved. [25]

He was also described as an active worker, an enthusiast who had the gift of making friends and keeping them. His influence was great and it was always exercised for good. 'Though for many years at the head of his profession he always remained among the most modest of men, finding dearly prized reward in the estimation in which he was held by those with whom he had laboured.' [26] Canon Scott Holland commented on Stainer's singular gifts for working with other men:

. . . his strong practical instincts, his readiness to give a helping hand to promising musicians and his deep belief in the musical capacity of the English nation made him a real power outside St. Paul's and go far to explain the position in the country which he, as a Church musician, attained. [27]

Scott Holland also wrote that Stainer used his freedom (at St Paul's) to the full without ever forcing it and that his delightful personal charm and intense enthusiasm won his way over all the obstacles created by the cathedral staff and tradition. W. G. McNaught, who spent many hours with Stainer (under trying conditions) travelling all over Britain, examining at the training colleges, said that Stainer's sphere of influence was countrywide. 'He first gained public attention by his musical capacity, but he held it afterwards by his capacity as a man of thought and feeling . . . Stainer was one of those men who make the life of other people worth living.'[28] An assessment by Sir Arthur Sullivan was given in an after-dinner speech when Stainer resigned as organist of St Paul's. Stainer was 'the great master on the king of instruments, the profound thinker, the earnest student, the zealous and enthusiastic teacher, the composer of power and imagination, and a man of blameless honour.'[29]

Stainer's humility could have its humorous side and the following is an example of these two aspects of his character; his holiday in Switzerland was somewhat interrupted:

Stainer was in the smoke-room of the hotel when the clergyman found him, and started the conversation with 'Do you play the harmonium?' 'A little', was the reply of the ex-organist of St Paul's Cathedral. 'Will you, then, be good enough to help us out of our difficulty on Sunday? We will read the psalms, and the hymns shall be the simplest I can select,' added the delighted parson. 'I will do my best,' said Stainer, with a smile. The service passed off all right; but the congregation, instead of rushing away at the close, listened to a brilliant recital. When the parson heard the name of his assistant, he asked him to dinner. 'Do you smoke?' he said at the close. 'I will do my best,' muttered Stainer, and the ensuing laughter was the prologue of an entertaining exchange of Oxford reminiscences.[30]

At times he appeared to exist on little sleep. But need arose, not only as a result of his work load, but also because of his naturally gregarious nature. He was a great conversationalist who 'knew more good stories than most men, and he could appreciate other people's good stories.'[31] Unfortunately Stainer's diaries and engagement books are believed to be no longer in existence; but those of Hubert Parry are, and they give some indication of Stainer in his professorial period and immediately following:

7 January, 1893:	Down to Oxford to Stainer. Lloyd and Strong to dinner. Sat up very late talking.
6 November, 1895:	Huge pile of work all day without stopping and up late smoking with the Stainers.
4 May, 1896:	Down to Oxford in time for dinner at the Stainers. Very kindly welcome.
3 November, 1896:	Down to Oxford. 14 candidates for Mus. Doc.!! and a huge lot of others. Very heavy work here; to dinner 7.30. Stayed with Stainers.
3 November, 1897:	Down to Oxford by last train. The kind Stainers welcomed me most friendly and we sat up smoking and talking till nearly 1.
3 May, 1898:	Down to Oxford by 9.15 train. Found Stainers all up in smoking room and we kept up late talking.
3 March, 1899:	Stainer kept me up till past 1 talking.
1 May, 1899:	By 5 o'clock train to Oxford. Charles Stainer at station to meet me. Parratt the only other guest at the Stainers. Impossible to get Stainer to bed as usual: up talking and smoking.
2 May, 1899:	Stainer kept us up very late again telling many stories of various peoples' wickedness.
6 November, 1899:	Down to Oxford by late train. To the Stainers who kept me up very late.
7 November, 1899:	Dinner at Stainers and the worthy man keeping me up very late again, though worn out.
5 November, 1900:	To Stainers by dinner time. Kept up late, as usual, smoking with Stainer.[32]

These extracts give some evidence of Stainer as a raconteur of no mean ability. But there must have been times when Parry would have willingly exchanged some of the social pleasure for an extra hour in bed to prepare for the work which, after all, was the main reason for him being in Oxford. Stainer, who was also engaged in the work, appeared to be unaffected.

During most of his professional career Stainer was compelled to spend periods away from home. While he was by all accounts a good and conscientious family man, he certainly had to neglect his family at times, as the following extracts from letters written to Mrs Stainer show:

As to your delightful proposal that I should come to Ventnor – I am afraid it is no good hoping against hope. I shall have my hands quite full – preparing for the little performance of Jairus at Morrish's Institute –

on the 15th of March and our Passion Service on the 23rd. On the 11th and 12th of March I have to be in Cambridge examining candidates for the Doctorate; and on the *4th of March* we produce Hiller's Song of Victory and Goetz 'By the waters of Babylon' at the Albert Hall. So you see my time is completely mapped out. I am very sorry as I am getting rather fagged from extra work and scanty sleep. For the past five or six nights I have not slept more than about *4 hours.* [33]

The second letter is sent from Caernarvon on notepaper bearing the insignia of the Royal Welsh Yacht Club:

All is going off well. But my whole day is occupied – the competitions take the whole morning till 3 or 3.30 then a long concert begins at 5.30!!! This morning at a Gorsedd of the Bards held in the inside of the castle – I was dubbed a 'Pencerdd' or Minstrel under the poetical name of Allaw'r Cyssegr (Musician of the Sanctuary) . . . [34]

Such was the manner and life of John Stainer: he had the 'simplicity of a scholar, a kindly disposition and manners eminently courteous' [35] coupled with a great capacity for work. No wonder that those who knew him and appointed him to St Paul's Cathedral could be guaranteed a successful outcome.

PUPILS

There are frequent reports of Stainer's giving great encouragement to young musicians. The following extracts reveal this:

Sir John's cheery presence will be much missed in Oxford, where he always had kindly words of encouragement for the young and struggling musician. [36]

There are few of his contemporaries, fewer still of his juniors, who have not had reason to be grateful for his advice, his help and his encouragement. [37]

Sir John Stainer was a very lovable Christian man, always accessible to any needing advice or encouragement, and many a young organist walked away with his head up the better for his interview. [38]

. . . he has a special claim to the respect and affection of musicians by reason of the lively interest he took in the work of younger men and the help and encouragement which he never failed to extend to them, especially if they were struggling. [39]

A very warm tribute, written in 1899, came from C. H. Lloyd:

Dr. Lloyd's recollections of his under-graduate period at Oxford in regard to music are of a specially interesting nature. The name of one good man and true is uppermost in his thoughts – that of John Stainer, then Organist of Magdalen College, who was the life and soul of all musical happenings in the University. 'I can hardly express my gratitude to Stainer' says Dr. Lloyd. 'He gave me a term's lessons in harmony, but beyond that I gained an experience of untold value to me in watching him as he played the organ and accompanied in his own inimitable manner.'[40]

When professor, Stainer examined and came into contact with men who were afterwards appointed to important positions in church music and academic life. Henry Coward (BMus 1889 and DMus 1894) was in charge of the music at the University of Sheffield and well known as a choral conductor in the north of England; the above mentioned C. H. Lloyd (DMus 1890) became, after cathedral appointments, Director of Music at Eton College; Charlton Palmer (BMus 1891 and DMus 1896) was Organist of Canterbury Cathedral; Percy Buck held posts in major public schools and finally became Professor of Music at the University of London; Hugh Allen (BMus 1892 and DMus 1896) remained at Oxford and later became professor; Ivor Atkins (BMus 1892) became a close acquaintance of Elgar and was Organist of Worcester Cathedral; T. H. Yorke Trotter (DMus 1892) is mainly remembered as an academic teacher; Ernest Walker (BMus 1893 and DMus 1898) stayed at Balliol College and became another Oxford musical historian; Harry Goss-Custard (BMus 1895) became Organist of Liverpool Cathedral; E. H. Fellowes (BMus 1896), in addition to his scholastic eminence, became a canon of Windsor; Basil Harwood (DMus 1896) was Organist of Christ Church, Oxford; C. H. Kitson (BMus 1897) is mainly remembered for his treatise on harmony; and John Borland was the first music adviser to the London County Council and a pioneer in the musical appreciation movement in schools in the first part of this century. Such were the men who must have benefited in one way or another from Stainer's own scholarship and musicianship.

At the time of his appointment as Professor of Music at Oxford, Stainer considered that England was 'striving earnestly to regain the position it has more than once held in the world of music'; and in view of the fact that the nation had better teachers, better performers and better educational institutions and that there was a widespread and active interest in music, he had great hopes for our future musical prosperity.[41]

George Thewlis, commenting on Stainer and his contemporaries, said that:

. . . when the unthinking modern man is tempted to sneer at their names, let him first learn the state of English music at this time and especially the appalling state of church music . . . The pioneer work done by Stainer was one upon which subsequent church composers built their edifice. It is impossible to overestimate the value of Stainer's influence on the music of his time: not only in Oxford but on the whole course of musical life in the country. His knowledge was as great as his predecessor's [Ouseley], his method of imparting it infinitely greater; and those who know him only as a composer know him not at all.[42]

Fellowes said much the same: 'Let us mainly forget him as a composer, but remember him for all time as an outstanding musician and a great leader in his day.'[43]

At St Paul's, in particular, Stainer's achievements merit recognition. Stainer began his period there with few of the advantages of a well-established and disciplined choir, yet through industry, determination and natural charm he brought the cathedral music to a standard excelled in England by no other similar body. It was an uphill struggle and very nearly broke him. When he took up his duties the organ was largely incomplete, the boys and men in the choir were badly disciplined, and the boys, of varying quality, knew only a small quantity of music because there was so much repetition of the service music and anthems. He reorganised the choir, regulated the system of deputies among the assistant vicars-choral so that there was always a good balance of voices, and instituted regular choir practices for the whole choir, not only the boys – something quite revolutionary and almost without precedent in cathedrals. A new choir school was built so that for the first time, whether from London or not, all boys lived and were educated together in one building. The psalms, previously unpointed and left to some kind of collective intuition in the attempt at unified performance, were pointed by Stainer, which led to a more thoughtful and intelligent interpretation. Eventually the whole range of Prayer Book services was published in a single volume. The musical repertoire was extended and weekly service lists were issued; in short, the whole place became alive, dignified and worthy of its purpose. For many of these improvements the credit must go to Stainer. Accordingly it is no surprise to have the comment of the *New York Times* that Stainer's efforts resulted in 'placing the music at St Paul's on the same level as that of St Peter's, Rome, and other churches of European renown'.[44]

What marks Stainer out for special discernment, however, is that he contributed so much in other areas of musical life. Remembering that broad musical interests and talents were not usually associated with cathedral organists, his achievements are all the more remarkable. According to Bumpus his ability and energy were known, 'but the world cannot know his pervading piety, his deep humility, and the springs of sympathy and loving kindness which lay so near the surface of his character, and gushed out so freely at the least touch of others' joys and sorrows'.[45] However, his interest in everything and everyone around him took its toll and after being so long in the public eye he wanted to sink, as far as possible, into obscurity. Latterly he refused all attempts by others to write a biography of him or to be drawn into any controversy. Had he lived longer, he would probably have devoted his working time to the Board of Education and at the same time lived a more relaxed kind of life. But such a pleasant way of living was to be denied him.

On the occasion of the centenary, in 1940, of Stainer's birth, another writer spoke of his outstanding contribution to music:

Stainer has claims that are too rarely possessed by the eminent in any branch of art. Without stint, he placed himself, his undoubted gifts, and his great power of work at the service of the public, and always in the most practical of ways; and it is as a great musical public servant that he will long be remembered with gratitude and honour.[46]

Today there seems no reason to qualify in any way this high estimation of Stainer's worth.

List of abbreviations

These abbreviations are used both in the text and notes.

BA Bachelor of Arts
BMus Bachelor of Music
c circa
Cath St Paul's Cathedral, London
Cath LSB St Paul's Cathedral, large scrap book of press cuttings collected by J. S. Bumpus, now housed in St Paul's Cathedral Library
CCER Committee of Council on Education Reports (Department of Education and Science Library)
Chapt St Paul's Cathedral Chapter Minutes
DMus Doctor of Music
DNB *Dictionary of National Biography*
Edw Letters from Sir John Stainer to F. G. Edwards (Edwards Papers, Egerton ms 3092, The British Library)
FTCL Fellow of Trinity College of Music, London
Hadow Papers of Sir Henry Hadow, Worcester College Library, Oxford
Hon Honorary
ISM Incorporated Society of Musicians
MA Master of Arts
MA The Musical Association
Mirror *The Mirror of Music* − P. A. Scholes
MS *The Musical Society*
ms manuscript
MT *The Musical Times*
MT Obit *The Musical Times* obituary article on Sir John Stainer, May 1901
MusBac Bachelor of Music
MusDoc Doctor of Music
MV Men's Voices
nd no date
NTSM National Training School for Music
OUG *Oxford University Gazette*
Oxon University of Oxford

RAM	Royal Academy of Music
RCM	Royal College of Music
RCO	Royal College of Organists
RMA	The Royal Musical Association
SATB	Soprano – alto – tenor – bass
Thew	Thewlis papers in possession of the widow of George Thewlis
UGM	Union of Graduates in Music
UL	University of London

Notes to chapters

1 *DNB*, under John Stainer
2 Unpublished notes of John and Edward Stainer, sons of Sir John Stainer (in the possession of J. R. Stainer)
3 ibid
4 *MT* Obit. Written by the Rev Arthur Whitley, a family friend of the Stainers and formerly Headmaster of Witton Grammar School, Northwich.
5 H. J. Gauntlett (1805–76) was an important church musician of his day and his advice on organ building was valued. He is mainly remembered now for his fine hymn tunes, notably *Irby, St Fulbert* and *St Albinus.*
6 William Pole (1814–1900), FRS, Professor of Civil Engineering, University College, London. With Stainer he helped to found The Musical Association and both were examiners for degrees in music at the University of London.
7 Pole, *Some short reminiscences*, 10
8 Edw 5 January 1901. F. G. Edwards (1853–1909) was editor of *The Musical Times* from 1897 to his death.
9 ibid
10 Pole, *Some short reminiscences*, 10
11 *The Guardian*, 10 April 1901. Obit article by Canon H. Scott Holland.
12 Cath Register Book of Almoner
13 Article by an unknown author in boys' paper *CHUMS* after Stainer's knighthood and probably just as he was to terminate his position at St Paul's (1888).
14 Grove, *Dictionary*, 1889 edition, article 'Sir John Stainer'
15 *CHUMS*
16 Edw 7 October 1896
17 Charles Steggall (1826–1905), Organist Lincoln's Inn Chapel from 1864 and Professor RAM
18 Edw 7 October 1896
19 *MT* Obit
20 ibid

21 Edw 6 October 1896

22 Edw 13 November 1896

23 *MT* Obit

24 *CHUMS*

25 George Cooper (1820–76) became sub organist in 1838 at the time Sir John Goss was appointed cathedral organist. Cooper also became Organist of the Chapel Royal in 1856.

26 *The Church Family Newspaper*, 4 April 1901

27 *MT* Obit

28 ibid

29 *RCO Calendar*, 1900–1

30 *DNB*

31 *RCO Calendar*, 1900–1

32 Edw 5 January 1901

33 Grove, *Dictionary*, article F. A. G. Ouseley. When Ouseley accepted these appointments they were little more than a sinecure but he was soon to change that in respect of the professorship. The post of precentor carried no emoluments and the sole duty was to preach the sermon at matins in the cathedral on Christmas Day.

34 *RCO Calendar*, presidential speech, 29 April 1889

35 *MA* Proceedings, 1889–90, *The Character and Influence of the late Sir Frederick Ouseley*

36 Bumpus, *English Cathedral Music*, 542

37 *MA* Proceedings, Character of Ouseley

38 Long, *Music of the English Church*, 325

39 *MA* Proceedings, Character of Ouseley

40 ibid

41 The contents of the present music library were not organised into a library until after 1918; in Stainer's time they were merely Ouseley's own books housed in his private quarters. When Ouseley was there the college possessed a general library of books on history, heraldry, orientalia, theology, travel, English and foreign literature, etc. One can safely assume that there was a large quantity of foreign antiquarian music in Ouseley's possession while Stainer was organist there, even though it seems impossible to detect exactly what.

42 *The Crucifixion* and hymn tunes apart, this anthem is the best known of Stainer's fuller scale works.

43 *MT* Obit

44 Ironically, *Praise the Lord, O my soul* was a text which Stainer later complained was used more often than any other, in his *A few words to candidates for the degree of Mus.Bac. Oxon.* The ms of Stainer's anthem is retained in the Bodleian Library, Oxford.

CHAPTER 2

1 Letter from Frederic Bulley, 20 December 1859 (in the possession of J. R. Stainer)

2 Letter from Bulley, 26 December 1859

3 Stainer matriculated at Christ Church on 26 May 1859 prior to becoming BMus on 10 June 1859. It is not clear why Bulley should suggest that Stainer matriculate again at St Edmund Hall. One assumes that the position was that while being Organist at Magdalen College, he eventually took up residence at St Edmund Hall.

4 Letter from Bulley, 23 January 1860

5 Tovey & Parratt, *Walter Parratt*, 49. It remains a mystery why Parratt should accuse Stainer of negligence: there is no other evidence for this and it seems to be uncharacteristic of Stainer. But there was some personal animosity between the two men, although just how much it is difficult to say and the assumption is made on shreds of evidence. P. M. Young in his book *George Grove* states (page 211) that 'there were tensions among the senior members of the teaching staff, and Stainer's dislike of Parratt made for a very frosty atmosphere at a Council meeting' – letter from Grove to his young friend and confidante, Edith Oldham.

6 Venables, *Sweet tones remembered*, 17

7 *Musical World*, 3 March 1855

8 *Oxford Chronicle*, 14 July 1860

9 *MT* Obit

10 *The Guardian*, 2 April 1901

11 *The World*, 12 January 1887

12 Letter from Bulley to Stainer, 7 November 1865

13 *Oxford Journal*, 11 November 1865

14 Source unknown, newspaper cutting dated 8 November 1865 (in the possession of J. R. Stainer)

15 *Oxford Times*, 11 November 1865

16 *University Herald*, 11 November 1865

17 *Oxford Chronicle*, 11 November 1865

18 Scholes, *Mirror*, 94

19 *The Orchestra*, 30 June 1866

20 Bramley in *Christmas Carols New and Old* and Tuckwell in *Magdalen Psalter* and *The Church Choir Chant Book*

21 *MT* Obit

22 *RCO Calendar*, 1900–1, 23

23 *DNB*

24 *The World*, 12 January 1887. Thewlis gave Stainer credit for the formation of the Oxford Philharmonic Society, a mixture of people

from 'town and gown' and quotes from an unnamed source, 'This result is entirely attributed to the exertions and personal good qualities of Dr Stainer, the popular organist of Magdalen College who has thus succeeded where all others have failed'. However, it appears that Stainer encountered some kind of opposition from the society's committee of influential ladies (according to Thewlis) and this was the reason for Stainer handing over the conductorship to James Taylor. Thus the Oxford Philharmonic Society and the Oxford Choral Society were rivals for a period. When Stainer returned as professor of music he managed to combine the two societies, a feat which required much tactical skill, and Varley Roberts, who succeeded Parratt as Organist at Magdalen College Chapel, took over the conductorship until 1893 when he resigned because of lack of men coming to practices. Later it was amalgamated with the Bach Choir (conducted at one time by Basil Harwood).

25 Exeter College Music Society, Oxford. Minutes of meetings, 1864–72.
26 Edw 6 June 1898
27 Graves, *Hubert Parry*, 115
28 Exeter College minutes
29 Thew, extract from press cutting of local newspaper (not identified)
30 Traditional story related to the author by Dr Watkins Shaw
31 Thew, assorted programmes
32 Thew
33 Stainer's eldest son complained that no copy existed in the British Museum Library (as it then was). It was issued by subscription and published by Houghton & Tuke, Oxford, 1864.
34 Thew
35 Unpublished material in Magdalen College Library, Oxford
36 Hall, *The Magdalen Vagabonds*, in the possession of Magdalen College Library, Oxford
37 Tuckwell, *Old Magdalen Days*, 49–50
38 *MT* Obit
39 Edw 19 January 1901
40 It is curious that Pole in his autobiography does not refer to The Musical Association, as it was in his time, although he does write about other learned bodies with which he was associated. Neither does he mention that he and Stainer subsequently became examiners in music to the University of London.
41 Edw 11 January 1901
42 *MT* Obit; Gadsby was a fellow chorister with Stainer
43 Young, *George Grove*, 103–4
44 *Musical World*, 14 November 1868

45 Graves, *Hubert Parry*, 62
46 ibid, 77
47 Hollins, *A blind musician*, 152
48 Pamphlet guide on St Cuthbert's Church, Doveridge
49 Scholes, *Mirror*, 663. Prout subsequently became professor at Dublin, Macfarren at Cambridge and Stainer at Oxford.
50 Contemporary account in newspaper; cutting leaves unclear which paper or when. (In possession of J. R. Stainer)
51 Edw 6 November 1899
52 Oakeley, *Hubert Oakeley*, 111
53 Edw June 1898, no day given
54 *MT* January 1904
55 *RMA* Proceedings, 1921–2, Music in the Universities – H. P. Allen
56 It is interesting that this letter, undated although the postmark on the envelope is 3 October 1871, presupposes Stainer's departure yet he was not seen for the St Paul's post until December 1871 and, as far as is known, Goss had made no announcement of his retirement as early as October.
57 Tovey and Parratt, *Walter Parratt*
58 *MT* Obit
59 *The Manchester Guardian*, 27 March 1872

CHAPTER 3

1 *MT* January 1904
2 ibid
3 Chadwick, *Oxford Movement*, 12
4 Grove, *Dictionary*, 1889 edition, article 'Novello, Ewer & Co'
5 Fellowes, *English Cathedral Music*, 10
6 Bumpus, *English Cathedral Music*, 335
7 West, *Cathedral Organists*, 93
8 Liddon, *W. K. Hamilton*, 23–4. Liddon held Bishop Hamilton in high esteem, not only as a reformer of cathedral worship but also as a man of great holiness. Liddon was appointed to a canonry at St Paul's in 1870 and Hamilton's example was evidently much in his mind in the part he played in the St Paul's reforms.
9 Hamilton, *Cathedral Reform*. In those days it was often the practice for clergymen to hold a number of livings, at the same time collecting the income from them; an assistant curate was paid to do the duty.
10 ibid
11 Jebb (1805–86) undertook a survey of all the choral foundations in

England and Ireland, publishing the results in *The Choral Service* (shortened title).

12 Wesley, *Cathedral Music*
13 Edward Copleston, Dean of St Paul's (1827–49). Like his two predecessors there he was also Bishop of Llandaff.
14 Jebb, *The Choral Service*, 377
15 Bumpus, *The Organists of St Paul's Cathedral*, 174
16 Gregory, *Robert Gregory*, 167. Robert Gregory (1819–1911) subsequently became Dean of St Paul's in 1890.
17 ibid, 158
18 ibid, 164
19 Bumpus, *The music at St Paul's*
20 Gregory, *Robert Gregory*, pages 168–9
21 *DNB* under H. P. Liddon
22 ibid
23 Chapt 26 January 1871
24 Chapt 11 January 1871
25 *MS* 3 February 1872
26 Church, *Dean Church*, 200
27 ibid, 238

CHAPTER 4

1 See Chapter 2, note 56. Because of the circumstances described, it is not possible to be certain whether negotiations had taken place prior to the resignation of Goss, but it seems reasonably certain that they had.
2 Chapt 2 December 1871
3 ibid
4 Chapt 22 December 1871
5 ibid
6 *MS* 20 January 1872
7 ibid
8 Henry Scott Holland (1847–1918), canon of St Paul's (1884–1911), precentor (1886–1911) and subsequently Regius Professor of Divinity at Oxford. As a student he was greatly influenced by H. P. Liddon.
9 *The Guardian*, 10 April 1901. Archdeacon Hale would have been the only member of the chapter who would have remembered Stainer as a chorister; although he had died before Stainer's appointment and Liddon's arrival, the eventual successor to Goss may have been discussed by Archdeacon Hale and Canon Gregory at some stage.
10 Chapt 28 December 1871

11 Frost, *Early Recollections*, 24
12 Chapt 28 December 1871
13 Matthews and Atkins, *St Paul's*, 272
14 *MT* February 1872
15 Cath LSB, 161
16 *The Times*, 3 January 1872
17 ibid
18 *The Choir*, 13 January 1872
19 *MS* 6 January 1872
20 ibid
21 Fowler, *J. B. Dykes*, 157
22 Letter in possession of J. R. Stainer
23 Chapt 22 December 1871
24 Gregory, *Robert Gregory*, 177
25 Chapt 18 January 1872. There was criticism of this ruling of the chapter (*MS* 24 February 1872) on the grounds that members of the chapter themselves held more than one clerical appointment. This was not true of this particular chapter.
26 Chapt 10 February 1872
27 Frost, *Early Recollections*, 26
28 ibid, 32
29 Charity schools were associated with parishes and had been started as early as 1698 by the SPCK. The pupils' attendance at church on Sundays was compulsory and in many cases they were compelled to sing in the choir. The charity schools paved the way for the monitorial system and generally became less effective during the nineteenth century. Eventually as church schools, they were absorbed into the state system.
30 Warner, *St Paul's Cathedral*, 233
31 Fellowes, *English Church Music*, XXI, no 1, article 'Sir John Stainer'
32 Frost, *Early Recollections*, 31–2
33 Fellowes, *English Church Music*, article *'Sir John Stainer'*
34 Chapt 18 April 1872
35 *Church Times*, 2 February 1877
36 HM Commissioners (1883) on *Cathedrals and Churches in England and Wales*, Appendix, para 4
37 *MS* 18 January 1873
38 Chapt 7 May 1872
39 *MS* 16 January 1886
40 *St Paul's Cathedral Bye Laws* – assistant vicars-choral
41 Chapt 25 January 1873
42 Johnston, *H. P. Liddon*, 141
43 ibid

44 Succentor's Report, 1885–7, 13
45 Church, *Dean Church*, 257
46 Massingham, *Dean Hole*, 159
47 *MS*
48 ibid
49 William Hawes succeeded John Sale as cathedral almoner in 1812 and chose to live in Craven Street, Charing Cross, which involved far too much travelling to be a convenient arrangement for the choristers who were, by that time, living with him. It seems probable that Hawes moved to Adelphi Terrace in 1817 and the choristers went with him, remaining there until they moved to the Chapter House in 1845. At first only the senior boys were fully boarded but by 1836 all the boys were boarded. In January 1831 Dr Copleston, Dean of St Paul's and Bishop of Llandaff, wrote to tell Miss Hackett that the Bishop of Chichester had consented to let the boys be instructed (although not necessarily live) in his house at Amen Corner. Unfortunately, Dr Carr was appointed Bishop of Worcester and gave up his house before this plan could be put into operation. Bumpus also offers some evidence that by the time of Trinity Sunday 1831 (the day that Attwood wrote his anthem *Come, Holy Ghost* in a gig travelling between his house in Brixton and the cathedral), eight of the St Paul's choristers, together with ten from the Chapel Royal, were living with Hawes in Adelphi Terrace.
   William Hawes (1785–1846) was Master of the Choristers at both St Paul's Cathedral and the Chapel Royal.
   (Bumpus, *A History of English Cathedral Music*, 407–8, and correspondence with headmaster of St Paul's Cathedral Choir School and Miss K. I. Garrett, lately principal cataloguer at Guildhall Library, London, January 1976).
50 Matthews and Atkins, *St Paul's*, 255–6
51 Johnston, *H. P. Liddon*, 142–3
52 ibid
53 *MT* May 1900
54 Johnston, *H. P. Liddon*, 142–3

CHAPTER 5

1 Chapt 15 October 1872
2 Frost reaffirmed the point when he said that 'Stainer engaged me to come and help, and knowing that he was paying the expenses, I offered to come for nothing but he would not consent' (*Early Recollections*, 40). The author is still doubtful as to whether the cathedral chapter would have allowed Stainer to bear the expenses

or, indeed, whether he could have afforded to meet such expenditure.

3 Chapt 18 December 1872
4 Grove, *Dictionary*, article 'Sons of the Clergy'
5 *The Church Review*, 19 May 1877
6 *MT* June 1877
7 *MT* June 1878
8 *The Times*, 13 May 1880. This setting by Stanford, still very popular was described as a 'novelty to be prized . . . Mr Stanford shows an evident leaning towards Mendelssohn but he writes well both for voices and instruments; his melody flows naturally and his harmony is unostentatious and pure'.
9 *MT* June 1881
10 Ferdinand Hiller (1811–85) was a pianist primarily but also conducted concerts in various towns in Germany, notably Cologne. He was a friend of Mendelssohn, Schumann, Chopin and other Romantic composers.
11 *MT* February 1883
12 *MT* February 1887
13 *Daily Chronicle*, 27 January 1885
14 Frost, *Early Recollections*, 68
15 *The Musical World*, 10 December 1887
16 *Daily Chronicle*, 6 December 1882
17 *MT* January 1879
18 Grove, *Dictionary*, article 'The Bach Society'
19 *Daily Chronicle*, 5 April 1882
20 Prefatory notes in Stainer's edition of *St Matthew Passion*, J. S. Bach
21 *Daily Chronicle*, 5 April 1882
22 Stainer's edition of *St Matthew Passion*
23 *MT* May 1921, commenting on the 1873 performance
24 *The Guardian*, 24 April 1878
25 Church Congress Paper, Leeds 1872
26 Sparrow Simpson, *Memoir*, 68–9
27 ibid
28 Chapt 11 June 1877
29 Sparrow Simpson, *Memoir*, 48
30 Sumner, *Organs of St Paul's Cathedral*, 19–21
31 In 1973 some work on the organ was undertaken by Noel Mander when it was intended, among other things, to restore the chancel organ as nearly as possible to its 1872 form. The choir organ also reverted to what it was in 1872, to serve as an accompanimental department; a new positive organ was installed thus giving the effects called for in the classical repertoire, lacking in the 1872 organ.

32 Sumner, *Organs of St Paul's Cathedral*, 19–21
33 Letter to Mr Tovey (in the possession of the late John Dykes Bower, 1973)
34 Chapt 15 March 1881
35 Rebuilt in 1970 by Noel Mander who installed a new tracker action, added a mixture on the great organ and made a case of classical design.
36 Bumpus, *The Organists of St Paul's*, 209. This account was written by Stainer.
37 Letter from W. L. Sumner to the author, September 1972
38 ibid, November 1972
39 Bateson, *Alcock of Salisbury*, 31
40 *The Times*, 11 June 1940
41 ibid
42 *MT* January 1904
43 Letter to Stainer from the Rev J. H. Coward (in the possession of the Rev J. Stainer)
44 *DNB*, 'Sir John Stainer'. The author's own view, one he believes shared by many, is that the art of improvisation and the ability to accompany the psalms beautifully and expressively, are the artistic qualities that mark the outstanding church organist; unfortunately, the art of improvisation is not treated seriously enough in contrast with the rest of Europe, alas, where the psalms are not sung to Anglican chant!
45 *MS* 14 February 1880
46 Graves, *Hubert Parry*, 62
47 Diary of Hubert Parry (in possession of Lord Ponsonby)
48 *The Guardian*, 10 April 1901, 492
49 ibid
50 *Oxford Magazine*, 24 April 1901, 288
51 Bumpus, *Organists of St Paul's*, 180
52 *MS* 15 October 1881
53 Letter from W. L. Sumner to the author, November 1972
54 Edw 12 October 1886
55 ibid
56 Edw 20 April 1887
57 Fellowes, *English Church Music*, article 'Sir John Stainer'
58 *MT* November 1875
59 *MT* June 1876
60 *The Daily News*, 7 February 1888
61 *Musical World*, 7 January 1888
62 Chapt 27 January 1888.
63 Dean Church was abroad at the time, recovering from illness.
64 Chapt 27 January 1888

65 *MT* June 1888
66 *MT* July 1888
67 Since Goss all retiring organists of St Paul's have been knighted. Stanley Marchant who resigned at the age of forty-nine to become Professor of Music at the University of London is the only exception; he resigned in 1936 during the brief reign of Edward VIII but was subsequently honoured in 1942.
68 *MT* August 1888
69 ibid
70 The choir school possesses an oil painting of Stainer, about 4 × 3ft and hanging in the gallery of the new choir school building. There is no evidence of a scholarship.
71 *The Guardian*, 2 April 1901

CHAPTER 6

1 Scholes, *Mirror*, 651
2 Crotch (1775–1847), BMus 1794, DMus 1799. Organist of Christ Church, Oxford, at the age of fifteen. Chiefly remembered for his oratorio *Palestine* (1812) which enjoyed considerable success even after his death; the movement *Lo, star-led chiefs* is still sung in churches today
3 *Oxford University Gazette*, 7 May 1889
4 *MS* 28 April 1889
5 *MT* Obit
6 *MA* Proceedings, 1889
7 *MT* May 1889
8 Edw 5 March 1899
9 Graves, *Hubert Parry*, 14
10 ibid
11 Hadow; Stainer persuaded Hadow to take the degree.
12 *MT* January 1909
13 *MT* July 1889
14 ibid
15 *MT* Obit
16 Fellowes, *Memoirs*, 56
17 *MT* Obit
18 *Oxford Magazine*, 27 November 1895. (A complete list of the lectures given during Stainer's professorship can be found on pages 205–208)
19 The choragus was the professor's assistant responsible for helping the professor in his lecture and appointed by the professor. Parry had succeeded Corfe in December 1883 as Ouseley's choragus and stayed on at Stainer's request.

20 *Oxford Journal*, 14 September 1889
21 *MS* 28 April 1889
22 Thew
23 In deference to Stainer's wishes, Hadow became BMus in 1890 but was never a professional musician in the strict sense of the word, ie that this was his main occupation. His contribution, however, to musical life within the university was far reaching. He became vice chancellor of the University of Sheffield (1919–31); in his efforts towards establishing the university's musical life nothing was too much trouble. During 1920–34 he was chairman of the consultative committee of the Board of Education and presented six reports, one of which became known as the Hadow Report, *The Education of the Adolescent* (1927).
24 *OUG* 11 October 1889
25 ibid, 16 January 1891
26 ibid, 22 January 1897
27 ibid, 15 October 1897
28 *Oxford Magazine*, 25 October 1893
29 Lecture entitled *Music as a branch of education*
30 *Oxford Chronicle*, 19 June 1897
31 *MT* August 1897
32 *Oxford Chronicle*, 31 July 1897
33 This information was contained in RCM minutes, but, in fact, Charles Wood proceeded to Selwyn College, Cambridge (1888–9) and then to Gonville and Caius College (1889–94) as organ scholar, where he read for both an arts and a music degree.
34 RCM minutes, March 1899
35 Stainer, *A few words*, 6. Although Stainer used the term MusBac in this instance, the correct form of all Oxford degrees is for the type of degree to precede the subject, hence BMus and DMus, which terms have been used throughout except where quotations are involved.
36 ibid, 7
37 ibid
38 ibid, 9
39 ibid, 16–17
40 ibid, 24
41 ibid, 22–3
42 ibid, 27
43 ibid, 28
44 Hadow, 27 October 1890
45 ibid, 1884
46 ibid
47 ibid, 11 May 1890

48 ibid, 22 November 1896. The work Hadow referred to was his *Primer* on Sonata Form.
49 ibid, 13 December 1891
50 ibid, 30 October 1897
51 ibid, 1 December 1893
52 *MT* January 1890
53 *MT* September 1889
54 Scholes, *Mirror*, 658. In present currency about £206.70 and £83.30.
55 Thew
56 Scholes, *Mirror*, 657
57 *Oxford Chronicle*, 8 October 1898
58 *MT* December 1898. Residence subsequently became compulsory in 1911.
59 Graves, *Hubert Parry*, 12
60 *OUG* 24 October 1899
61 *MT* July 1899
62 *MT* July 1899. Parry was professor from 1900 to 1908 (he died in 1918); his successor, Sir Walter Parratt, Organist of St George's Chapel, Windsor, held the chair from 1908 to 1918; neither lived in Oxford. Sir Hugh Allen followed and was professor from 1918 to his death in 1946; he was also Director of the RCM from 1919 to 1937, so for part of the time (from 1922) he did not reside in Oxford either, although he retained his rooms in New College where he spent weekends and stayed when he came up to Oxford to perform his professorial duties. In the space of almost one hundred years Stainer was the only professor to reside permanently in Oxford during his professorship.
63 Hadow, 7 May 1899
64 ibid, 3 December 1899
65 Diary of Hubert Parry, 9 November 1899
66 *OUG* 24 October 1899
67 *MT* April 1900
68 Edw 30 July 1897
69 *MT* December 1882
70 W. G. McNaught was editor of the *School Music Review*, founded in 1892, and succeeded F. G. Edwards as editor of *The Musical Times* from 1909–18. On Stainer's death it had been expected that McNaught, then having nearly twenty years' experience as assistant inspector and recognised as the country's great expert in school music, would be appointed as his successor; he resigned when the less experienced Arthur Somervell was appointed.
71 CCER, 1883
72 ibid

73 ibid, 1888
74 Apart from London, which comes at the end, the list is reproduced in the order it is printed in the board's report.
75 CCER, 1891. The word 'schools' is actually mentioned in the report from which it can be assumed that Stainer had visited schools and heard their pupils' performances. This must have been the beginning of instrumental work in schools which came into full fruition in the first two decades of the next century.
76 *Edw* 27 February 1901
77 Bridge, *A Westminster Pilgrim*, 260
78 Chapt 2 December 1871
79 MA Proceedings, 1894–5
80 Grove, *Dictionary*, article 'Royal Musical Association'. The association received the 'Royal' prefix in 1944
81 A full account can be found in P. A. Scholes, *The Mirror of Music*, 685ff.
82 *MT* Obit
83 Edw 6 November 1899
84 ibid, 1 December 1900
85 ibid, 19 October 1898
86 ibid, 21 October 1899. A short precis of this argument is that Stanford and Parry were anxious to improve the state of music in cathedrals without considering the resources available. Some provincial cathedrals had only 6 men (2 of whom ought to be pensioned off according to Stainer), some 5 and some only 4, so Palestrina's 8-part motets were clearly out of the question. Parry criticised those composers who gathered in royalties for writing 'cheap twaddle', which comment Stainer thought unworthy of a man in Parry's position. Stanford's subsidiary argument was that the precentor should hand over his duties to a trained musician, ie the cathedral organist.
87 *MA* Proceedings, 1900–1
88 Edw 23 August 1900
89 Edw November 1900
90 *MT* April 1901
91 *MT* Obit
92 ibid
93 Diary of Hubert Parry, 6 April 1901
94 *Oxford Chronicle*, 12 April 1901
95 *MT* February 1907
96 *MT* February 1906
97 *MT* January 1904

CHAPTER 7

1 Thew
2 Routley, *The Musical Wesleys*, 236
3 Bumpus, *The Organists of St Paul's*, 176
4 *Oxford Magazine*, 24 April 1901
5 Fellowes, *English Church Music*, article 'Sir John Stainer'
6 ibid
7 *Musical Mirror and Fanfare*, October 1932; letter from Sir Richard Terry, Organist and Master of the Music, Westminster Cathedral, 1901–24.
8 ibid
9 Stainer lecture, *The present state of music in England*, delivered to the University of Oxford, 13 November 1889
10 Thew
11 Hutchings, *Church Music*, 127–8
12 ibid
13 *The Guardian*, 10 April 1901
14 Long, *Music of the English Church*, 330–1
15 ibid
16 Phillips, *The Singing Church*, 8
17 Scholes, *Mirror*, 556
18 Long, *Music of the English Church*, 330
19 Letter from Mrs E. C. Stainer to J. S. Egerton, 13 March 1879 (in the possession of J. R. Stainer)
20 Stainer lecture, *The present state of music in England*
21 Lowther Clarke, *Hymns Ancient and Modern*, 34
22 ibid, 40
23 Stainer, *Hymn Tunes*, Preface
24 Hadow, 14 October 1900
25 Hadow, 4 November 1900
26 Stainer, *Hymn Tunes*, Preface
27 ibid
28 *The Guardian*, 31 October 1900
29 ibid
30 Stainer, *Hymn Tunes*, Preface
31 All these hymn tunes with the exception of *All for Jesus* and *Day of Wrath* appeared also in *Hymns Ancient and Modern Revised* (1950)
32 Bumpus, *The Organists of St Paul's*, 194
33 *Musical Mirror and Fanfare*, October 1932
34 Long, *Music of the English Church*, 30
35 *The Cathedral Prayer Book*, Appendix

CHAPTER 8

1 *MT* October 1878
2 *The Times*, 16 September 1878
3 *MT* October 1878
4 Published by Novello in 1878
5 *The Times*, 6 September 1883
6 *MS* 6 September 1883
7 *The Daily Telegraph*, 6 September 1883
8 P. A. Scholes even failed to include *St Mary Magdalen* in his general lists of oratorios, see *Oxford Companion*, article 'Oratorio'
9 *MT* March 1887
10 *The Sunday Times*, 27 February 1887
11 Unknown press report in the possession of J. R. Stainer
12 *MT* March 1887
13 *The Citizen*, 26 February 1887
14 Fellowes, *English Cathedral Music*, 223
15 *English Church Music*, article 'Sir John Stainer'
16 Press cutting, see note 11
17 Long, *Music of the English Church*, 365
18 Routley, *The Musical Wesleys*, 82
19 Fellowes, *English Cathedral Music*, 223
20 Stainer, *Hymn Tunes*, Preface
21 *Ilford Recorder*, 21 February 1952
22 Scholes, *Oxford Companion*, article 'Hymns and hymn tunes'
23 There are currently two excellent performances of the work on disc. In earlier days HMV recorded it (1930) and Robin Legge wrote at the time in *The Daily Telegraph* (10 May 1930): 'Stainer's Masterpiece: There is a good deal of justification for the claim put forward by the HMV Co. that Sir John Stainer's oratorio 'The Crucifixion' was the first universally popular oratorio for English-speaking people. It has never been claimed for it that it ranks with the great 'Passions' or Handel's oratorios. It is direct, sincere and simple music, which seeks not to be dramatic in a modern sense. In consequence, it makes an appeal to a multitude numerically far beyond that to which Bach and Handel appeal'.
24 Scholes, *Oxford Companion*, article 'J. H. Maunder'

CHAPTER 9

1 *Aids to the Student of the Holy Bible* and *The Bible Educator*
2 *MT* August 1879
3 Walker, *Music in England*, 330
4 E. W. B. Nicholson (1849–1912), member of Trinity College,

Oxford from 1867; Librarian of the London Institution (1873–82). Appointed Librarian of The Bodleian Library in 1882. A man of many and varied interests.

5 Stainer, *Dufay and his contemporaries*, vii
6 ibid, 1
7 Arrangements by Sir John and his two children
8 MA Proceedings, 1895–6
9 *Catalogue of English Song Books, forming a portion of the Library of Sir John Stainer, with Appendices of Foreign Song Books, Collections of Carols, Books on Bells, etc*
10 The contents of Harding's library are now in the Bodleian Library, Oxford. It is not expected to have the whole catalogued for many years. Of the Stainer collection they are thought to be almost exclusively song books.
11 *The World*, 12 January 1887
12 *The Book Collector*, vol XI, article 'British Song Books and kindred Subjects' – W. N. Harding
13 CQ Press Cable dated 14 December 1973 (in the possession of the author)

CHAPTER 10

1 *The Times*, 8 June 1940
2 *The Morning Leader*, no date. Press cutting in the possession of J. R. Stainer.
3 *The Pilot*, 20 April 1901
4 Thew
5 *The Guardian*, 10 April 1901
6 *The Morning Post*, 2 April 1901
7 Bumpus, *The Organists of St Paul's*, 180
8 *Oxford Magazine*, 24 April 1901, article 'Sir John Stainer'
9 ibid. It is believed that W. H. Hadow was the author of this article.
10 *Musical Mirror and Fanfare*, October 1932
11 ibid
12 *The Church Family Newspaper*, 4 April 1901
13 Letter from Stainer to J. F. Bridge, 11 September 1869 (in the possession of J. R. Stainer)
14 Letter from Stainer to his wife, 4 August 1880
15 Stainer lecture, *The present state of music in England*
16 ibid
17 *Oxford Mail*, 6 January 1964, article 'Stainer's contribution' by Sir Thomas Armstrong
18 ibid
19 Knight & Reed, *Treasury of English Church Music*, vol 4, 207

20 ibid Introduction by George Guest
21 Johnston, *H. P. Liddon*, 220
22 see page 19
23 Stainer lecture, *The present state of music in England*
24 *The Pilot*, 20 April 1901
25 *MS* 6 April 1901
26 ibid
27 *The Guardian*, 10 April 1901
28 *School Music Review*, May 1901
29 *The Pilot*, 20 April 1901
30 *The Church Family Newspaper*, 4 April 1901
31 *School Music Review*, May 1901
32 Diary of Hubert Parry (in the possession of Lord Ponsonby)
33 Letter from Stainer to his wife, 12 February 1880 (in the possession of J. R. Stainer)
34 ibid, 26 August 1880
35 *The Athenaeum*, 6 April 1901
36 *The Morning Post*, 2 April 1901
37 *Oxford Magazine*, 24 April 1901
38 *The Times*, 11 June 1940, letter from Sir Walter Alcock
39 *MT* June 1899
40 ibid
41 Stainer lecture, *The present state of music in England*
42 Thew
43 Fellowes, *English Church Music*, article 'Sir John Stainer'
44 *New York Times*, 2 April 1901. Stainer would not have cared for this comparison as he thought not too highly of the musical services in St Peter's, Rome.
45 Perkins and Bumpus, *Westminster Abbey*, 274
46 *MT* July 1940

Appendix A

Summary of lectures given to the University of Oxford during the professorship of Sir John Stainer, 1889–99.

1889–90

Stainer	The present state of Music in England.
Parry	The Middle-age Theorists and the first Experiments in Harmonic Construction. The Troubadours, Trouvères, Jongleurs and their influence. The Parisian School and the general progress of the art up to AD 1400.
Stainer	The Characteristics of Schumann's Songs; list given of songs to be analysed and sung as illustrations.
Parry	The Progress of Pure Choral Music in Italy. The Culmination of Pure Choral Music.
Stainer	Mendelssohn's oratorio, 'Elijah'.

1890–1

Stainer	Carols, English and Foreign, with illustrations.
Parry	Instrumental Music prior to the Musical Revolution, and its share in the influences which led to it, with illustrations. Further lecture in continuation of this.
Stainer	Origin and development of the Ground-Bass, with illustrations – 'owing to the character of the illustrations, the lecture will probably occupy 1½ hours'.
Parry	The beginnings of Opera and Oratorio. Monteverde and his School. Carissimi and his influence.
Stainer	The Styles of Composers, as exhibited by various settings of the same lyric, with illustrations.

1891–2

Stainer	Mozart's Requiem.
Parry	Music for Viols of the seventeenth century, illustrations by Arnold Dolmetsch, Miss Dolmetsch and others.
	Lulli and the beginnings of the French opera.
Stainer	Canons as a Form of Composition, with choral illustrations.
Parry	Purcell (two lectures).
	String Quartets with special reference to Haydn in G, op 77 no 1, and Beethoven in C, op 59 no 3.
Lloyd	Wagner's Siegfried Idyll.
Hadow	Parry's English Symphony.
Stainer	Music in its relation to the Intellect and Emotions.

1892–3

Stainer	Lute, Viol and Voice, with illustrations.
Hadow	Beethoven's 7th Symphony.
Piggott	Japanese Music, with illustrations on the Koto.
Stainer	Palestrina's Mass, Aeterna Christi Munera, also sung by the Choir.
Hadow	Schubert, Symphony in C.
Stainer	Composer and Performer.

1893–4

Stainer	Song and Dance – some old tunes sung by the Choir.
Hadow	Beethoven's Symphony no 3.
Stainer	Mendelssohn's oratorio, St Paul, with illustrations.
Hadow	Brahms Sestett in B flat.
Cohen	Musical traditions of the Synagogue, with illustrations.
Stainer	Composer and Hearer – a sequel to Composer and Performer. 'At 3.15 p.m. the music cast in 1612 on the fourth bell of St. Mary's Church (the Music Bell) will be explained and afterwards played by a string quartet.'

206

1894–5

Stainer	The Choral Responses of the English Liturgy, with illustrations.
Cunningham-Woods	Schumann's Symphony in B flat.
Bridge	Early English Dramatic Music, from the Miracle Plays to the Masque of Comus, with illustrations by some members of Westminster Abbey Choir.
Stainer	Handel's oratorio, 'Messiah'.
Hadow	Structure in Musical Composition.
Birkbeck	Music of the Russian Liturgy.
Varley Roberts	Madrigals with illustrations.
Stainer	Influences which affect Melodic Form.

1895–6

Stainer	Purcell, including the Te Deum.
Hadow	Concerto Form.
Stainer	Tye's Mass, Euge bone, with illustrations.
Hadow	Brahms' Pianoforte Quintet in F minor.
Stainer	The secular compositions of Dufay, with illustrations.

1896–7

Stainer	Song-writers of the Classical Period, with illustrations.
Hadow	Classic and Romantic ideals in music.
Stainer	Early harmonisation of Psalm-Tunes, and their treatment in motet form, with illustrations.
Hadow	Beethoven's Violin Concerto.
Garwood	The cultivation of the Speaking voice, with special reference to reading in Church.
Stainer	Music as a branch of education.

1897–8

Stainer	Morley's Plaine and Easie Introduction to Practicall Musicke (1597), with illustrations.
Hadow	The National Element in the Music of Haydn.
Garwood	Some famous speakers and their methods.
Stainer	Hans Leo Hassler (b 1564), with illustrations by the choir.

Buck	The Influence of Troubadours on Musical Art.
Hadow	Musical Form and Criticism.

1898–9

Stainer	Psalm and Hymn-tunes (continued) with illustrations by the choir.
Iliffe	'48 Preludes' in J. S. Bach's 'Well-Tempered Clavier'.
Stainer	Madrigalian Composers of the Gallo-Belgian School, with illustrations by the choir.
Stainer	The Influence of Fashion on the Art of Music.

Sir John Stainer, Professor
C. Hubert Parry, Choragus
C. H. Lloyd, Christ Church
W. H. Hadow, Worcester College
F. T. Piggott
The Rev F. L. Cohen
Dr J. F. Bridge
Dr F. Iliffe
W. J. Birkbeck
Dr Varley Roberts, Magdalen College
W. Garwood

Appendix B

Complete list of known works by John Stainer.
All published works are *London, Novello* unless otherwise stated.

Section A: Sacred Music

LARGER-SCALE CHORAL WORKS
Gideon: DMus exercise, 1865. Performed (in part) 8 November 1865. Unpublished. SATB soli and SATB chorus; instrumental scoring not known. Vocal score deposited in Bodleian Library, Oxford: Bod: Ms Mus Sch Ex d, 169.

The Daughter of Jairus: written for Worcester Triennial Festival, 1878. First Performed 14 September 1878. STB soli and SATB chorus; instrumental scoring: flute 2, oboe 2, clarinet 2, bassoon 2, horn 4 (1st and 2nd horn for valve horns in G: 3rd and 4th for valve horns in E flat – *composer's note*, 'The 3rd and 4th horn parts have also been written out for F valve horns. The 3rd and 4th cornists can, therefore, use whichever instrument they may prefer.'), trumpet 2, trombone 3, timpani, strings and organ. Text from Gospels of SS Matthew, Mark and Luke. Selected by John Stainer with assistance from H. Joyce. Vocal score and instrumental parts printed separately, London, 1879. Orchestral accompaniments arranged for harmonium and for piano by W. Hodge, London, 1879. Full score in ms now in possession of J. R. Stainer. Performing time c 1 hour. Movements published separately: *Love Divine*, 1885; arranged for SS or SA by J. Holler, New York, 1942. *Sweet tender flower*, 1893. Overture arranged for organ by W. Hodge, 1880.

St Mary Magdalen: written for Gloucester Triennial Festival, 1883. First performed 5 September 1883. SATB soli and SATB chorus; instrumental scoring: not known. Text compiled and written by W. J. Sparrow Simpson. Vocal score and instrumental parts printed separately, 1884. Full score in ms, whereabouts unknown. Performing time c 2 hours. Movement published separately: *Come, ye sin-defiled*, 1909 and *MT* vol 50 no 793.

The Crucifixion: inscribed to W. Hodge and the choir of Marylebone Church and first performed there on 24 February 1887. TB soli, SATB chorus with organ accompaniment. Text selected and written by W. J. Sparrow Simpson. Vocal score, 1887. Ms in possession of J. R. Stainer. Performing time c 1 hour. Movements published separately: *Could ye not watch*, H. W. Gray Co., New York, 1956; *Fling wide the gates*, New York, 1933; *God so loved the world*, *MT* vol 33 no 588 and London, 1892; arranged for three-part choir by V. Knight, Curwen, London, 1966; for SSA by C. H. Trevor, London, 1970; for TTBB by H. A. Chambers, 1954. *Procession to Calvary* arranged by John Stainer for organ and published in *The Village Organist* series, book 44, no 6, London, 1906.

CHURCH ANTHEMS
In the following list the date given in brackets is the year or estimated year of composition. *MT* reference gives detail of anthem published as *MT* supplement.

Anthems prior to 1872:
I saw the Lord (1858) nd. Isaiah, vi, 1–4: SATB double chorus and verse. Anthem for Trinity Sunday.
The righteous live for evermore (1858) 1858. Wisdom, v, 15–16: SATB chorus and verse.
The morning stars sang together (1858) nd. Job, xxxviii, 7; Luke, ii, 11; Isaiah, lxvi, 10–12: SATB chorus and SATTB verse. Anthem for Christmas Day. First contained in Ouseley's collection (1866) and published by Novello in 1873. Written following Stainer's arrival at Tenbury (1858) and dedicated to George Cooper.
Praise the Lord, O my soul (1858). BMus exercise and not subsequently published. Oxford, Bod: Ms Mus Sch c, 57.
For a small moment have I forsaken Thee (1862) 1895. Isaiah, liv, 7, 8 and 10: SATB quartet and chorus. Dedicated to Dr C. W. Corfe, Organist of Christ Church, Oxford.
They were lovely and pleasant in their lives (1866) 1901. 2 Samuel, i, 23; Wisdom, iii, 5–6; Ecclesiasticus, xxiv, 24: SATB verse and chorus and duet for bass voices. Anthem for the feast of St Simon and St Jude. First contained in Ouseley's collection (1866).
Drop down, ye heavens (1866) 1901. Isaiah, xlv, 8; Luke, i, 28, 31–3; Psalm xlv, 2: SATB chorus, verse and soprano solo. Anthem for the feast of the Annunciation. First contained in Ouseley's collection, *Special Anthems for Certain Seasons*, vol II (1866).
The Lord is in His holy temple (1866) 1901. Habakkuk, ii, 20: SSATB chorus. Anthem for the feast of the Purification. First contained in Ouseley's collection (1866).

Lead, kindly light (1868) nd. Text by Cardinal Newman. SATB chorus with treble (or tenor) solo. Dedicated to Herbert A. B. Wilson.

Awake, awake; put on thy strength (1871) nd and *MT* vol 59 no 909 (1918). Isaiah, iii, 1–2, 7–10: SATB chorus and semi-chorus. Dedicated to Rev J. R. G. Taylor, Hereford.

What are these? (1871) nd. Revelation, vii, 13–17: SATB chorus. Written for the Dedication Festival of All Saints' Church, Lathbury, Bucks.

Anthems 1872–88:

Sing a song of praise (1872) nd also York Series, York, 192–. Ecclesiasticus, xxxix, 19; v, 14–15; ii, 11 and 1, 29: SATB chorus and semi-chorus. Dedicated to the Rev W. Rayson, Sacrist of Worcester Cathedral and hon secretary for the Worcester Choral Association, for whom it was written. Date of composition uncertain but between 1872–7.

O clap your hands (1873) nd. Psalm 47, verses 1 and 2; Isaiah, xl, 31; xxvi, 4: SATB chorus and semi-chorus with orchestral accompaniment. Dedicated to Captain Malton and composed for the Eleventh Annual Festival of the Richmond and Kingston Church Choral Association.

O Zion that bringest good tidings (1874) 1874 and *MT* vol 16 no 381 (1874). Isaiah, xl, 9 and part of hymn 'Of the Father's Love begotten': SATB chorus. Anthem for Christmas. Dedicated to the Rev Dr Sparrow Simpson.

They have taken away my Lord (1874) 1875 and *MT* vol 16 no 385 (1875). John, xx, 13, 15 and 16; 1 Corinthians, xv, 55 and 57: SATB chorus. Anthem for Easter. Dedicated to the Rev Dr Troutbeck.

Hosanna in the highest (1875) 1875 and *MT* vol 17 no 392 (1875). Luke, xxi, 9; Isaiah, lxiii, 1–4 and part of a hymn: SATB chorus. Anthem for Advent Sunday.

I desired wisdom (1876) nd. Ecclesiasticus, li, 13–15; iv, 14; Matthew, ii, 1, 2, 9 and 10 and verse from *Adeste Fideles*: SATB chorus and trio for three trebles. Anthem for the feast of The Epiphany.

Leave us not, neither forsake us (1877) 1877 and *MT* vol 18 no 410 (1877). Psalm 27, 11; Psalm 16, 12; Acts i, 11 and Psalm 68, 18: SATB full anthem for use at Ascensiontide.

Ye shall dwell in the land (1877) 1877 and *MT* vol 18 no 414 (1877). Ezekiel, xxxvi, 28, 30, 34–5; Psalm 136, 1 and hymn by Chatterton Dix. SATB chorus, treble (or tenor) and bass solos with orchestral accompaniment. Harvest anthem.

I am Alpha and Omega (1878) 1878 and *MT* vol 19 no 423 (1878).

Revelation, i, 8 and Sanctus. SATB chorus and soprano (or tenor) solo. Anthem for Trinity-tide.

Grieve not the Holy Spirit (c 1880) nd. Ephesians, iv, 30–2; SATB verse and chorus.

Thus speaketh the Lord of hosts (1880) 1880 and *MT* vol 21 no 453 (1880). Zechariah, vi, 12–13 and part of a hymn: SATB chorus. Anthem for Christmas.

Let the peace of God rule your hearts (c 1882) nd. Colossians, iii, 15–17; SATB chorus and soprano (or tenor) solo.

And all the people saw thunderings (1883) nd. Exodus, xx, 18–19; hymn by John Keble 'When God of old' and 1 John, iv, 7 and 12: SATB chorus, duet for tenor (or treble) voices and recit for tenor and bass. Anthem for Whitsuntide or general use. Composed for the London Church Choir Festival.

There was a marriage in Cana of Galilee (1883) nd. John, ii, 1 and 2 and hymn: SATB chorus, bass solo, soprano voices (or tenor) in duet. A wedding anthem written for the marriage of Mrs Paget (the daughter of the Dean of St Paul's) and the Dean of Christ Church, Oxford.

Let every soul be subject (1887) 1887 and *MT* vol 28 no 527 (1887). Romans, xiii, 1; Psalm 118, 1–5 and 19 and two verses of a hymn: SATB chorus, soprano and tenor solo. Composed for Jubilee of Queen Victoria.

Lord, Thou art God (1887) and one movement 'The Lord our God be with us' in *MT* vol 54 no 843 (1913). 1 Chronicles, xvii, 26–7; 2 Samuel, xxii, 2–4; 1 Kings, viii, 57, 60; a versicle and response from the office of matins (or evensong) and verse one of the National Anthem. Tenor solo, SATB chorus and orchestral accompaniment. Written for Jubilee Year of the Sons of the Clergy Festival.

Lo! Summer comes again (c 1888) nd. Text by the Dean of Wells. SATB chorus and semi-chorus. Anthem for harvest festival or general use. Dedicated to the Rev F. H. Hichens.

The hallowed day hath shined (1888) 1888 and *MT* vol 29 no 550 (1888). Text from 'an ancient Office and part of a hymn by the Very Rev E. B. Plumptre'. SATB chorus with tenor solo. Christmas anthem.

Anthems from 1889:
Honour the Lord (1892) 1892. Proverbs, iii, 9–10, 19–20; Deuteronomy, xxxiii, 27–9: SATB chorus with tenor and bass solo. Harvest anthem.

There was silence in Bethlehem's fields (1893) 1894 and *MT* vol 35 no 622 (1894). Text by W. Chatterton Dix. SATB chorus. Christmas anthem. Unison arrangement, New York, 1893.

And Jacob was left alone (1894) 1894. Genesis, xxxii and part of a hymn by Charles Wesley: SATB chorus with two basses (Narrator and The Angel) and tenor (Jacob) solos.

Behold, two blind men (1895) 1895. Matthew, xx, 30 and two stanzas of the hymn 'O lift the veil': STB solos and SATB chorus.

Let not thine hand be stretched (1895) 1895 and *MT* vol 36 no 628 (1895). Ecclesiasticus, iv, 31; xxxv, 10; vii, 35 and xviii, 25: SATB chorus with soprano (or tenor) solo. Anthem for Hospital Sunday 'or any other occasion of almsgiving to the poor'.

Mercy and truth are met together (1895) 1895 and *MT* vol 36 no 633 (1895) Psalm 85, 10–11 'and from the Offices of the Greek Church': SATB chorus with soprano solo. Anthem for Christmas.

Behold, God is my helper (c 1896) nd and 1926. Psalm 54, 4 and 6: short general anthem for SATB chorus.

Blessed is the man (c 1896) nd and 1926. James, i, 12: short general anthem for SATB chorus.

Deliver me, O Lord (c 1896) 1901. Psalm 143, 9–11: SATB chorus. Short general anthem.

Seven Greater Antiphons (1896) 1896. O Wisdom; O Lord and Ruler; O Root of Jesse; O Key of David; O Dayspring; O King and Desire; O Emmanuel. SATB chorus.

It came upon the midnight clear (1899) 1899 and *MT* vol 40 no 681 (1899). Hymn by the Rev E. H. Sears. Bass solo and SATB chorus. Christmas anthem.

Thou Lord in the beginning (1899) 1899. Psalm 102, 25–7; Revelation, xxi, 1–4 and a stanza and doxology from 'Urbs beata': SATB chorus, quartet and soprano solo. Anthem for Septuagesima, St John or general use.

Day of Wrath (1900) 1900. Text translated by the Rev W. J. Irons from Thomas of Celano. SATB chorus and quartet.

O bountiful Jesu (1900) 1900 and *MT* vol 41 no 684 (1900). Text from part of a prayer from the primer 'set forth by order of King Edward VI in 1553'. SATB chorus.

O Saving Victim (1900) 1900. Text from writings of St Thomas Aquinas. SATB chorus and verse. Short anthem or introit.

SERVICE MUSIC

Set no 1 in E flat: SATB with organ accompaniment. *Holy Communion office:* Introit, Kyrie, responses before and after Gospel, Credo, Offertory sentences (4 sets), Sursum Corda, Sanctus, Gloria in excelsis (1874) nd. Benedictus and Agnus Dei (2 sets) (1899) 1899. *Matins:* Te Deum, Benedictus, Jubilate (1874) nd. *Evensong:* Magnificat, Nunc Dimittis (1870) nd.

Set no 2 in A and D: SATB with organ accompaniment. Sir George Martin orchestrated the Sanctus and Gloria in excelsis from the *Holy Communion office* when they were sung at the Coronation of Edward VII in 1902. An orchestral accompaniment was also available for the *evening canticles* but it has not proved possible to find out details of instrumentation. *Holy Communion office:* Kyrie, Credo, Offertory sentences (4 sets), Sanctus, Gloria in excelsis (c 1876) nd. Benedictus and Agnus Dei (2 sets) (1899) 1899. *Matins:* Te Deum, Benedictus (c 1876) nd. *Evensong:* Magnificat, Nunc Dimittis (1877) nd. Composed for the Festival of the Sons of the Clergy, 1873.

Set no 3 in B flat: SATB with organ accompaniment. *Holy Communion office:* Kyrie, responses before and after Gospel, Credo, Sursum Corda, Sanctus, Benedictus, Agnus Dei, Gloria in excelsis (c 1884) 1884. This setting is sometimes referred to as the service in F major and was published thus, 1886 and 1958. *Matins:* Te Deum, Benedictus (c 1884) 1884. *Evensong:* Magnificat, Nunc Dimittis (1877) nd. Composed for the Fifth Annual Festival of the London Church Choir Association, 1877.

Service in D major: MV, ATTB with organ accompaniment. *Holy Communion office:* Kyrie, responses before and after Gospel, Credo, Offertory sentences (4 sets), Sursum Corda, Sanctus, Gloria in excelsis (c 1895–1900) 1900. *Matins:* Te Deum, Benedictus (c 1895–1900) 1900. *Evensong:* Magnificat, Nunc Dimittis (1873) 1898.

Miscellaneous settings of the Holy Communion office:
'Magdalen' setting in A (1864). SATB with organ accompaniment. Unpublished; ms in possession of J. R. Stainer.
Setting in A major: SATB with organ accompaniment. Kyrie, Credo, Sanctus, Gloria in excelsis (c 1895) 1900.
Setting in C major: SSATBB, unaccompanied. Composed expressly for St Paul's Cathedral Choir (1899). Kyrie, Credo, Sanctus, Gloria in excelsis. 1901.
Kyrie Eleison, 4 sets, 1899. John Stainer contributed no 3 in A major to this set of 4.

Miscellaneous settings of canticles for Matins:
in C major: SATB with organ accompaniment, mostly in unison and intended for choir and congregation use. Te Deum (after 1877) nd.
in G major: SATB with organ accompaniment, for congregational use. Te Deum (after 1877) 1893.
A flat major: SATB with organ accompaniment, chant form. Te Deum (after 1877) 1899.

in D major: SATB with organ accompaniment. Chant form, Benedicite (after 1877) 1894.

in F major: SATB with organ accompaniment, chant form, chants by John Stainer and B. Blaxland, Benedicite (after 1877) 1896.

in G major: SATB with organ accompaniment, chant form, chants by John Stainer and J. Turle, Benedicite (after 1877) 1915 and *MT* vol 56 no 864 (1915).

Miscellaneous settings of canticles for Evensong:
'Magdalen' service in A major: SATB with organ accompaniment. Unpublished; ms in possession of J. R. Stainer (c 1864).

in D and F majors: SATB with organ accompaniment, chant form (after 1877) 1894.

in E major: SATB with organ accompaniment (after 1877) 1894.

in F major: SATB with organ accompaniment (after 1877) 1895.

MISCELLANEOUS CHURCH COMPOSITIONS
Sevenfold Amen, SATB, unaccompanied in A major (1873) nd. Also arranged for three treble voices with optional organ accompaniment, by H. Blair, 1909, and ATTB by G. J. Bennett, 1909.

Fourfold Amen, SATB, unaccompanied (?) 1909.

Miserere, setting of Psalm 51. SATB, unaccompanied (1873) 1894.

Twelve Sacred Songs for Children (illustrated when originally published as *Holy Gladness*) (c 1875) 1889. Unison songs (apart from no 1 which is a duet) with organ or piano accompaniment. Words by Edward Oxenford.

1 Listening Angels
2 Morning Hymn
3 Hour by Hour
4 The Beautiful Land
5 The Crown is Waiting
6 The Cross of Life
7 We will praise Thee
8 Sabbath Bells
9 The Good Shepherd
10 The Haven of Glory
11 The Golden Shore
12 Evensong

HYMN TUNES: a collection of most of John Stainer's hymn tunes assembled in one volume (1867–1900) 1900. All are SATB except where stated.

1867:   Sudeley

1868: Magdalena, Charity, Iona
1869: Dies Judicii, Damiani
1870: Matins, Dawn, Celano, Christmas Day, The Haven, Wondrous Love
1871: Columba Sancta
1872: Crux Beata
1873: Rest, The Athanasian Creed (this tune may have been written in 1883)
1874: Lux, Sebaste, Harland, Vesper, St Paul's, Jejunia, St Cyprian, St Francis Xavier, Ascendit, The Roseate Hues, The Blessed Home, Credo, Eucharisticus, Author of Life, Jerusalem, Pastor Bonus
1875: Watchword, Raise the Song (written for the London Church Choir Association Festival), Stella in Oriente, Ad Perennis Vitae Fontem, In Memoriam, A Child's Evensong
1879: Christmas Morn, Gazing Upward
1883: St Paul
1885: Holy Mirth, Aletta, Angelina (written for the marriage of Sir Reginald Dyke Acland)
1887: Sursum Corda, Rex Regnum (written for Dr Stephenson's Children's Home Jubilee Festival), Jaazaniah, Cross of Jesus (from *The Crucifixion*), Plead for Me (from *The Crucifixion*), Etiam pro nobis (from *The Crucifixion*), All for Jesus (from *The Crucifixion*), Adoration (from *The Crucifixion*), Stola Regia, Sons of Labour (written for the Church of England Working Men's Society), Sabaoth, Kind Shepherd
1888: Covenant, Woodlynn, Redeemed, Matrimony, Up in Heaven
1889: Love Divine, The Good Shepherd, Hour by Hour, The Golden Shore, The Beautiful Land
1890: Dominus Misericordiae, Crucifixion, Veni, Oxford, Verborgne Gottesliebe, Just as I am, Lynton, Breast the Wave, Christian, Jerusalem Coelestis, Oblations, Offerings of Flowers
1892: O Holy Star!, Sweet Christmas Bells
1893: There was silence in Bethlehem's fields (music also arranged as a Christmas anthem), Christmas Dawn
1894: Come, Gracious Saviour, Day of Wrath, The Golden Crown, Crux Salutifera, Paschale Gaudium, Where Thou Art, Gratias Agimus, A Little While, In manus tuas, Harvest Offerings
1895: Self-Sacrifice
1896: Te Deum Laudamus, Vale
1897: Repose, Mane mecum, Nazareth, Following, Patience, Obedience (in canon), Adoremus, St Faith, God in Nature, Seasons, Children's Offerings
1898: Gloaming, Protection, Totland, Venit hora, Veni spiritus,

216

Creator Spiritus, Per Recte et Retro, Tenbury, Grandpont, Pilgrim Band, Mors et vita, Gathered in, Simplicity, St Benedict, Evening Prayer (unison with organ accompaniment), The River of Life, Joy Bells

1899: Deum videbunt, On brothers on!, Venturus est, Iam fulget oriens, The Child Jesus, Surrexit, Spiritus Vivificans, Transfiguration, Laudate Dominum Coelorum, Homeland, Where Brethren Meet, Apart with me, Weep not for me, Faithful unto Death, Exivit Sonus Eorum, Holy Offerings, Exsurgat Deus, Studland, Swanage, Whom Thou lovest

1900: Coelestis Curia, From Strength to Strength (written for the Truro Festival), Scientia Salutis, Haec est dies, Surge, O Zion, In Majestate, New Year's Eve, Non te negabo, Fiat voluntas tua, Per Crucem tuam, Love is of God, Go forth with Joy, St Peter and St John, Omnium Dominator (written in aid of the Transvaal War Fund)

Year unknown: Vespers

Miscellaneous hymn tunes not included above:

Emmanuel (1868) and Nativitas (1868): both contained in *Hymns Ancient and Modern*, 1868 edition.

Litany (1875) contained in *Hymns Ancient and Modern*, 1875 edition.

Eternal Wisdom (1889) written for use in Hockerill Training College, Bishops Stortford, 1889.

Soumission, Consolation, Piete and Joie Sainte (1895) contained in *Day School Hymn Book*, 1896.

Burslem (?) written for an edition of *Church Hymns* but not used. Whereabouts unknown.

Two hymn tunes, not named, set to existing words *Now once more we greet Thee* and *O God, our Hope, our Strength, our King* (written for the children of the Royal Albert Orphan Asylum). Whereabouts unknown. (This information and also that regarding Burslem is contained in notes by J. F. R. Stainer written on the inner cover of *Hymn Tunes*, in possession of J. R. Stainer.)

Hymn tunes set to existing words: *God of Supreme Dominion*, 1887 – Stainer's contribution to a small collection of hymns written for the eightieth birthday of Queen Victoria; *Stars, that on your wondrous way*, 1894; *Behold, the Lamb of God*, 1903; *At home with Christ*, 1905; *The Boys and Girls of England Hymn*, 1913; *We'll sing and praise our God*, 1930.

Christmas Carols New and Old, 1871 – carols by John Stainer not previously listed: *The Child Jesus* (another version), *Jesu, hail! O God most holy*; harmonies written for following carols based on ancient or traditional melodies: *A Babe is born all of a Maid, As it fell out one May morning, I saw three ships, The Angel Gabriel from God, 'Tis the day, What soul-inspiring music, The Coventry Carol.*

Anglican chants – Single chants: 17. A flat (1), A major (2), A minor (1), C major (5), D major (2), E major (1), F major (2), G major (3).
Double chants: 15. C major (2), C minor (1), D flat major (1), E flat major (2), E minor (2), F major (2), G major (3), G minor (1), A flat major (1).
Triple chants: 5. C major (1), F major (1), C minor (1), G minor (2).

ARRANGEMENTS OF MISCELLANEOUS SACRED AND CHURCH MUSIC
J. S. Bach *St Matthew Passion*, abridged version with English translation (1873) nd. Vocal score with piano accompaniment.
Come unto me, double choir with organ accompaniment, being the last chorus of *St Matthew Passion* – J. S. Bach, adapted to text from St Matthew, xi, 28–30 (c 1890) nd.
Schubert *The Lord is my Shepherd*, SATB with organ accompaniment. Arranged before 1880 and later published 1898.
W. Hayes *Save Lord, and hear us* and W. Croft *Sing praises to the Lord* (c 1875, no trace of publication).
J. G. Naumann, 'Dresden' Amen, arranged SSATB (? prior to 1880) 1904.

Arrangements of canticle settings to Gregorian tones:
(All arranged for unison voices with faux-bourdons and organ accompaniment)
Canticles of Church arranged to Gregorian tones, series 1–4 (c 1876–7) 1878. Subsequently published separately:
Te Deum, 1st set, 1895
Te Deum, 2nd set, 1896
Te Deum, 3rd set, 1896
Te Deum, 4th set, 1895
Benedictus, 1st set, 1895
Benedictus, 2nd set, 1895
Benedictus, 3rd set, 1896
Benedictus, 4th set, 1897
Magnificat and Nunc Dimittis, 1st set, 1896
Magnificat and Nunc Dimittis, 2nd set, 1896
Magnificat and Nunc Dimittis, 3rd set, 1896
Magnificat and Nunc Dimittis, 4th set, 1895
Gregorian tones with their endings harmonised in various ways being the accompanying harmonies to the Merton Psalter (prior to 1872) 1879.

Magnificat arranged to 1st Parisian tone (?) Oxford, nd.
Nunc Dimittis arranged to 2nd Parisian tone (?) Oxford, nd.
Magnificat arranged to St Saviour's Tone (c 1875) nd.
Ambrosian Te Deum (after Merbecke) (c 1875) nd.
Holy Communion office – John Merbecke, arranged with organ accompaniment (c 1875) 1898
Lord's Prayer from previous setting (c 1875) 1895
Athanasian Creed – plainsong, arranged for unison voices with organ accompaniment (c 1873) 1882
Preces, Responses and Litany as used in St Paul's Cathedral (Ferial), arranged SATB (1873) 1886
Versicles and Responses with harmonised confession, arranged ATTB (? 1873) 1899
Preces and Responses with harmonised confession (Ely use) – Tallis, arranged SATB (1873) 1900
Hymn, *All blessing, Honour, Glory, Might*, arranged from Mendelssohn, 1901

Editions of miscellaneous church music in which John Stainer was editor or co-editor:
A Choir Book of Office to Holy Communion, 1874
The Cathedral Psalter, nd.
St Paul's Cathedral Chant Book, 1878
Cathedral Prayer Book – sets of canticles for use with cathedral psalter, London and New York, 1894
Order for the Burial of the Dead, together with a selection of suitable hymns, 1898
The Cathedral Psalter Chant Book, with S. Flood Jones, J. Turle, J. Troutbeck and J. Barnby (prior to 1882) nd.
The Cathedral Prayer Book, incorporating previously mentioned arrangements and editions, with W. Russell (various times) 1891
The Church Hymnary, Frowde, Edinburgh, 1898
The Hymnal Companion, ed C. Vincent with assistance from John Stainer, 1890
Magdalen Psalter, pointed and arranged with L. S. Tuckwell, Oxford, 1875
Church Choir Chant Book, ed with L. S. Tuckwell, 1899
Christmas Carols New and Old, with H. R. Bramley, 1871
Manual of Plainsong, H. B. Briggs and W. H. Frere under general superintendence of J. Stainer, 1902
Church of America Altar Book, plainsong, edited and arranged by John Stainer, New York, 1896
Words of Anthems, with W. Rayson and J. Troutbeck, 1875

Magnificat and Nunc Dimittis in E minor – Daniel Purcell. Service edited and restored (prior to 1872) 1900

Edited the following non-liturgical services:
Jubilee: A Service of Praise and Thanksgiving for the times (1887) 1887
The Story of the Cross, 1893 and *MT* vol 35 no 611 (1894)
A Christmas Service of Song, 1894
The Story of the Advent of Jesus, 1900
At the Manger, A Litany of the Incarnation, 1901

Section B: Secular Vocal Music

SOLO SONGS

To sigh, yet feel no pain, soprano solo with piano accompaniment, dedicated to Eliza Randall (to become Mrs Stainer) (1865). Words unknown. Unpublished ms in possession of J. R. Stainer.

Insufficiency, tenor solo with piano accompaniment, words by Mrs H. Browning (1869) nd. Dedicated to Walter Goolden.

Loyal Death, Bass/baritone solo with piano accompaniment, words by P. S. Worsley (1870) nd. Dedicated to J. Swire.

Jilted, soprano/tenor solo with piano accompaniment, words by W. A. Barrett, (1870) nd. Dedicated to T. M. Everett.

My Little Pet, soprano/tenor solo with piano accompaniment, words by W. A. Barrett (1870) nd. Dedicated to Miss Clara Findeisen.

Unbeloved, bass solo with piano accompaniment, words by Gerald Massey (1871) nd. Dedicated to Frank Pownall.

My Maker and My King, soprano solo with piano accompaniment, words from Dr Watts (1873) nd. Dedicated to Mrs W. Margetson.

Slumber Song, soprano solo with piano accompaniment and ad lib 'cello part, words translated from Körner (1873) nd. Dedicated to Miss Mary Stewart.

Seven Songs, mezzo-soprano, contralto or baritone, with German and English translation apart from song no 6, 1892. 'Affectionately inscribed to Cecie and Ellie.'
1   Das Ferne Land, words by Joh Heinrich Voss, F major
2   Der Rosenstrauch, words by Ed Ferrand, D flat major
3   Das Meer der Hoffnung, words by Fr Rückert, C minor
4   Poesie, words by Justinus Kerner, F sharp minor
5   An Leukon, words by Joh Wilh. Ludwig Gleim, A flat major
6   Quand je te vois comme une fleur, translation of 'Du bist wie eine Blume' – Heine, by Jules Bue, D flat major

7   Daheim, words by Joh Georg Fischer, G minor
To a violet, unison song for school use, with piano accompaniment
(1894) 1894. Words unknown.
A Soldier's Life, unison action song for boys from *Six Unison Action Songs*, with piano accompaniment (?) nd. Words by John Stainer.

MADRIGALS AND PART-SONGS
Like as a ship, madrigal SSAATTBB, *A cappella*, words by Edmund
Spencer from Amoretti Sonnet xxxiv. Written for prize competition of
Bristol Madrigal Society, 1865. Not awarded a prize. Ms in possession
of J. R. Stainer.
Bind my brows, glee ATTB, *A cappella*, text arranged from Anacreon's
Fifth Ode by T. Moore. 1879.
The desert island, catch ATTBB, *A cappella*, words by John Stainer.
1880.
The Triumph of Victoria, madrigal SSATB, *A cappella*, in imitation of
'The Triumphs of Oriana' published in honour of Queen Elizabeth.
No details of author. 1893.
Flora's Queen, madrigal SSATBB, *A cappella*, no details of author.
1899.
Cupid look about thee, a fa la for ATTB, *A cappella*, no details of author.
1900.
I prythee send me back my heart, glee for ATTB, *A cappella*, words by
Dr Henry Hughes (1650). 1904.
Prithee, why so pale? madrigal SSATBB, *A cappella*, no details of
author. 1906.
The Queen of May, madrigal SSATTB, *A cappella*, words from seventeenth-century ballad. 1906.

Although it has not been possible to ascertain dates of composition of the
previously mentioned madrigals and part-songs, it is believed that some,
if not all, were written before 1872 for use with madrigal societies in
Oxford under Stainer's direction.

ARRANGEMENTS OF SECULAR VOCAL MUSIC
Six Italian Songs, English words written and adapted by John Stainer.
For mezzo-soprano voice, piano accompaniment and violin obbligato.
Nos 2 and 3 are also published in a separate volume. 1895.
1   Dolce Amor − P. F. Cavalli, G minor
2   Non Dar Piu Pene − A. Scarlatti, G major
3   Fier Destin − F. Gasparini, D major
4   L'Immago Tua Vezzosa − Emanuele, Baron D'Astorga, G major
5   Danza Fanciulla − F. Durante, A minor
6   La Pastorella − B. Galuppi, C major

The School Round Book – a collection of one hundred rounds, catches and canons; words edited by Rev J. Powell Metcalfe and music edited by John Stainer. 190–.

Section C: Instrumental Music

Six Pieces for the Organ, 1897
    Andante, A flat major
    Prelude and Fughetta, C major
    Adagio (ma non troppo), E flat major
    On a bass, G minor
    Impromptu, E minor
    Reverie, A flat major
Twelve Pieces for the Organ (Book II), 1900
    Andante Pathetique, E major (written in Florence, 1898)
    Praeludium Pastorale (super gamut descendens), C major (written in Oxford, 1898)
    A Church Prelude, E flat major (written in Mentone, January 1899)
    Introduction and Fughetta, E minor (Mentone, January 1899)
    Fantasia, C major
    Finale Alla Marcia, D major
Jubilant March for Organ in D major, nd.
A Song of Praise (1897) – *The Village Organist* series, book 1 no 9, 1897.
Procession to Calvary from *The Crucifixion* – *The Village Organist* series, book 44, no 6, 1906.
The Village Organist, joint editor with F. Cunningham Woods and J. E. West, 1897–. 48 volumes.
Quartett for Two Violins, Viola and Violoncello, E minor, dedicated to Professor W. F. Donkin, Savilian Professor of Astronomy. Unpublished, no date, ms in possession of J. R. Stainer.

Section D: Published Educational Works and Miscellaneous Items

BOOKS
A Theory of Harmony founded on the Tempered Scale, 1871. Dedicated to Professor Müller.
Dictionary of Musical Terms, with W. A. Barrett, 1876; revised and edited by John Stainer, 1898 and 1912. Compressed edition, 1880.
A Manual of Singing, for the use of choir-trainers and schoolmasters – Richard Mann, new edition with revisions by John Stainer, 1876?
Novello's Music Primers and Educational Series, 1877–. John Stainer

acted as editor. He also wrote four: *The Organ* (1877) *Composition* (1877); *Choral Society Vocalisations* (1877); and *Harmony* (1878).
Dictionary of Musical Terms was also issued as a Primer (1880); *Choral Society Vocalisations* was arranged for female voices by A. W. Marchant, 1897; *The Organ* was revised by F. Flaxington Harker, Schirmer, New York, 1901.

The Music of the Bible, 1879. New edition with additional material supplied by Rev. F. W. Galpin, 1914.

Tutor for the American Organ, London Metzler, 1883.

Catalogue of English Song Books, forming a portion of the Library of Sir John Stainer, with Appendices of Foreign Song Books, Collections of Carols, Books on Bells, etc., 1891.

A few words to candidates for the degree of Mus.Bac. Oxon., 1892.

Music in relation to the Intellect and Emotions, 1892. Subsequently repeated in *Primer* series, 1911, and translated into French by Louis Pennequin, Paris, 1911.

Dufay and his contemporaries, 1898, with J. F. R. and C. Stainer.

Early Bodleian Music, 1901, edited John Stainer.

VARIOUS PUBLISHED PAPERS, ARTICLES AND MISCELLANEOUS ITEMS

'On the rhythmical form of the Anglican chant' – *MT* January 1872.

Church Music, Church Congress, Leeds, 1872.

On the Progressive Character of Church Music, Church Congress, Brighton, 1874. 'On the principles of Musical Notation' – *MA* April 1875.

Aids to the Student of the Holy Bible, 1878, sometimes referred to as *Bible Educator* series; Part II, *Music of the Bible.*

'How can Cathedrals best further the Culture of Church Music?' – *Quarterly Church Review*, January 1879.

'Sir John Goss' – obit notice *MT* June 1880.

'The Principles of Musical Criticism' – *MA* January 1881.

An Address to the Scholars of the National Training School for Music, September 1881.

Handbook of St Paul's Cathedral, with G. Phillips Beavan, 1882.

Great Paul – S. J. Mackie: Preface written by John Stainer, 1882.

The present state of music in England, Oxford, 1889.

'The Character and Influence of the late Sir Frederick Ouseley' – *MA* December 1889.

'Julian's Dictionary of Hymnology' – review article *MT* April 1892.

'Technique and sentiment' – monthly journal ISM, February 1893.

Music considered in its effect upon, and connexion with, the worship of the Church, Church Congress, Exeter, 1894.

Does Music train the Mind? Address given to ISM Conference, Dublin, January 1895.

'Address of Welcome to American Musicians' – *MA* July 1895.

'A Fifteenth Century Ms Book of Vocal Music in the Bodleian Library, Oxford' – *MA* November 1895.

'Musical Directions in early English Psalters' – *MA* November 1900.

Musical illustrations of Sir John Stainer's lectures at Oxford: In the Old Library of Magdalen College there are some printed notes giving certain musical illustrations of Sir John's lectures. There are no details of publication and the notes were issued to those attending the lectures. It is not clear, however, how much Stainer or his choragus was responsible for the actual notes and musical illustrations. What was available in the library is as follows:

Origin and Development of the Ground Bass, February 1891: Specimens of Ground Basses.

Mendelssohn's oratorio, St Paul, February 1894: various versions of chorales used in the oratorio.

Tye's Mass, 'Euge Bone', March 1896: thematic material with brief summary of Tye's career.

Morley's 'Plaine and easie introduction', December 1897: details of music performed.

Madrigalian composers of the Gallo-Belgian School, March 1899: details of music to be performed – Jannequin, Jacobin, Claude de Sermisy.

Ms notes by John Stainer in *On purity of Musical Art* – A. F. J. Thibault (1877).

Bibliography

The place of publication is London unless otherwise stated

Bateson, J. *Alcock of Salisbury* (Salisbury, 1949)
Bumpus, J. S. *A History of English Cathedral Music* (1889)
— *The Organists and Composers of St Paul's Cathedral* (1891)
Chadwick, O. *The Mind of the Oxford Movement* (1960)
Dictionary of National Biography (1912)
Fellowes, E. H. *English Cathedral Music* (1941)
— *Memoirs of an Amateur Musician* (1946)
Fowler, J. T. *Life and Letters of J. B. Dykes* (1897)
Frost, W. A. *Early Recollections of St Paul's Cathedral* (1925)
Graves, C. L. *Hubert Parry, His Life and Works* 2 vols (1926)
Gregory, R. *Robert Gregory* (1921)
Greville, C. F. *Journals of the Reign of William IV* (1874)
Grove, G. (ed) *Dictionary of Music and Musicians* (1889, 1900 and
    1954 editions)
Hamilton, W. K. *Cathedral Reform* (1855)
Hollins, A. *A blind musician looks back* (1936)
Hutchings, A. *Church Music in the 19th Century* (1967)
Jebb, J. *The Choral Service of the United Church of England and
    Ireland, being an Enquiry into the Liturgical System of the Cathedral
    and Collegiate Foundations of the Anglican Communion* (1843)
Johnston, J. O. *Life and Letters of H. P. Liddon* (1904)
Joyce, F. W. *The Life of Rev Sir F. A. G. Ouseley, Bart* (1896)
Knight, G. H. and Reed, W. L. (ed) *Treasury of English Church Music*
    vol 4 (1965)
Liddon, H. P. *W. K. Hamilton* (1869)
Long, K. R. *The Music of the English Church* (1971)
Lowther Clarke, W. K. *100 Years of Hymns Ancient and Modern*
    (1960)
Massingham, B. *Turn on the Fountains – the life of Dean Hole* (1974)
Matthews, W. R. and Atkins, W. M. *A History of St Paul's* (1957)
Oakeley, E. M. *The Life of Sir Hubert Oakeley* (1904)
Perkins, J. and Bumpus, J. S. *Westminster Abbey and St Paul's
    Cathedral* (1914)
Phillips, C. H. *The Singing Church* (1945)
Pole, W. *Some short reminiscences of events in my life and work* (1898)

Routley, E. *The Musical Wesleys* (1968)

Scholes, P. A. (ed) *The Mirror of Music* (1947)

— (ed) *The Oxford Companion to Music* (1955)

Sinclair, W. *Memorials of St Paul's Cathedral* (1909)

Sparrow Simpson, W. J. *Memoir of the Rev W. Sparrow Simpson* (1899)

Stainer, J. *A few words to candidates for the degree of Mus.Bac. Oxon.* (1892)

— *Catalogue of English Song Books, forming a portion of the Library of Sir John Stainer* (1891)

— *Hymn Tunes* (1900)

Stainer, J. and Russell, W. (ed) *The Cathedral Prayer Book* (1891)

Sumner, W. L. *Organs of St Paul's Cathedral* (1931)

Tovey, D. F. and Parratt, G. *Walter Parratt, Master of the Music* (Oxford, 1941)

Tuckwell, L. S. *Old Magdalen Days – Reminiscences of Oxford* (1907)

Venables, E. M. *Sweet tones remembered* (nd)

Walker, E. *A History of Music in England* (Oxford, 1952)

Warner, W. A. *St Paul's Cathedral* (nd)

Wesley, S. S. *A Few Words on Cathedral Music and the Musical System of the Church, with a Plan of Reform* (1849)

West, J. E. *Cathedral Organists* (1921)

Young, P. M. *George Grove* (1980)

Periodicals

Athenaeum, The 6 April 1901

Book Collector, The vol XI (1962)

Choir, The various editions

CHUMS c 1888

Church Congress Papers 1872, 1874 and 1894

Church Family Newspaper, The 4 April 1901

Church Review, The 19 May 1877

Church Times, The 2 February 1877

Citizen, The 26 February 1887

Committee of Council on Education Reports various editions

Daily Chronicle, The various editions

Daily News, The 7 February 1888

Daily Telegraph, The various editions

Doveridge, St Cuthbert's Church guide (nd)

English Church Music vol XXI no 1

Guardian, The various editions

HM Commissioners, enquiring into the condition of Cathedral Churches in England and Wales, 1883

Ilford Recorder 21 February 1952

Manchester Guardian, The various editions

Morning Leader, The (nd)
Morning Post, The 2 April 1901
Musical Association Proceedings, The various editions
Musical Mirror and Fanfare October 1932
Musical Standard, The various editions
Musical Times, The various editions
Musical World, The various editions
Orchestra, The 30 June 1866
Oxford Chronicle, The various editions
Oxford Journal various editions
Oxford Magazine various editions
Oxford Mail, The 6 January 1964
Oxford Times, The 11 November 1865
Oxford University Gazette various editions
Pilot, The 20 April 1901
Royal College of Organists Calendars 1889 and 1900
Royal Musical Association Proceedings, The 1921–2
St Paul's Cathedral Bye-laws – assistant vicars-choral, 1872 and 1888
St Paul's Cathedral, Succentor's Reports various editions
School Music Review May 1901
Sunday Times, The 27 February 1887
Times, The various editions
University Herald 11 November 1865
World, The 12 January 1887

Unpublished Material
Edwards, F. G. – letters from Sir John Stainer over approximately the last fifteen years of his life. (Edwards Papers, Egerton ms 3092, The British Library)
Exeter College Music Society, Oxford, minutes of meetings – Exeter College Library, Oxford
Hall, E. Vine, The Magdalen Vagabonds, a history of their wanderings and their doings – Magdalen College Library, Oxford
Maltese Glee Club – reminiscences; Magdalen College Library, Oxford
National Training School of Music, minutes of committee of management
Diary of Sir Hubert Parry, in the possession of Lord Ponsonby
Royal College of Music, minutes of council and executive committees
St Paul's Cathedral Chapter Minutes
St Paul's Cathedral Register Book of Almoner
Stainer, Sir John, biographical notes compiled by John and Edward, sons of Sir John, in the possession of J. R. Stainer
Thewlis, George, notes of Oxford musical life, in the possession of his widow, Mrs G. Thewlis

Acknowledgements

I am grateful to the librarian of the University of Cambridge Library for allowing me the use of books and music; the ease and speed in obtaining books was always much appreciated. Similar acknowledgement is given to the librarians of the British Library, the City of Cambridge Public Library and the Archbishop of Canterbury's Library at Lambeth Palace.

I wish to express my thanks also to friends, colleagues and former pupils who have helped me in many ways relevant to my research, and to the following in particular. Dr W. L. Sumner encouraged me in the early stages of this work and supplied me with various useful pieces of information as did John Stainer, lately Registrar of the Royal College of Music, a grandson of Sir John. Dr E. D. Mackerness, formerly Reader in English Literature at the University of Sheffield and Dr Watkins Shaw read the draft of the work at an early stage and offered useful advice; Sir John Dykes Bower was of much assistance in the chapters which deal with St Paul's Cathedral. Lord Ponsonby was kind enough to allow me to use extracts from Sir Hubert Parry's diaries, and Mrs George Thewlis of Oxford permitted me to refer to the unpublished notes of her late husband. Mr A. R. B. Fuller, Librarian of St Paul's Cathedral, was most helpful in arranging for me to see the Cathedral Chapter Minutes, the large and small scrap books of press cuttings accumulated by John S. Bumpus, and other documents. Dr Bernard Rose, Magdalen College, Oxford, was also helpful in a variety of ways and Mrs Janet Hopewell supplied me with some useful information on the librettist of *The Crucifixion*. I acknowledge also the assistance given by various officers of the Royal College of Music and the Royal College of Organists. During my summer holidays I took refuge in the Benedictine monastery at Einsiedeln in Switzerland and no expression of thanks would be complete without mention of the kindness of the Abbot, and Fr Wolfgang Renz, OSB, Guestmaster of that particular community. It gives me pleasure also to acknowledge the constant attention, assistance and kindness of Dr David Charlton, my supervisor when the work was presented as a doctoral thesis, and to John Lloyd who has been invaluable in reading the work in its present form and offering so much helpful and detailed criticism and many suggestions.

Index